RELATIONSHIP MANAGEMENT IN BANKING

OTHER BOOKS AVAILABLE IN THE CHARTERED BANKER SERIES

Chartered **Banker**

RELATIONSHIP MANAGEMENT IN BANKING

PRINCIPLES AND PRACTICE

STEVE GOULDING
AND RICHARD ABLEY

KoganPage

Publisher's note
Every possible effort has been made to ensure that the information contained in this book is accurate at the time of going to press, and the publisher and authors cannot accept responsibility for any errors or omissions, however caused. No responsibility for loss or damage occasioned to any person acting, or refraining from action, as a result of the material in this publication can be accepted by the editor, the publisher or the authors.

First published in Great Britain and the United States in 2019 by Kogan Page Limited

2nd Floor, 45 Gee Street	c/o Martin P Hill Consulting	4737/23 Ansari Road
London EC1V 3RS	122 W 27th St, 10th Floor	Daryaganj
United Kingdom	New York NY 10001	New Delhi 110002
www.koganpage.com	USA	India

© Stonecross Education Solutions Ltd, 2019

ISBN   978 0 7494 8283 1
E-ISBN 978 0 7494 8284 8

British Library Cataloguing-in-Publication Data

A CIP record for this book is available from the British Library.

Library of Congress Cataloging-in-Publication Data
Names: Goulding, Steve (Management consultant), author. | Abley, Richard, author.
Title: Relationship management in banking : principles and practice / Steve Goulding and Richard Abley.
Description: London ; New York : Kogan Page, [2019].
Identifiers: LCCN 2018034346 (print) | LCCN 2018036036 (ebook) | ISBN 9780749482848 (ebook) | ISBN 9780749482831 (pbk.)
Subjects: LCSH: Banks and banking–Customer services–Great Britain. | Bank management–Great Britain. | Customer relations–Great Britain.
Classification: LCC HG1616.C87 (ebook) | LCC HG1616.C87 G68 2019 (print) | DDC 332.1068/8–dc23

Typeset by Integra Software Services, Pondicherry
Print production managed by Jellyfish
Printed and bound by 4edge Limited, UK

CONTENTS

PREFACE

The authors have, together, spent over 65 years in banking, working in a number of different banks in both retail and business divisions. They have detailed knowledge and experience of relationship management across a wide variety of customer types, across all industry sectors and business sizes, from new start-ups to large corporates.

Throughout their careers they have always shared a passion for staff development and education by sharing their knowledge and experiences of dealing with all different types of banking customers. They have written a number of books across a diverse range of banking topics, including credit and lending, risk management, banking operations and relationship management.

Their journey through their own careers in relationship management will help you through your own journey. This book will provide you with both theoretical and practical applications of relationship management. It is presented in a concise and logical way enabling you to develop your own knowledge, skills and competences when dealing with customers. Whether you are an experienced relationship manager or someone new to a relationship role, this book will help guide you through your own journey in relationship management.

Introduction

This book explains the role of relationship management for personal as well as business customers and demonstrates what it is customers are looking for from both their bank and their relationship manager. It describes the skills required to do the job as well as the competences needed that will enable you to have a successful career in relationship management.

It details the different types of customers you will encounter and the products and services they require.

The book also discusses what happened before, during and after the global financial crisis of 2007–09. It explains how regulators, legislators and the banks themselves are repositioning the banking sector, so that the events that damaged the reputation of banks and bankers will never be repeated again. It discusses the importance of ethics and professionalism and how they can be used to restore trust within the banking sector. You have an important role to play in this.

The book provides you with a number of practical tools and techniques that you can use with customers to help them to manage risk as well as enabling you to have better conversations and discussions with your customers whenever you meet.

It also covers customer service and service quality including what to do when things do go wrong before any problems turn into complaints. It also provides a step-by-step guide to complaint handling and service recovery.

It considers the key relationship strategies of customer retention, development and acquisition. It explains how portfolio planning and management can help you to develop your own appropriate relationship strategies to use with customers.

The final chapter in the book, entitled 'Gaining New Business', is an extended case study providing you with an example of how a relationship manager takes the opportunity to secure a new business customer from a competitor bank. This chapter will enable you to consolidate all the learnings from the book and use them in a practical, non-threatening and real-life environment. It will demonstrate how to become your customer's own trusted financial professional and an exemplar in the role.

That is what relationship management in banking is all about.

Business customers

This chapter looks at the most common business customer types you will encounter throughout your career. Each business type has its own legal structure, obligations and reporting requirements.

LEARNING OBJECTIVES

By the end of this chapter you will be able to:

- differentiate between a range of different customer types;
- evaluate the benefits of customer segmentation;
- assess the ways in which a bank might segment its customers and analyse why different banks might take different approaches;
- assess the legal aspects which need to be considered when dealing with different customer types.

Introduction

There are a number of different business customers you will encounter, whether you work in the retail side of your bank, in private, corporate or commercial banking, or any of the other divisions that employ a relationship management model. In this chapter we examine the different characteristics of each business type and we look at the advantages and disadvantages of each. We also explore how important business customers are to the banks and how important it is for you to understand how different business customers are organized and function.

Before we start this chapter, how would you mark yourself, on a scale of 1–10, about your knowledge of the different types of business customers and the different ways they operate?

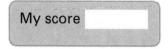

We'll come back to this at the end of the chapter, but for now let's examine the most common business customer types you may come across.

Types of business customers

A number of business structures are used by both large and small business customers, including:

- sole traders;
- partnerships;
- private limited companies;
- public limited companies;
- limited liability partnerships (LLPs);
- other non-personal accounts including charities, trusts, clubs and societies and 'not-for-profit' organizations.

At a corporate level, the largest and most important groupings are limited companies (both public and private), but the other groupings cannot be ignored as they too can fall into the corporate bracket. For example, large firms of lawyers or accountants commonly operate as partnerships or LLPs, and some of the UK's largest 'not-for-profit' organizations also fit comfortably in the corporate arena.

Small and medium enterprises (SMEs)

There is a wide variety of business customers from new start-ups to small, medium or large corporate customers. In order to distinguish between large and smaller businesses, the European Commission introduced the concept of small and medium enterprises (SMEs). This differentiates businesses by employee headcount and annual turnover or balance sheet value. The UK adopts this principle and defines SMEs as shown in Table 1.1.

Table 1.1 SME definition

Category	Employee headcount	Annual turnover (up to and including)	or	Balance sheet value (up to and including)
Micro	Less than 10	€2 million		€2 million
Small	Less than 50	€10 million		€10 million
Medium	Less than 250	€50 million		€43 million

Employee headcount is compulsory and the turnover and/or balance sheet values are secondary. For example, a business with nine employees that turns over £11m with a balance sheet value of £5m would fall into the 'small' business category.

SMEs in the UK account for more than half of UK private sector employment and play a vital role in overall UK productivity and economic growth. The Department for Business, Innovation and Skills (BIS) publication, *Business Population Estimates for the UK and Regions 2016*, reported:

- in 2016, there were 5.5 million private sector businesses in the UK, up by 97,000 or 2 per cent since 2015;

- since 2000, the number of businesses in the UK has increased each year, by 3 per cent on average;

- over 99 per cent of businesses in the UK are small or medium-sized businesses;

- micro-businesses accounted for 32 per cent of employment and 19 per cent of turnover.

SOURCE BIS, 2016

ACTIVITY 1.1

Read the BIS publication and assess how vital SMEs are to the UK economy.

SMEs make a significant contribution to the economy and banks commit huge levels of resources to them. However, not all SME customers warrant or need a dedicated relationship manager; some customers may only need a relationship manager at a particular time in their development. Indeed, it is not economical for the bank for every business customer to have a dedicated relationship manager appointed. Nevertheless, SME customers may still need access to business banking managers to talk to when visiting branches, so many branches have SME-dedicated areas and personnel who can deal with their problems or requirements.

Branches are still very important for SME customers, especially for those, like retailers, who still transact in cash (notes and coin).

Segmentation

Depending on how banks segment their business customers (and no two banks are the same), some business customers may be serviced in a retail branch, a call centre, online, or, dependent on size and complexity, by a dedicated relationship manager or relationship management team. Private banking managers may also look after their private banking customers' businesses.

ACTIVITY 1.2

Find out how your bank segments its business customers, then compare this to how a competitor segments theirs.

Why do you think their methods are different?

How banks segment their business customers is left to each individual bank to decide. None of the UK banks adopt the same criteria; they usually segment initially by turnover, but the levels of turnover differ to suit each bank's individual structure and resources.

To manage the segmentation of customers, banks also segment their people resource. Whilst each business customer will be managed by somebody, the way banks deliver the relationship varies according to each individual bank.

For example, larger corporate customers will have relationship teams to look after them, whereas at the smallest end, the bank services and products may be delivered remotely, using low-touch techniques such as telephone, internet banking or mail.

Some banks also segment their business customers according to the industry or sector in which they operate.

Sector specialists

A quick search through banks' websites reveals a wide variety of sectors in which the banks specialize. They include:

- agriculture (farms and farming, agri-food and equipment finance);
- education (state-funded, independent schools and academies);
- not-for-profit and charities (government and local authorities, social housing, housing associations, churches);
- environment (clean-tech, renewable energy, low-carbon energy and environmental projects);
- financial institutions (funds, specialist finance, FinTechs, insurance);
- healthcare (high-street healthcare, NHS, private acute care hospitals and social care);
- hospitality and leisure (leisure operators, restaurants and the licensed trade, hotels, professional sport, travel);
- manufacturing, transport and logistics;
- aerospace and defence;
- power and utilities (mining and metals, oil and gas);
- professional services (accountants, lawyers, insolvency practitioners, pension administrators);
- real estate (commercial real estate, residential real estate, property investment and development);
- retail and wholesale (clothing, accessories, footwear and department stores);
- household (food and drink, motor);
- technology, media and telecoms.

ACTIVITY 1.3

Compare your bank to another competitor bank.

Does your bank provide specialist managers? If so, which sectors do they cover?

Do your specialist managers work with your bank's relationship managers or do they manage the relationships themselves? Who can you call upon for their expertise?

Most banks provide sector-specialist relationship managers who concentrate their efforts and resources by serving particular segments and industry sectors. This gives the banks a deeper and broader understanding of industry sectors, enabling specialist relationship managers to better understand sector participants' specific needs. Often, specialist managers are supported by in-depth analysis of sector trends via in-house research teams.

Segmentation has a number of benefits for the banks and their customers. The main advantages include the concentration of specialist knowledge which:

- allows a deeper understanding of the idiosyncrasies and trends of each individual sector or industry;
- enables specialist managers to keep up to date with changes in the sector;
- offers more experienced staff members to deal with more complex cases;
- provides wider career opportunities as relationship managers move up the career ladder, gaining valuable experience as they progress.

With the emergence of challenger banks and other new entrants it is clear to see that some of these new entrants segment their relationship management strategies differently from the larger, more traditional banks.

This new breed of banks tend to have flatter organizational structures and are able to differentiate how they manage their customer relationships and service levels. For example, some may provide customers with a dedicated relationship manager or may offer access to virtual, remote relationship managers based in a branch or call centre, where contact is made via telephone or the internet.

This allows for **scalability** whilst controlling servicing costs.

> **Scalability** A system or model that describes an organization's capability to cope and perform under an increased or expanding workload.

In this context, scalability describes a new entrant's ability to grow without being hindered by its structure or available resources, and to maintain or improve profit performance when sales volumes increase.

The main problem for these new challengers is how to lure customers away from the traditional high-street banks and achieve attractive returns by doing so. One answer is to identify and target different segments of the SME market.

The traditional high-street banks generally tend to be product-centric in their approach. Banking relationship management is primarily organized on a geographical basis, rather than on industry sector or life stages. This creates an opportunity for challenger banks if they are able to develop a deeper understanding of the dynamics and risks SMEs face at each stage of their development. For example, a new business start-up will have differing banking needs than a more mature established business. So challenger banks and new entrants may target specific segments within the SME market and offer a differentiated proposition which could be based around industry sectors and/or life stages.

Different industry sectors have different specialized needs. Agriculture, real estate and financial services are examples of sectors with specific SME needs. A farmer will have different banking needs to a house builder. This is evident in the way the traditional high-street banks are employing sector experts in their relationship management populations.

Many SMEs are businesses in early stages of growth and need different banking products than their more mature larger counterparts. A start-up business will not necessarily require forex hedging products or interest rate management products, whereas a large corporate might.

Creating sector specialisms is a good opportunity for challenger banks to penetrate the SME market. Handelsbanken, Aldermore and Shawbrook have all started to implement these types of strategies.

Aldermore Bank is a retail bank offering financial services to small and medium-sized businesses. It provides retail and business savings products, asset finance and sales receivables financing (invoice discounting/factoring) as well as SME commercial and residential mortgages. It does not operate a branch network and serves customers and intermediary partners online, by telephone or face-to-face through its regional offices. As a specialist asset financier it is able to price its assets' finance products more accurately and competitively than a traditional bank with only a general knowledge of specialist asset finance.

Shawbrook Bank Limited is a retail and commercial bank. It has developed a number of niche products for secured lending and other specific areas of consumer finance. The bank offers loans to small and medium-sized businesses that are unable to obtain finance from the main commercial banks.

Another interesting retail strategy is to leverage an SME corporate banking strategy to develop a high-end retail niche. Handelsbanken has attracted highly affluent retail customers who were first introduced to the bank through its SME operations.

CASE STUDY
Handelsbanken

Handelsbanken commenced operations in the UK in 1982 and manages a decentralized network of over 200 branches across the country. Its founding philosophy was to change its objectives from volume to profitability and to move its focus from products to customers.

Handelsbanken's goal is to have higher profitability than the average of banks in home markets. It has a unique approach to geographic location and how its serves local communities. It operates a 'church spire' principle: 'You should not conduct banking operations over a larger area than can be seen from the top of a church spire':

- each branch has a well-defined market area;
- each branch is located where its customers are;
- it is staffed with people who know the market area well;
- it provides a personalized service based on customer requirements and is relationship driven;
- the customer meets a decision-maker with greater local market knowledge;
- it does not use any call centres: the branch is the bank.

Its business model provides local branch managers with full autonomy and accountability. Each branch manager is empowered to make all decisions regarding:

- recruitment;
- costs;
- marketing;
- customer selection and management;
- credit (within their individual discretionary powers);
- pricing.

The measures used by the bank to assess each branch include:

- return on equity;
- cost-to-income ratio;
- profit per employee;
- total profitability.

Staff are paid salaries based on market conditions and individual performance. Branch staff have no sales or activity targets or bonuses. All staff members share in its profit-sharing scheme, Oktogonen. If Handelsbanken achieves its RoE targets all staff receive an allocation of profits paid into the Oktogonen Foundation. Each staff member receives the same allocation of shares and they are only able to withdraw their allocated units when they reach the age of 60.

Customer acquisition is based predominantly on viral marketing (word of mouth) and customer referrals.

It has never needed state liquidity support or capital injections before, during or after the global financial crisis.

Question

Read the following presentation by Mikael Sorensen CEO, Handelsbanken UK, where he explains Handelsbanken's business model. In what ways does it differ from your own bank's business model?

https://nordicfinancialunions.org/wp-content/uploads/NFU-Conference_MikaelSorensen.pdf

Sole traders

Sole traders are businesses that are run by a single proprietor who manages and runs a business in their own name. There is no legal difference between the owner of the business and the business itself. They may or may not have employees.

A **sole trader** has unlimited liability for all the debts and liabilities of the business and is in complete control of his or her business.

In order to set up as a sole trader, all that an individual needs to do is open a separate business bank account and inform HM Revenue & Customs that they are operating a business. They can be individuals trading in their own name or using a registered trading name, for example, Georgina Formby trading as Formby's Window Cleaning Services.

Sole traders do not need to produce financial accounts in a way that a limited company does. However, they do need to keep accurate records of business income and expenditure in order to calculate their tax liabilities. Sole traders are taxed on the profits the business generates, not on what the proprietor takes out of the business. They can, however, offset some business expenses against the tax paid on their profits.

> **A sole trader** A self-employed person who is the sole owner of their business. Sole traders may or may not have employees.

Advantages of being a sole trader

- Sole traders are independent and responsible for their own business decisions (rather than as an employee).
- The business is easy to set up, with few or no formalities.
- All profits go to the proprietor.
- They do not have to file their accounts in the public domain.

Disadvantages of being a sole trader

- Proprietors are personally liable for any debts incurred by the business and have no protection for their own personal assets.
- They pay tax on their profits, not on what they take out of the business.
- Because there is no financial information in the public domain, access to credit may be more difficult.
- Problems can occur if the proprietor falls ill or is absent from the business.
- If the proprietor dies, the business dies with them.

Partnerships

Partnerships are determined by the Partnership Act 1890, which defines a **partnership** as two or more people who come together to conduct business with the *aim* of making a profit. Note: it is the intention to make a profit that is important; if they do not actually make a profit, this does not disqualify them as a partnership.

The partners form a partnership, or firm, and in England and Wales it is the partners who are liable for obligations such as debt. The partnership itself is not a legal entity and there are no formalities for a business relationship to become a partnership.

Even if the individual members of the firm don't intend to form a partnership, if that is how they hold themselves out to the public, then their relationship will be deemed a partnership and all partners will be liable for the obligations of the partnership.

> **Partnership**   A legal business structure that is formed by two or more individuals to carry on a business as co-owners.

Whilst it is not essential to have a **partnership agreement**, it is desirable, because the partnership agreement sets out the relationship the partners have between themselves.

If there is no written partnership agreement, then the partnership is governed by the rules of the Partnership Act 1890. If it does have a written partnership agreement, then the partnership is governed by the rules contained within that agreement.

Partnership agreements usually state the number of partners, the partnership name and the arrangements they have agreed, such as how profits (and losses) of the firm will be apportioned. It should also set out what is to happen in the event that one or more partners leave (including on retirement or death) or if new people join the partnership. It should include how the partnership's assets will be divided in the event of the firm being dissolved.

> **Partnership agreement**   A written document that establishes the rights and responsibilities of each party within the partnership.

Upon the death of a partner or a partner leaving the partnership, the outgoing partner (or their estate) is liable for debts incurred by the partnership before the date of death or leaving. An incoming partner will only be liable for debts incurred after the date of entry.

ACTIVITY 1.4

Contact your advances/securities department and ask them to send you an example of a partnership agreement. Read the agreement to see what areas it covers.

What would happen in the event of the death or incapacitation of one of the partners?

Joint and several liability means that all of the parties are jointly liable for the debts equally or as an individual for the whole debt. Should any partner be unable to meet their share, then the others would have to meet the deficit.

For example, Sue and Mel operate a partnership and are equal partners. They have a business loan with a debt of £250,000. Sue's net worth is fairly modest at £20,000 and Mel is much wealthier, with a net worth of £1m.

If they default on their borrowing, the lender would not seek to reclaim half the debt from each partner; it can and would approach all of them to repay the whole amount. Although they are equal partners, one might end up paying more than the other because the bank would pursue both jointly and individually (severally) until the entire debt is repaid. If, however, the partnership was a 50/50 split, and in the example Mel paid more than 50 per cent of the debt to the bank, she would have a right to sue Sue for the difference.

When opening a bank account for a partnership, the bank's mandate (account opening documentation) will include a joint and several liability clause rendering each partner liable for the debts of the partnership to the bank. All partners must sign the bank account mandate, but in that mandate they can set out their own signing arrangements for payments from the account, for example 'any two partners to sign'.

> **Joint and several liability**   When two or more people agree to pay a debt (or similar obligation). It is a joint promise that, if and when the need arises, the partners all agree to pay off the debt together. This means each partner is liable to pay the full amount of the debt, not just his or her own share.

As any one partner can bind (ie commit) the partnership, if it is in the ordinary course of business, then prudence would dictate that all partners sign a facility letter (the formal lending agreement) when borrowing. This will also provide some additional protection to the lending banker should there be a future legal dispute.

A partnership is permitted to trade using all the surnames of the partners or it may trade under a business name and, if it does, it must comply with the provisions of the Business Names Act 1985, which sets out the requirements for business names and prevents certain words that could cause confusion or offence from being used in business names.

If the word 'company' or an abbreviation of it such as 'Co' is used in a business name, it is deemed to be a partnership. However, should the word 'limited' follow the word 'company', or any abbreviated version, then it is a limited company. For example:

Goulding, Abley Co = a partnership

Goulding, Abley Co Ltd = a limited company

Partners are taxed as individuals on their share of the profits and not what they take from the business. The business entity itself does not pay tax.

Advantages of a partnership

- Partnerships are easy to set up and run (few formalities are required).
- Raising capital (funds) may be easier with more owners.
- Partners are taxed as individuals and not as a business entity.
- Employees may be attracted to work for the partnership if they have an opportunity to become a partner.

Disadvantages of a partnership

- Like sole traders, the partners are individually liable for the partnership debts.
- Partners are subject to the actions of other partners.
- Shared decision-making means individual partners do not have full control, which could lead to disagreements.
- Complications could arise in the event of the untimely death of a partner.
- Repayment of debt is on a joint and several basis, even if the partners operate on an equal basis.

Limited companies (corporate personality)

One of the main advantages of incorporation (becoming a **limited company**) is that the process involves the creation of a separate legal entity. This was determined in the legal case *Salomon v. Salomon* (1897) which established the principle of separate corporate personality.

CASE STUDY
Salomon v. Salomon (1896)

In 1892, Mr Salomon transferred his boot-making business, initially run as a sole trader, to a limited liability company (Salomon Ltd) with the shareholders comprising himself and his family. The company had been formed by Mr Salomon with the clear intention of taking advantage of the limited liability afforded by the Companies Act 1862, which required a private limited company to have seven members/shareholders (the later Companies Act 2006 requires only one).

In order to achieve this, Mr Salomon offered one share in the company each to six of his relatives, and took 20,001 shares for himself. It was apparent, therefore, that he had no intention of affording control of the company to anyone other than himself. On incorporation, Mr Salomon gave the company a £10,000 loan, secured by a floating charge over the assets of the company.

Soon after Mr Salomon incorporated the business, the business failed and it defaulted on its interest payments to its largest (secured) creditor, Broderip. The company was put into liquidation.

Broderip sued to enforce its (debenture) security in October 1893. Broderip was repaid £5,000. This left £1,055 company assets remaining, which Salomon claimed under his original debentures. This left nothing for the unsecured creditors who were owed £7,773. When the company failed, the company's liquidator contended that Mr Salomon's debentures should not be honoured, and Mr Salomon should be made personally liable for the company's debts.

Mr Salomon sued.

The High Court and Court of Appeal granted the liquidator's claim, holding that the other shareholders were Mr Salomon's 'proxies' and had no part to play in running the business.

Mr Salomon appealed to the House of Lords.

On appeal, the House of Lords unanimously held that the company was duly incorporated and that the limited company was an independent, legal entity and was therefore separate and independent from its shareholders. It therefore upheld Mr Salomon's appeal.

Lord Macnaghten made the observation that the judgments of the lower courts surmised that the company was not valid because its members (other than Mr Salomon) took no role in the running of the business, but that this was a misconception because the Companies Act contained no such requirement. Indeed, Mr Salomon had done no more than the Act required him to do, and was therefore entitled to take full advantage of its protection.

With the decision in the *Salomon v. Salomon* case study, the House of Lords firmly established the principle of separate corporate personality. This case also determined that in a limited company, the shareholders (owners) are only liable to any amount which remains unpaid on their shares. If shares have been fully paid up, then the shareholders have no further liability for the debts of the company. The case also established that a company as a separate legal entity has perpetual succession which means that the company lives on in perpetuity no matter what happens to its shareholders.

> **A limited company**   A type of legal structure that provides limited personal liability to the owner(s) of the business.

REGULATION
The Companies Act 2006

The Companies Act 2006 is the main piece of legislation which governs company law in the UK. The Act applies to all companies whether they are private limited companies, public limited companies or not-for-profit companies, such as charities. To source updates, visit: www.legislation.gov.uk/ukpga/2006

Private limited companies (Ltd Company) and public limited companies (PLCs)

The main distinction between a private limited company and a public limited company is that public limited companies must have shares that are capable of being transferred without any restriction. So, whilst only public companies can be quoted on the stock exchange (a quoted company), they do not have to be quoted. Indeed, many PLCs are not publicly quoted; they take the status to add prestige to the business, which can lead to increased credibility and confidence in the business. A PLC must have a minimum issued share capital of £50,000, of which 25 per cent (£12,500) must be fully paid up. It must have a minimum of two directors, and a suitably qualified company secretary.

> **Board of directors**   The individuals who run the organization on behalf of its shareholders.

Directors

The Companies Act 2006 codified the rules on directorships stating:

- A company is managed by the **board of directors** and the directors run the business on behalf of the shareholders.
- All companies are required to have at least one director but a public company must have two.
- A company director must be at least 16 years of age on the date of appointment.

If a person has a job title with the word 'director' included in it, it would suggest that they are a director of the company. This is not always the case. You may come across titles such as finance director or sales director; it does not necessarily mean they have a seat on the board of directors.

Interestingly, the Companies Act does not actually specify what a director is. However, the law states that if a person participates in the decision-making process of a company then they are a director of the company whether they have the title of director or not.

Shadow directors

The term 'shadow director' is regulated and defined by the Companies Act 2006. The Act states that a shadow director is 'a person in accordance with whose directions or instructions the directors of a company are accustomed to act'. This definition can apply to individuals or to corporate bodies (companies).

However, a person will not be deemed to be a shadow director of a company if they are a professional advisor to a company and its directors act on the basis of advice given to them solely in that capacity. So, an accountant who advises a company's directors on issues relating to compliance with their various responsibilities will not be considered to be a shadow director.

Where a company is a parent company, there is a real possibility of it being deemed as acting as a shadow director of its subsidiary companies if it has overall control of its subsidiaries. If its subsidiary's directors are wholly accustomed to acting on the parent's instructions then it could be classed as a shadow director. However, if the subsidiary's directors do not always act on the instructions of the parent, then the parent company will not be considered a shadow director.

Restrictions on becoming a director

The Company Directors Disqualification Act 1986 provides that persons who are undischarged bankrupts or subject to a **bankruptcy** restrictions order may not act as directors of limited companies. It is an offence for persons to act in contravention of these provisions (www.legislation.gov. uk, 2017).

You may come across occasions where somebody is purporting *not* to be a company director, but in practice they are. Remember, the Companies Act 2006 states that if a person participates in the decision-making process of a company then they are a director of the company whether they have the title of director or not. You must always be on your guard.

A (TRUE) CASE STUDY
Shadow directors and the importance of the Disqualified Directors Register

My role, as a lending banker, was titled 'relationship director'. This did not mean I was a director of the bank; it was simply a title the bank chose for some of their more senior relationship managers. I had inherited an account from another relationship director who had left the bank. I arranged to visit the company to introduce myself and to review their banking facilities.

I met the managing director who also introduced me to her husband who was the sales manager. The MD kept deferring to her husband, particularly when we were renegotiating the banking facilities.

I left the meeting and was driving back to the office. Something did not feel right. I telephoned my assistant manager and enquired about the sales manager as the previous relationship director's files were silent about his involvement in the business.

When I returned to the office, my assistant met me with the news that he had searched the Disqualified Directors Register at Companies House and discovered the person in question was an undischarged bankrupt. As an undischarged bankrupt he could not be a director of the company without the Court's permission. This made him, in my view, a shadow director.

I telephoned the husband and asked him whether he was an undischarged bankrupt. He admitted he was, but had not informed the bank or the court as he was 'embarrassed' about his past business failures.

I reported our findings through the bank's internal channels and the Official Receiver's office was notified. Following an initial investigation by the Insolvency Service and a full criminal investigation, he was prosecuted by the Department for Business, Innovation and Skills (BIS). I was brought before the Court to provide evidence and he was subsequently convicted and imprisoned. The business failed soon after and the company was dissolved.

Questions

1 Why do you think that I felt something wasn't right?

2 Why do you think my assistant examined the Disqualified Directors Register?

3 Why do you think I needed to report this case to the authorities?

Bankruptcy   A way for individuals to deal with debts they cannot pay. It only applies to personal customers (including sole traders) and not companies or partnerships.

Formation procedures

Limited companies have three key documents:

- the certificate of incorporation (its birth certificate) which is issued by the Registrar of Companies (**Companies House**) – in the case of PLCs the certificate of incorporation is known as a trading certificate;

- the **Memorandum of Association** which determines the company's relations with the rest of the world;

- the **Articles of Association** which regulate the company's internal operations such as the borrowing powers of the directors.

> **Companies House** The UK's registrar of companies. All companies have to be incorporated and registered with Companies House. All registered limited companies must file their annual accounts and annual returns with the registrar. All of these documents are in the public domain.

Memorandum of Association

The 2006 Act radically revised the requirements in the Memorandum of Association which now has only two clauses:

- a statement that the company has been formed;
- a statement that the subscribers (the founding shareholders) have taken at least one share of a specified value in the new company.

Prior to the 2006 Act, the Memorandum was more encompassing. It set out:

- the name of the company;
- its location (within the UK);
- its objects (or objectives);
- its authorized capital (the maximum that it would be able to raise).

Companies founded before the 2006 Act can continue to have these clauses in their Memorandum. However, the 2006 Act states that these clauses will now be regarded as forming part of the Articles of Association.

Articles of Association

The Articles of Association form the basis of the shareholders' relationship with the company and also govern the relationship of the shareholders with each other. The Articles sets down clauses relating to:

- share capital;
- share certificates;
- transfers of shares;
- alterations of capital;
- company meetings;
- voting rights;
- directors;
- financial accounts;
- audit.

The 2006 Act has published model Articles of Association in a standard form. A company can choose to:

- adopt these as they stand;
- adopt them and alter any Articles as appropriate; or
- prepare their own Articles of Association.

The legal powers of the board of directors are simply to act on behalf of their company. Their powers are not independent of the company and they may not carry out, in the name of the company, any activity that the company itself is not entitled to perform.

In the past, a company's activities were subject to the rule of 'ultra vires' (beyond the powers of). This meant that a company was only entitled to carry out activities that were, expressly or implicitly, provided for in the objects clauses of their Articles. That led to companies drafting very lengthy objects clauses as they sought to give themselves a wide range of powers to ensure that their activities would never be called into question.

The Companies Act 2006 now provides that, unless a company's Articles specifically restrict the objects of the company, the company's objects are unrestricted.

The 2006 Act adds that where a third party deals with a company in good faith, the power of the directors to bind the company, or to authorize others to do so, is deemed to be free of any restriction. So any third party (including the bank) is not bound to enquire as to whether there is any constitutional limitation on the directors' powers. That said, when lending to a limited company, most banks still obtain a board resolution from the company confirming that it is acting under the correct authorities.

Group structures

Some large and medium-sized companies operate within a group structure. Typically, this would have a holding company at the top and operational subsidiaries, which would be separate limited companies, underneath. Such separation of subsidiaries may be for geographical, regulatory, marketing or functional reasons.

The holding, or parent, company has to report consolidated accounts in its annual return to Companies House, together with a breakdown of the results of its subsidiaries. Each subsidiary also has to make an annual return to Companies House.

The majority of subsidiaries are wholly owned, which means the parent company owns 100 per cent of the shares. Where investments are not wholly owned they are classified as:

- *A simple investment* whereby the holding company exercises limited influence on the investment or an investment which is expected to be held over a short term.
- *Associates* when the holding company has a participating interest and exercises significant influence.
- *Joint ventures* when a holding company holds a long-term interest and shares control under a contractual agreement.
- *Subsidiaries* when the holding company has the ability to direct their operating and financial policies with a view to gaining economic benefits.

Figure 1.1 presents a typical group structure.

Figure 1.1 An example of a group structure

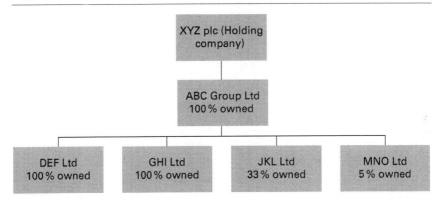

Question

Which businesses are controlled by XYZ Ltd?

ABC Ltd	Yes/No
DEF Ltd	Yes/No
GHI Ltd	Yes/No
JKL Ltd	Yes/No
MNO Ltd	Yes/No

Write down your answer before referring to the answer provided in Appendix 1.1.

Advantages of a limited company

- separate corporate personality;
- perpetual succession;
- limited liability;

Disadvantages of a limited company

- formal and costly procedures for incorporation and ongoing administration;
- information has to be disclosed and held in the public domain;
- more onerous accounting requirements with annual submissions of financial information (unless exempt);
- more onerous record-keeping and greater legal duties, responsibilities and formalities for its directors.

Limited liability partnerships (LLPs)

LLPs are governed by the Limited Liability Partnerships Act 2000 and the Limited Liability Partnerships Regulations 2001.

A **limited liability partnership (LLP)** is an alternative business structure that provides the benefits of limited liability to its members, those who own the LLP. It is a legal entity that is separate from its members in that each member acts as an agent of the LLP.

LLPs can be described as hybrid entities between normal partnerships and limited companies. The main difference between LLPs and limited companies is the treatment of tax. Profits are shared amongst members of an LLP, and individual members (not the LLP) pay income tax on these profits.

The members subscribe to an incorporation document and this is filed with the Registrar of Companies in the same way as a company. As such, the details of the LLP are in the public domain. LLPs also have to file their accounts with Companies House in the same way as a limited company.

The LLP is a separate legal entity from its members and is responsible for its own debts. When lending to an LLP it should be treated in the same way as a limited company. As the LLP has a separate legal personality there is no recourse against the members of the LLP. If a lender wanted to secure the borrowings of the individual members of the LLP, they would have to take personal guarantees from each of the members of the LLP, in the same way as they would when dealing with the directors of a limited company.

LLPs have become a common form of business structure; for example, solicitors, auditors and surveyors often constitute themselves as limited liability partnerships. They use LLP status as this allows them to limit their liability against any potential litigation claims that may be significant enough to threaten the partners' own personal assets.

Limited liability partnership (LLP) A legal structure that provides its members limited liability for the debts and obligations of the partnership. It is therefore a hybrid between a partnership and a limited company.

Advantages of an LLP

- the LLP establishes limited liability for its members;
- its members are taxed as individuals and not as a company;
- the LLP continues in the event of the death of one of its members.

Disadvantages of an LLP

- an LLP is more formal and costly to run than a traditional partnership;
- complications can arise in the event of disputes between its members;
- information about the business is held in the public domain including its financial accounts which have to be sent to Companies House.

Published accounts

Under the 2006 Act every company (private limited companies, PLCs and LLPs) must keep adequate accounting records. These records must contain:

- details of income and expenditure over a period (normally produced on an annual basis);
- a record of the company's assets and liabilities (what the company owns and what it owes).

These records must be kept at the company's registered office for at least three years from the date on which they are made (in the case of a private company) and for six years (in the case of a public company).

The Act requires all private and public limited companies to prepare annual accounts which should comprise:

- a Statement of Comprehensive Income (income and expenditure) formerly known as the profit and loss account;
- a Statement of Financial Position (assets, liabilities and capital) formally known as the balance sheet;
- a Statement of Cash Flows formerly known as the cash flow statement;
- notes to the accounts;
- a directors' report.

Publicly quoted companies that have a full listing on the UK Stock Exchange must also prepare a remuneration report containing details of the remuneration policies and practices in relation to the directors and senior staff.

Filing accounts

It is the responsibility of a company's directors to ensure that its accounts and reports are filed with the Registrar of Companies within set deadlines. Different deadlines apply to private and public companies (UK Government, 2017):

- Private companies are required to file their accounts and reports no more than nine months after the end of their last accounting period.
- Public companies are required to file their accounts no more than six months from the end of the accounting period.

Reporting regimes

There is a separate reporting regime for micro-, small and medium-sized businesses. The 2006 Act created a separate reporting regime for 'small companies' (which includes micro-enterprises) and medium-sized businesses. To qualify, a company must satisfy at least two of the following size criteria in both the reporting year and in the previous financial year:

- its turnover must not exceed £10.2 million;
- its Statement of Financial Position total must not exceed £5.1 million;
- it must have no more than 50 employees.

Filing accounts under the small companies' regime

Companies within the small companies' regime need not file full accounts with the Registrar. They are only obliged to file their Statement of Financial Position and, if the accounts have been audited, a copy of the auditor's report (unless they are exempt from audit), together with the notes to the accounts.

They may choose to file a Statement of Comprehensive Income (profit and loss account) and a directors' report, although they are not obliged to do so. If a company chooses not to file its Statement of Comprehensive Income and directors' report the Statement of Financial Position must contain a statement to the effect that the company's annual accounts and directors' report have been prepared in accordance with the provisions of the small companies' regime.

Abbreviated accounts

Before January 2016 companies within the small companies' regime may have made an additional choice to file abbreviated accounts with the Registrar. Abbreviated accounts comprise a Statement of Financial Position and notes to the accounts drawn up under the rules laid down under the 2006 Act.

Where abbreviated accounts were prepared on this basis and where the company's full accounts have been audited, they must include an auditor's statement that in the opinion of the auditors the company was entitled to file abbreviated accounts.

Companies which qualified as medium-sized could also choose to file abbreviated accounts with the Registrar rather than their full accounts.

A company would qualify as being medium-sized if it met two out of three of the following conditions in the reporting year and the previous financial year:

- turnover: not more than £3 million;
- Statement of Financial Position total: not more than £18 million;
- number of employees, not more than 250.

Abbreviated accounts abolished

The Companies, Partnerships and Groups (Accounts and Reports) Regulations 2015 abolished abbreviated accounts. This means that abbreviated accounts cannot be filed for accounting periods beginning on or after 1 January 2016.

This introduced the concept of **abridged accounts** which have replaced abbreviated accounts. For accounting periods that start on or after 1 January 2016 small companies basically have three choices:

- they may prepare micro-entity accounts (if they are within the threshold);
- they may prepare abridged accounts; or
- they may prepare a full set of accounts.

In all cases a small company can choose whether or not to file their directors' report and Statement of Comprehensive Income. Companies that do not opt to file their directors' report and Statement of Comprehensive Income are said to be filing 'filleted' accounts. In every case, however, the company must file at least the Statement of Financial Position and any related notes to the accounts.

The difference between abridged and abbreviated accounts

You may think abridged accounts are the same as abbreviated accounts, but they are not; there are some subtle differences.

Previously, the directors would prepare full accounts for the members and would then decide whether or not to abbreviate them for the public record. Abridged accounts now mean that companies must prepare and file the same set of accounts for their members and for the public record. This means that a company will decide at the point they are preparing their accounts whether or not to abridge them (or to prepare micro-entity accounts).

If they opt to file abridged accounts they must include a statement in the Statement of Financial Position that the members have agreed to the preparation of abridged accounts for the accounting period.

The decision to abridge all or part of the accounts cannot be taken by the directors alone; it must be agreed by all members without any dissent and consent must be obtained each time the accounts are produced. A statement by the company that all members have consented must be filed with the Registrar of Companies each time the accounts are produced (UK Government, 2016).

> **Abridged accounts**   Financial statements that cover a full accounting period but omit detailed financial information.

Appointment of auditors

Normally a company must appoint an auditor for each financial year.

In the case of a public company, the appointment is made at the company's AGM where the company's annual accounts and financial reports are presented to its members (shareholders).

The 2006 Act also sets out disclosure requirements either in the notes to the company's accounts, in the directors' report or in the auditor's own report. It must include:

- the terms on which the auditor is appointed, remunerated or performed their duties;
- non-audit services provided by the company's auditor and the amount of remuneration paid for those services.

Audit exemptions

Small companies may claim exemption from audit. If the company meets the qualification criteria for the exemption, it may submit unaudited accounts. In this case they must make the following disclosures in the notes to their accounts:

- the auditor's name (if the auditor was a firm, the name of the senior statutory auditor);
- whether the auditor's report was qualified or unqualified, and, if the report was qualified, what the qualification was.

The contents of accounts

Micro-entity accounts

A micro-entity is required to prepare accounts that contain:

- a Statement of Financial Position (compulsory);
- any notes to the accounts (compulsory);
- a Statement of Comprehensive Income (optional);
- a directors' report (optional);
- an auditor's report (unless the company is claiming exemption from audit as a small company).

The Statement of Financial Position must contain a statement that the accounts have been prepared in accordance with the micro-entity provisions. This statement should appear in the original accounts as well as the copy sent to Companies House.

Micro-entities do not have to deliver a copy of the directors' report or a Statement of Comprehensive Income to Companies House. However, if they opt not to deliver a copy of the Statement of Comprehensive Income the company must state this on the Statement of Financial Position.

Small company accounts

Generally, small company accounts prepared for members include:

- a Statement of Financial Position (compulsory);
- notes to the accounts (compulsory);
- a Statement of Comprehensive Income (optional);
- a directors' report (optional);
- an auditor's report (unless the company is claiming exemption from audit as a small company).

The Statement of Financial Position must contain a statement that the accounts have been prepared in accordance with the special provisions applicable to companies subject to the small companies' regime.

Small companies do not have to deliver a copy of the directors' report or a Statement of Comprehensive Income to Companies House. If they opt not to deliver a copy of the Statement of Comprehensive Income or directors' report, the company must state this on the Statement of Financial Position.

Medium-sized company accounts

Medium-sized accounts must include:

- a Statement of Financial Position (compulsory);
- notes to the accounts (compulsory);
- a Statement of Comprehensive Income (optional);
- group accounts (if appropriate);
- a directors' report including a business review or strategic report;
- an auditor's report that includes the name of the registered auditor (unless the company is exempt from audit).

Exemptions available to medium-sized companies

Medium-sized companies may omit certain information from the business review or strategic report in their directors' report if they consider it to be commercially sensitive information and prejudicial to their trading activities. There are no special rules for medium-sized groups. A medium-sized parent company must prepare group accounts and submit them to Companies House.

Before we look at other non-personal accounts, consider the business structures in the following case study.

CASE STUDY
Bernadette and Sam

Bernadette and Sam work together writing books for ABC Global Publishing Inc. Bernadette drafts the core text and Sam edits the content and provides academic oversight. They share their income earned on a 50:50 equal split. Sam owns a limited company and the company invoices the publishers for the full amount agreed. Once payment is received, Bernadette (who does not operate a company) submits an invoice to Sam's company for payment.

Questions

What business types are Bernadette and Sam? Write down your answer before referring to the answer provided in Appendix 1.2.

Other non-personal accounts

Banks also deal with a number of other non-personal accounts. These include accounts for:

- clubs, associations and societies;
- charities and not-for-profit organizations;
- executors and administrators;
- trustees.

Clubs, associations and societies

Clubs, associations and societies involve groups of people with a common goal, for example a social club or sports club. They are generally run by committees and have their own rules and regulations.

The club, association or society has no separate legal identity and therefore cannot be sued for any debts. Think of a cricket club, for example: the individual members are not liable for any debts the club incurs at the instigation of the ruling officers or committee members. That is why, when a bank lends to a club or society, it will ensure that someone is liable for the debt. Such an advance would be made into a separate account opened by the responsible officers or in the name of the club, with the officers often personally guaranteeing some or all of the borrowings.

Charities and not-for-profit organizations

A **charity** is a **not-for-profit organization** established to benefit the public. Its purpose and activities have to meet certain legal criteria in order to be defined as charitable. In the main, charities have to be registered with the Charity Commission, which grants them charitable status and issues a registered charity number. The Charity Commission is a government organization and exists to give the public confidence in the integrity of organizations that hold charitable status.

> **Charity** or **not-for-profit organization**   A legal structure where the organization does not earn profits for its owners. All of the money earned by or donated to it is used in pursuing the organization's objectives.

There are a number of advantages to registering as a charity:

- registered charities can claim back tax paid by donors, using schemes such as Gift Aid or payroll giving (ie Give As You Earn);
- many charitable foundations will only donate to registered charities;
- charitable status enhances the credibility of the organization when asking for donations from the public.

A disadvantage of registration is the bureaucracy involved. Charities need to send regular (usually on an annual basis) information to the Charity

Commission and conform to its requirements. Many of these requirements are basic good practice, and a charity's auditor would make sure that it complied with the Commission's requirements as part of the audit process.

Some charities, for example some universities, museums, churches and schools, may enjoy exempt status. This is because they are deemed to be adequately supervised by, or accountable to, another body or authority. These charities do not have a registered number.

Some charities can also be limited by guarantee. They adopt this structure because it limits the liability of the management committee, normally its trustees, just as it would if it were a limited company. Choosing to be limited by guarantee means that the members guarantee to meet the debts of the charity, if necessary, but only up to an agreed limit, usually just a nominal £1.

An organization can be a not-for-profit organization without being a registered charity.

Executors and administrators

Executors and administrators are the personal representatives tasked with carrying out the procedures necessary to distribute the estate of someone who has died or is otherwise incapacitated.

If a deceased person has left a will, they are said to have died *testate*. The people administering the estate, as detailed in the will, are known as the executors. If the deceased did not leave a will, they are said to have died *intestate*. In this situation, the people administering the estate are known as the administrators.

Sometimes lending facilities are required to pay death duties prior to the winding-up of an estate. These are commonly known as probate loans, and if the personal representatives borrow, they are personally liable for the debt, although repayment is usually sourced from the sale of assets from the deceased's estate.

Trusts

A **trust** (also known as a settlement) is a method by which the owner of an asset (the settlor) can distribute that asset for the benefit of another person or persons (the beneficiaries) but without allowing them to exert control over the asset.

The settlor is the person who creates the trust and who originally owned the assets placed in the trust (the trust property).

A trust can arise from the death of the settlor and can be created under the terms of a will, or from a wish by the settlor to establish a trust whilst they are living. In this case, once the trust is created, the settlor has no rights to the property after that date (although a settlor may be a trustee and exercise their rights as a trustee).

The beneficiaries are the people or organizations that will benefit from the trust property. They may be named specifically or more generally as a group, such as 'all of my children'. The trustees are the people, appointed by the settlor, who will take legal ownership of the trust assets and will administer the assets under the terms of the trust deed. The trustee(s), who can include the settlor, are named in the trust deed.

Trustees must:

- Act in accordance with the terms of the trust deed; if the trust deed gives them discretion to exercise their powers, the agreement of all of the trustees is required before a course of action can be taken.

- Act in the best interests of the beneficiaries, balancing fairly the rights of different beneficiaries.

The banking needs of the trustees will depend on the nature of the trust itself.

> **Trust**   A legal structure that is designed to hold and administer money or other assets on behalf of another party. There are three key people involved in any trust: the settlor, the person who puts the assets or money into the trust; the beneficiary, the person who benefits from the trust; and the trustee, the person who manages the trust.

As we started this chapter, you were asked to score yourself about the knowledge you had on the different types of business customers. How would you score yourself now?

> My score [   ]

How have your views changed? Are there any areas you need to review, revisit or discuss further with a colleague or with your line manager?

Chapter summary

In this chapter we have explored:

- how banks segment their customers;
- the types of business relationship managers can encounter;
- the legal regimes under which corporates and other business types operate;
- the considerations when lending money to differing business types.

Objective check

1 What are the different types of business customers?

2 What are the benefits of segmenting customers?

3 Think about how a bank might segment its customers. Why might different banks take different approaches to segmentation?

4 What legal aspects need to be considered when dealing with different customer types?

Further reading

A Guide to Corporate Governance Practices in the European Union [online]. Available at: https://www.ifc.org/wps/wcm/connect/c44d6d0047b7597bb7 d9f7299ede9589/CG_Practices_in_EU_Guide.pdf?MOD=AJPERES

Running a Limited Company, UK government information on running a limited company [online]. Available at: https://www.gov.uk/browse/business/ limited-company

Set up a Business, UK government guidance on setting up a business [online]. Available at: https://www.gov.uk/set-up-business

Visit the major bank websites and read through their SME/corporate offerings

www.legislation.gov.uk (2017) *The Companies Act 2006* [online]. Available at: https://www.legislation.gov.uk/ukpga/2006/46/contents [accessed 26 November 2017]

References

Department of Business, Innovation and Skills (BIS) (2016) *Business Population Estimates for the UK and Regions, 2016* [online]. Available at: https://www.gov.uk/government/uploads/system/uploads/attachment_data/file/559219/bpe_2016_statistical_release.pdf [accessed 26 November 2017]

UK Government (2016) *Accounts Advice for Small Companies* [online]. Available at: https://companieshouse.blog.gov.uk/2016/10/06/accounts-advice-for-small-companies/ [accessed 26 November 2017]

UK Government (2017) *Life of a Company: Annual Requirements* [online]. Available at: https://www.gov.uk/government/publications/life-of-a-company-annual-requirements [accessed 26 November 2017]

Appendix 1.1

	Control	Reason
ABC Ltd	Yes	(100% owned)
DEF Ltd	Yes	(100% owned)
GHI Ltd	Yes	(Majority owned)
JKL Ltd	No	(Minority owned)
MNO Ltd	No	(Minority owned)

Appendix 1.2

Bernadette operates as sole trader. She invoices Sam's limited company in her own name.

Sam operates through a limited company.

Whilst they may work in partnership together, they are not partners because Sam's limited company has established separate corporate personality. Partnership would only exist if Sam did not use the limited company.

If Sam did not use a limited company and chose to invoice in his own name, neither would be classed as sole traders as they would be considered to be in partnership. Remember: even if you don't intend to be a partnership, if that's how you hold yourself out to the public, then your relationship will be deemed to be a partnership and all partners would be liable for the obligations and debts of the partnership.

02

Products and services

This chapter reviews some of the most common products and services used by retail and business customers. It examines how customers use these products and why.

LEARNING OBJECTIVES

After completing this chapter, you will be able to:

- analyse the benefits of products and services available to personal and business customers;
- analyse the ways in which a business's working capital needs can be met;
- evaluate the different lending facilities available to a business that is looking to invest in non-current assets;
- assess how businesses trading outside of the UK can be supported with products designed specifically to meet the needs of importers and exporters;
- review the risks involved when trading outside of the UK.

Introduction

Over time banks have developed a huge range of products and services to meet customer needs and wants. Sometimes customers may be unaware that they actually have a need or that the bank can provide a product or service to help them. Products and services are designed to help your customer to mitigate risk.

Some products and services are quite technical and complex and will be made available through specialist managers, such as sales receivables personnel (invoice discounting or factoring), international trade managers (currency risk mitigation), treasury managers (interest rate hedging) and private banking relationship managers (private banking products).

On these occasions you will need to involve these specialist providers and whilst you do not need to be an expert, you still need to have a basic understanding of how they work. That is how you can best help your customers and your bank by meeting their needs.

Before we start, how would you mark yourself on a scale of 1–10 about your understanding of the products and services banks provide to both retail and business customers?

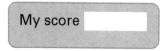

We'll come back to this at the end of the chapter, but for now let's start by looking at the common products and services that are available to retail bank customers.

Bank accounts

In order to access the products and services banks offer, you must have a bank account.

There are many different types of bank accounts, but the most common are a traditional current account or a basic bank account.

Current accounts

This is a bank account where customers can receive deposits and access different payment systems. Its features include:

- a safe and secure depository for money;
- interest may or may not be paid on credit balances;
- a cheque book is provided to make payments;
- a cash card is provided enabling cash to be withdrawn via ATM networks 24/7 and, if eligible, a debit card is also supplied which allows customers to transact in shops or online;

- provision of statements (online or paper) enabling customers to track deposits and withdrawals;
- allows for payments via standing orders or direct debits;
- can provide access to credit.

Banks can also provide customers with bank accounts that offer additional features. For a small monthly fee customers can receive additional benefits such as annual travel insurance, gadget insurance (eg mobile phones) and preferential rates on overdraft. These are known as 'packaged accounts'.

The basic bank account

This is an initiative by UK banks, the government and voluntary organizations to help the financially excluded. Financial *exclusion* is a term used to describe a lack of access to, and use of, a range of financial services. Basic bank accounts aim to support financial *inclusion* for those without a bank account.

The financially excluded are people who are most likely to be on the margins of financial services and may include people who are unemployed, unable to work through sickness or disability, pensioners and some people living on benefits.

Basic accounts are designed for people who might not meet the bank's criteria for opening a standard current account or who want to ensure that they cannot overdraw their account. Account features typically include the ability to receive payments, eg pensions and benefits, credited directly to the account, and to make withdrawals by plastic cards through cash machines. They also offer the facility to pay bills by direct debit and standing orders. They do not provide a cheque book and do not offer overdraft facilities.

There are two types of basic banking accounts: those operated through bank branches and ATMs, and those that can also be operated through post office counters.

Basic accounts are regarded as a convenient stepping stone to fuller-featured accounts for people without previous banking relationships. Banks will, when appropriate, move customers from a basic account to a standard current account, when circumstances warrant.

Savings and investments accounts

Depositors can accumulate funds and receive a return on this investment. Interest paid for these credit balances can be variable or fixed for a period.

Variable rates fluctuate with base rate, fixed rates do not. The same fixed rate applies for the duration of the investment, whether base rates go up or down. Fixed rate deposits can have restrictions on withdrawals and are subject to an agreed notice period. Because customers are 'tying their funds up', they expect a higher rate of return for their investments.

At July 2018, interest rates for these accounts are at an all-time low due to an extended period of low interest rates following the global financial crisis.

Premium banking

Premium bank accounts, also known as packaged accounts, are provided to mass-affluent customers. They are current accounts that come with a 'package' of extra features such as mobile phone insurance, travel insurance or car breakdown services, all for a monthly fee. Banks provide these accounts at a much lower price point, at lower cost and level of service than traditional private banking, which is offered to high-affluent customers at a much higher cost and level of service.

The premium accounts do not generate as much revenue as traditional private banking, but given the volumes of customers, they still provide significant revenues to the bank. In essence, it is wealth management but at a much smaller scale.

Private banking

Private banking is for high-affluent, wealthy customers. It offers an integrated proposition to meet the client's own personal needs, the needs of family members and their business needs. Private banking requires a deep understanding of a client's needs and risk appetite, providing unbiased advice and tailoring their solutions accordingly.

Private banking advisors can help their clients by:

- finding investment opportunities that aim to grow the client's wealth over the long term;
- creating tax-efficient savings;
- providing credit with tailored lending and finance;
- staying on top of tax matters;

- reviewing a will and providing advice on trusts;
- putting plans in place with the aim of financially supporting the client's family and businesses should anything unexpected happen;
- helping to create a flexible strategy for retirement;
- taking a holistic view of the client's business and personal finances;
- managing the client's wealth internationally.

Of course, some of the products available to this set of customers will be available to other customers, but not via the private banking arm of the bank. Often, preferential rates and a much deeper level of service are available once the wealth management criteria are met.

Private banking relationship managers are tasked with structuring bespoke lending solutions that are unique to the client's circumstances, for example, providing lending for equity partnerships. They use their expertise with alternative securities and are able to work across geographical borders and jurisdictions to meet a lending need. They can arrange credit secured against most asset types, whether the client needs a mortgage, a personal loan or wants to borrow against an investment portfolio.

Many private banking clients use specialized lending services to invest in property abroad, which is something normally outside the remit of a traditional bank branch. We discuss private banking and wealth management in more detail in Chapter 6.

Personal overdrafts

Standard current accounts can provide customers with access to credit. One of the most common forms is a personal overdraft. An overdraft is a form of **revolving credit**. A limit is agreed and the customer can use the facility, allowing them to go overdrawn for an agreed period. Overdrafts are a convenient form of temporary borrowing for occasions when expenditure exceeds income.

Revolving credit   A type of credit where the debt is not repaid by instalments. A credit limit is agreed and the customer can use the funds up to and including the credit limit agreed.

Features of an overdraft

Features of a personal overdraft include:

- Overdrafts are simple and easy to arrange.
- Overdrafts are agreed in advance (authorized overdraft).
- Interest is calculated on a daily basis on the amount of the overdrawn balance.
- Overdrafts are 'on demand' which technically means the lender can demand repayment of the facility if circumstances demand.
- They are accessed by credit scoring where a system-driven limit is automatically set to agreed parameters based on operation of the bank account and credit history.
- Affordability is based on:
  - the borrower's income and expenditure;
  - the borrower's previous credit footprint;
  - the stability of the borrower's employment.
- Overdrafts are regulated by the Consumer Credit Acts of 1974 and 2006 and the Standards of Lending Practice (covered in more detail in a later chapter).

Unauthorized overdrafts

Unauthorized overdrafts occur when an authorized overdraft has not been agreed in advance. If the bank allows the customer to go overdrawn without prior agreement it will levy a higher rate of interest and additional fees. Banks can and do return items to prevent an account from going overdrawn.

Lenders who provide overdrafts will expect to see the account 'swing' from debit to credit during the duration of the facility. If the facility does not swing from debit to credit the overdraft may be termed as being 'hard-core'. This may concern the lender as it suggests the overdraft is not being operated in line with the original purpose. In some cases the hard-core element could be transferred to a loan account to enable a formal repayment programme to be put in place.

> **Hard-core borrowing** A term used to describe the part of an overdraft facility that is not cleared each month by payments into the account.

Personal loans

Personal loans can be agreed in the same way as an overdraft. Whereas an overdraft is a revolving credit facility, a loan is not. The loan balance has to be repaid in instalments as detailed in the loan agreement. Personal loans are unsecured facilities where the borrower does not have to pledge any assets as security for the loan.

Typically, personal loans can be used for holidays, car purchases, home improvements or the purchase of white goods (appliances); they can also be used to consolidate debts.

Loans have the following features:

- They are for a fixed amount.
- They are for a fixed period of time.
- They have a fixed interest rate.
- They have scheduled repayments that repay capital and interest.
- They are accessed centrally by credit scoring.
- Like overdrafts, affordability is based on:
  - the borrower's income and expenditure;
  - the borrower's previous credit footprint;
  - the stability of the borrower's employment.
- Like overdrafts, loans too are regulated by the Consumer Credit Acts of 1974 and 2006 and the Standards of Lending Practice.

Following a successful application the lender will produce a loan agreement which sets out all the terms and conditions the customer must adhere to for the duration of the loan. The loan is created by debiting the new loan account and crediting the borrower's current account. The agreed repayments are debited each month from the borrower's current account and credited to the loan account.

Loan interest is calculated by applying a rate to the amount of the loan for the whole period. The loan capital and interest is divided equally over the specified period. Details of the repayment schedule will be contained within the loan agreement.

Credit, debit and charge cards

Plastic cards are a convenient way to buy goods and services. They enable consumers to spend without having to use cash or cheques. They can also be used over the internet or by mail order.

Like an overdraft, credit cards are another form of revolving credit. The customer has an agreed credit limit and can use the cards to pay for goods and services up to that limit. Transactions are authorized (online) up to the amount of the credit card limit; should the buyer attempt to overspend this limit the transaction will be rejected.

The customer is allowed to spend and can repay all or some of the outstanding balance on a monthly basis. If the balance is cleared in full, no interest will be charged. If the outstanding balance is not cleared in full then interest will be charged.

The customer receives a monthly statement detailing the transactions made; these can be produced in paper form or accessed online or by mobile. The statement shows the outstanding balance and what minimum payment needs to be made (typically between 3 and 5 per cent of the outstanding balance). It also details when the payment needs to be made.

Credit cards also provide a facility for drawing cash from ATM machines and the cardholder will be charged extra for this cash advance. Borrowing by credit cards is much more expensive than overdrafts or personal loans.

Debit cards enable customers to pay for goods and services by presenting the card and entering their PIN (Personal Identification Number) in the same way as credit cardholders do. The funds are then transferred electronically from the cardholder's bank account to the account held by the retailer. Debit cards also enable the cardholder to withdraw cash from ATM networks.

Charge cards operate in a similar way to credit cards, the difference being that the amount outstanding has to be paid in full each month. This provides interest-free credit for the time the transaction occurs to the day the balance is paid in full.

House purchase loans

Banks entered the mortgage market in the 1970s and have now captured a significant part of the market. Mortgage lending is a lucrative and popular area of bank business.

Mortgage lenders will often look for the customer to make a contribution towards the cost of the property being purchased. Although there has been, in the past, a market for 100 per cent mortgages (a loan for house purchase where no contribution is made by the purchaser), lenders now expect to see a prospective borrower contribute some of their own resources into a property purchase. In addition to the deposit, the borrower will also need to have funds to cover upfront costs such as legal fees, valuation fees and a number of incidental costs in setting up or moving house.

The maximum mortgage offered to an applicant must be based on an assessment of affordability. The Mortgage Conduct of Business (MCOB) rules insist that consideration must be given to the applicant's regular income, committed expenditure and some estimate of discretionary expenditure and living costs. (MCOB rules are covered in more detail in Chapter 5). In addition, the lender must also anticipate possible future changes that may affect the ability to repay, such as changes in interest rates or stability of employment. Before sanctioning a mortgage, lenders need to know that the loan will be serviced on an ongoing basis and that it will be repaid on expiry of the agreed term of the mortgage.

Question

What different types of mortgages does your bank provide? Speak to one of your mortgage advisors to understand which is the most popular type of mortgage, and why.

Types of mortgage

Despite a plethora of mortgage products available on the market, there are only two ways in which a house purchase loan can be paid off: either by making regular payments covering capital and interest; or by repaying the mortgage on an 'interest only' basis.

Repayment mortgages

With a repayment mortgage, the borrower repays some of the interest and capital element of the mortgage each month. At the end of the period, often 25–30 years, the borrower will have repaid the mortgage and will then own the property outright.

With this type of mortgage the interest repayment element makes up a much larger part of the repayment than the capital element in the early stages of the loan. It is only later on in the life of the mortgage that repayments begin to reduce the total amount of capital. Most mortgage lenders use software to demonstrate this reduction to customers at the time the mortgage is arranged. It shows how the repayment of the capital element accelerates as the mortgage gets closer to its repayment date.

It is also standard practice for lenders to look for the customer to provide some form of life assurance to guarantee the repayment of the mortgage in the event of the borrower's death.

This type of mortgage is suitable for borrowers who want to be certain their house will be paid for at the end of the mortgage.

Variable rate mortgages

Every lender has a standard variable rate (SVR) mortgage. This is their basic mortgage. The interest rate goes up and down as the base rate changes.

This type of mortgage is suitable for borrowers who think base rates will reduce over the period.

Fixed rate mortgages

Fixed rate mortgages occur when the mortgage rate is fixed for a set number of years. As the mortgage rate is fixed, borrowers know exactly what they have to pay each month and this will not change during the period of the fix, no matter what happens to base rates.

The disadvantage of fixed rate borrowing is that the borrower may be fixed with a high rate when base rate falls. Borrowers can break a fixed rate but there will be penalties for switching before the end of the fix period.

This type of mortgage is suitable for borrowers who need to budget carefully and want to know exactly how much they will be paying over the period of the fix.

Interest only mortgages

Interest only mortgages are when the borrower and lender agree that interest is covered during the lifetime of the mortgage and the capital element is repaid at the end of the term in full. This is known as a bullet repayment. Bullet repayments may come from a variety of independent sources such as endowment polices, investments, pensions, etc.

Borrowers and lenders must have certainty of repayment and the ability of the borrower to repay the capital at the end of the term. If at the end of the term, the borrower is unable to repay the capital in full, the lender is entitled to sell the property to repay their debt. When house prices are rising many borrowers assume they will always be able to repay or re-mortgage the property; but property prices can also fall as was evident in the housing crash that occurred during the 2007–09 financial crisis.

The main advantage of interest only mortgages is that monthly repayments are lower than with any other mortgage because the borrower is only paying the interest element for the duration of the mortgage. Like a capital and interest loan, the only change in repayments occurs if there is a change to base rates.

This type of mortgage is suitable for borrowers who want the lowest monthly repayments and are confident they will have enough money to repay the debt at the end of the mortgage.

Capped rate mortgages

This is an SVR mortgage but one with a ceiling (a cap) on how high the interest rate can rise. Borrowers will have the comfort of knowing that their mortgage repayments will never exceed a certain level but can still benefit when rates go down.

This type of mortgage is suitable for borrowers who believe mortgage rates are going to rise.

Discounted interest rates

These are variable rate mortgages with favourable introductory rates which are discounted for the early part of the mortgage term. For example, the discount could be 1 or 2 per cent for the first one or two years. These mortgages are provided to give new borrowers an incentive to choose a particular lender.

This type of mortgage is suitable for those who want to pay less in the earlier term of the mortgage.

Cashback mortgages

This is a marketing incentive sometimes offered by lenders. When borrowers take out their mortgage, the lenders give them money back, typically a percentage of the loan. This may not necessarily be as attractive as it first looks and borrowers should look carefully at the interest rate being charged and any additional fees, as they are likely to find cheaper mortgage rates without cashback.

This type of mortgage is suitable for borrowers who need a lump sum of money to help with moving house.

Offset mortgages

Offset mortgages are linked to a savings or current account and combine surplus funds and mortgage together. Each month, the lender looks at how much is outstanding on the mortgage and then deducts the amount held as surplus funds. Borrowers pay mortgage interest on the difference between the two. For example, if a borrower has a mortgage of £100,000 and surplus funds of £20,000, the mortgage interest is calculated on £80,000 for that month. This reduces the amount of interest the borrower has to pay. Surplus funds can still be accessed but the more that is offset, the quicker the borrower may repay the mortgage. When the surplus funds are offset the surplus funds will not earn any interest on them.

This type of mortgage is suitable for borrowers with surplus funds.

Bridging loans

Bridging finance is required when a major purchase precedes a major sale. The result of this timing difference is that there will be a large shortfall for the purchaser to finance, but usually only for a short period of time.

Bridging finance is commonly encountered in house purchase and sale transactions. The customer may purchase their new home before receiving the sale proceeds from their old home; therefore they will need to finance both homes for the period between the purchase of the new home and the receipt of the sale proceeds of the old home.

Bridging finance can be either open bridging or closed bridging. Open-ended bridging covers the situation where the date of the sale of the asset that is to repay the bridging loan has not been agreed, ie where the customer has bought their new property, but has not yet sold the previous property. This represents a far higher risk for the bank, as the lender has no certainty of when they are going to receive repayment of the bridging loan.

Closed bridging occurs when the date of the sale of the asset that is to repay the bridging has been confirmed. Therefore, in a house purchase it is when there is an agreed completion date for the sale of the property and contracts have been exchanged. The lender will know how much the house has been sold for, and when the funds are due to be paid.

Probate loans

Another form of bridging loan is a **probate** loan. Sometimes lending facilities are required to pay death duties prior to the winding-up of a deceased person's estate. The death duties are paid from a probate loan then repayment is sourced from the sale of the assets from the deceased's estate.

> **Probate** Grants authority for an executor or administrator to administer the estate of a deceased person.

Further advances

A further advance is a way to release the equity in a borrower's residential property. The equity element is the difference between the value of the property and any outstanding loans secured on it. For example, a house might be worth £170,000 with an outstanding mortgage of £60,000. The equity element is £110,000. This might enable the borrower to increase their mortgage or take up a new loan, subject to the lender's credit assessment criteria.

Second mortgages

A second mortgage is slightly different. It is created where a borrower seeks a new second mortgage from a different provider and that new provider seeks a second charge behind the first lender.

Business lending products

Banks have a number of lending products and services to suit any type of lending request. These products and services have developed over the years and it is essential that you match the most appropriate product to the specific lending situation.

The most common types of business lending products include:

- overdrafts;
- loans;
- credit and charge cards;
- sales receivables financing (factoring and invoice discounting);
- asset finance (HP and leasing).

Bank lending products tend to fall into three main categories:

- providing short-term liquidity for cash flow including the financing of imports and exports;
- financing the purchase of fixed assets;
- covering contingent liabilities, which is a future liability that may or may not be incurred, eg guarantees.

In providing lending facilities, you must ensure that the risks are fully understood. Once lending facilities have been provided, they should be monitored to ensure that the original plans and basis of support are still relevant. The longer the duration of the facility, the more important monitoring is, because there is more time for things to go wrong.

Lending facilities need to be reviewed on at least an annual basis to ensure there is no actual or potential deterioration in the business's risk profile. The business environment is constantly changing and you must remain vigilant to the risks that could affect your customers.

Business overdrafts

As with personal overdrafts, some businesses may experience a mis-match in timing of income and expenditure. Not many businesses are paid in advance for providing their products or services; most have to negotiate credit terms with both their suppliers and their customers. A cash flow problem may occur when money has to be paid out before payments owed to the business have been received.

There are several issues you need to consider when assessing the appropriateness of an overdraft as a source of finance. The customer must demonstrate:

- why the overdraft is needed;
- the duration or time period for which the facility is required;
- their ability to operate within the overdraft limit;
- their ability to service the debt, ie pay the overdraft interest.

The amount of an overdraft allowed at any one time will depend on the cash flows of the business, ie the timing of receipts and payments, and/or if there are any seasonal trends in the sales of the business. This can be illustrated by the cash flow statement shown in Figure 2.1.

Figure 2.1 Bank account conduct: monthly range balances (£)

	January	February	March	April	May	June	July	August	September	October	November	December
Opening bank balance	20,000.00	60,000.00	65,000.00	70,000.00	72,000.00	47,000.00	-11,000.00	-23,000.00	-18,000.00	-18,000.00	7,000.00	47,000.00
Sales receipts in	120,000.00	100,000.00	115,000.00	112,000.00	95,000.00	92,000.00	98,000.00	100,000.00	110,000.00	120,000.00	125,000.00	100,000.00
Payments out	80,000.00	95,000.00	110,000.00	110,000.00	120,000.00	150,000.00	110,000.00	95,000.00	110,000.00	95,000.00	85,000.00	80,000.00
Closing bank balance	60,000.00	65,000.00	70,000.00	72,000.00	47,000.00	-11,000.00	-23,000.00	-18,000.00	-18,000.00	7,000.00	47,000.00	67,000.00

In the example shown in Figure 2.1, the business has an overdraft requirement for the months June through to October because sales income dips during May to July at a time when payments out rise. The situation restores itself in November and the business ends up with more cash in its bank account then it started with in January.

Question

What is the peak overdraft requirement in the example shown in Figure 2.1?

The obvious answer is £23,000 (July). However, this may not always be the case.

The cash flow statement shows the monthly position; however, if the payments out are made before the sales receipts are received, the overdraft requirement might be understated *during* the month.

Let's take July as an example.

The bank account starts at –£11,000. If the business makes its payments out before any sales receipts are received, the overdraft requirement changes significantly:

Opening bank balance	–£11,000
Payments out	–£110,000
Bank balance	*–£121,000*
Sales receipts in	+£98,000
Closing bank balance	–£23,000

In this example the peak overdraft requirement is an overdraft of £121,000 and not £23,000.

As such, it is crucial for you to understand the cash dynamics of the business to ensure that the right level of overdraft is provided.

Hard-core debt

Like personal overdrafts, business overdrafts are expected to fluctuate between debit and credit at some point during the period agreed; if the facility does not return to credit during the period then it may be described as being hard-core debt. Generally, as a rule of thumb, if credit turnover in any given month exceeds the overdraft limit then it might not be classed as hard-core and would be acceptable to a lending banker because the business is generating sufficient cash to cover the amount of the overdraft.

Sales (receivables) financing

There are two forms of sales financing: factoring and invoice discounting. These are available to businesses trading with other businesses on credit terms, and so are not normally available to retailers or to cash traders as they tend not to have trade debtors. Furthermore, certain industry sectors such as construction, in which staged payments are made, are also unsuitable for this type of finance.

Factoring and invoice-discounting facilities are designed to replace overdraft funding as they provide fast payment against the sales ledger, enabling a business to improve its cash flow.

Factoring

Debt factoring involves a business selling its invoices (money that is owed to it) to a factoring company. In return, the factoring company will process the invoices and allow funds to be drawn against the money owed to the business. Factoring companies also provide a debt collection and ledger management service as well as financing the debtor book.

Although factoring is commonly used to improve cash flow, it can also be used to reduce administration overheads as the factoring company undertakes the credit control function on behalf of the business.

When a business enters into a factoring agreement, the factor will agree to advance up to 85 per cent of approved invoices, subject to the quality of the debtor book. Payment is usually made within 24 hours, with all sales invoices being passed through the factor who will collect the debts.

The business's invoices to its customers instruct them to pay the factor directly. The factor then pays the agreed percentage of the invoice to the business. It issues statements to customers on the business's behalf and operates the credit control procedures, including chasing payments if necessary.

When the business's customer pays the invoice direct to the factor, the factor then pays the balance of the invoice to the business, minus its own fees and any interest that has accrued.

Recourse and non-recourse factoring

With recourse factoring, the factor does *not* assume the risk of bad debts. They will reclaim their money from the business if its customer does not pay.

With non-recourse factoring, the factor takes on the bad debt risk. The factor takes over all of the rights to pursue the customer for payment, which can include the right to take legal action.

Recourse factoring is cheaper than non-recourse factoring because the business, and not the factor, is taking on the bad debt risk.

Invoice discounting

Invoice discounting is another way of providing funds against a company's sales ledger. Unlike factoring, the business retains full control over the administration of its sales ledger.

When providing an invoice-discounting facility, the discounter will first check the business, its systems and its customers. It will review the credit history and profit track record of the business. Once it has satisfied itself, it will then agree to advance a percentage (normally 80–90 per cent) of the total of the approved sales ledger.

The invoice discounter also undertakes regular audits of the business to ensure that its internal procedures remain effective. The business continues to collect its debts and undertake credit control.

A monthly fee is paid to the invoice discounter, together with interest on the net amount advanced. There are normally additional fees and charges attached for credit management and administration. The amount of these fees is typically linked to levels of turnover and will increase as the business increases its turnover (sales). It is also dependent on the volume of the invoices being discounted and the number of customers a business has.

Like factoring, invoice discounting can be made available on both a recourse or non-recourse basis. Both factoring and invoice discounting can also be used for financing international trade debts and they are common ways of advancing funds against an overseas sales ledger.

ACTIVITY 2.1

Speak to one of your sales financing colleagues to find out which types of customers use invoice discounting and factoring. Understand what levels of advance percentages they use, and why.

Loan accounts

Loans are committed term facilities provided by the banks for asset purchases, rather than for liquidity purposes such as working capital funding (overdraft/sales receivables financing). Funds are provided for an agreed period, usually linked to the useful lifetime of the asset being funded, and are most often subject to capital repayments. The interest margin can be fixed for the duration of the facility or allowed to move in line with base rate changes.

Loan repayments

Interest for the loan facility accrues on the daily debit balance outstanding, and the loan repayments will incorporate an element of both interest and capital. In some circumstances the loan capital can be repaid in full by a single repayment at maturity of the facility (bullet repayment).

Secured and unsecured loans

Loans can be provided on a secured or unsecured basis, although if the loan is for an asset purchase it is common practice to take a charge over the underlying asset (eg taking a legal charge when financing property purchase).

Unsecured loans would be priced more expensively than secured facilities, with the loan terms and conditions likely to be more stringent to align with the higher risk to the bank.

Second mortgages

This is a loan provided for business when the security provided is a domestic property. For example, an owner of the business seeks to raise additional finance for their business by pledging their domestic property as security for the advance. The property may be subject to an existing mortgage with sufficient equity to raise funds for the business.

A lender may consider providing finance by taking a second legal charge over the domestic residence. In such circumstances the first lender's charge takes precedence and retains all the rights they had prior to the second charge, and the first lender has to consent to the second mortgage before the second lender provides the additional loan.

In the event that the property is sold, then the first lender is repaid in full and the second lender's charge becomes a first legal charge enabling the second lender to exercise their rights to the remaining sale proceeds. Lenders will apply a **loan-to-value** ratio (LTV) restriction as part of their security calculations.

> **Loan-to-value**   The ratio of the loan to the value of the property.

LTVs vary from bank to bank. Let's assume the first lender applies an LTV of 70 per cent and the second lender an LTV of 60 per cent.

In the example above the house is worth £170,000 with an outstanding mortgage of £60,000 and the borrower wants to borrow £20,000 from the second lender.

The first lender's security calculation is:

Value   £170,000

LTV   70 per cent

Security calculation is £170,000 × 70% = £119,000

The first lender then deducts the outstanding mortgage of £60,000 = £59,000.

The second lender applies their LTV of 60%

£59,000 × 60% = £35,400.

For the second lender this is the value of their security for the £20,000 additional loan. Note that the lenders apply their LTV *before* deducting the outstanding mortgage.

Consider the alternative if they deducted the outstanding mortgage before applying their LTV ratio:

Value   £170,000

LTV   70%

Security calculation would be £170,000 – £60,000 = £110,000 × 70%

The 'security cover' would be £77,000 and not £59,000

As property values change over time, where property values fall, the borrower and the lender could find themselves in a **negative equity** situation.

Prudence therefore dictates that lenders apply their LTVs before deducting outstanding loans.

> **Negative equity**   Occurs when the market value of a property falls below the outstanding amount of a mortgage secured on it.

Loan covenants

Unlike an overdraft, which is a **demand facility**, a loan account is a **committed facility**. As the bank is making a term commitment for the loan facility, it is normal practice to adopt loan covenants that are designed to ensure that the borrower meets certain agreed conditions for the duration of the loan.

> **Demand facility**   An uncommitted lending facility where repayment of the debt can be called upon demand. An overdraft is a demand facility.
>
> **Committed facility**   A lending facility whereby terms and conditions are clearly defined by the lender and imposed on the borrower. A loan is a committed facility.

If the borrower breaches a loan covenant, the loan is considered to be in default. The lender then has the right to demand payment or take the opportunity to restructure and/or renegotiate the terms of the facility. Covenants can be either financial or non-financial covenants; in practice, they tend to be a combination of both.

Financial covenants are determined by the customer's own unique financial performance, such as its levels of profitability, cash generation and net worth. The covenants can be expressed as ratios or absolute numbers and will set triggers based on forecast financial performance criteria negotiated and agreed with the borrower.

Non-financial covenants are designed to protect the lender against any actions by the borrower that might weaken the bank's security position. It may include the level and frequency of information provided by the customer to test the ongoing financial performance of the business, for example, production of regular management information such as the current trading figures.

ACTIVITY 2.2

Obtain a copy of a business loan agreement that includes both financial and non-financial covenants. Speak with the lending manager to ascertain why they have applied the covenants to the loan and how they monitor them.

Asset finance (hire purchase and leasing)

A business can obtain the resources and equipment it needs in two ways: buying the asset outright; or through hire purchase or leasing.

Purchasing an asset outright is a good option if the business has cash available, but not all businesses do.

Asset finance (hire purchase or leasing) is a way of purchasing equipment, machinery or other assets without having to pay the full cost of the asset up front.

Using hire purchase or leasing allows a business to use an asset over a fixed period in return for regular payments. It enables the business to choose the equipment it needs, with a finance company purchasing the asset on behalf of the business.

Hire purchase

A hire purchase (HP) agreement is a way to finance the purchase of fixed assets that allows the cost of the asset to be repaid over a fixed period of time. Only when all the payments are made does the asset belong to the business; until that point, the asset belongs to the lender. However, the business can claim valuable tax allowances from the beginning of the HP contract.

There are various different HP structures that can be used and the attraction of each one will vary according to the specific requirements of the business and its tax position.

The types of assets that can be purchased on HP include:

- computers;
- industrial machinery;
- equipment;
- furniture.

Leasing

Leasing arrangements are similar to hire purchase agreements. When a business leases an asset, the leasing company purchases the equipment on behalf of the business and the business then pays for it by regular instalments over a fixed period of time. A lease agreement is drawn up between the business (the *lessee*) and the lender (the *lessor*).

Leasing means that the business never owns the asset outright, although some lease arrangements do allow the customer to buy the asset at the end of the agreement.

The range of equipment that can be bought under a lease includes:

- telephone systems;
- office computers;
- company cars;
- forklift trucks.

Not only do banks and a number of specialized finance houses offer this service, but a growing number of equipment manufacturers have also entered this lucrative market.

Types of leasing

There are three different kinds of lease arrangements:

- finance leasing;
- operating leasing;
- contract hire.

Finance leasing

With finance leasing, the business takes a long-term lease intended to run over the expected life of the equipment, usually three years or more. After this period has elapsed, a nominal rent is paid or the business can sell or scrap the equipment, as the leasing company will not want it any more. The leasing company recovers the full cost of the equipment, plus charges, over the period of the lease.

Although the business does not own the equipment, it is responsible for maintaining and insuring the asset. A leased asset must be shown on a business's Statement of Financial Position (balance sheet) as a capital item, as if the item has been bought by the company.

Operating leasing

An operating lease is taken out if the equipment is not needed for its entire working life. The leasing company is responsible for maintenance and insurance of the asset and takes it back at the end of the lease. The business does not have to show the asset on its Statement of Financial Position (balance sheet), because the lessor (the lender) retains ownership.

Contract hire

Contract hire is often used for company vehicles. The leasing company takes responsibility for management and maintenance, such as repairs and servicing. As with an operating lease, assets are not shown on a business's Statement of Financial Position (balance sheet).

International trade finance

International trade finance has a function and terminology of its own, but the principles of lending are no different from any other lending process or decision. There are additional risks associated with businesses trading overseas, not least in terms of receiving timely payment in the appropriate currency from customers.

Methods of payment

Four main payment methods are adopted for overseas trade:

- payment in advance;
- documentary letters of credit;
- documentary collections;
- open account trade.

Payment in advance

This involves obtaining payment for goods and services before the goods are sent to the customer. Using this method, an exporting business bears no risks or financing costs, and it is used when there are concerns about a customer's ability to pay. However, customers might not want to pay in advance unless the products are unique and in high demand.

Documentary letters of credit

These are commonly known as 'letters of credit' and are used by exporters. Documentary letters of credit are one of the safest ways to be paid by an overseas customer.

The overseas customer arranges a letter of credit with their bank. The bank then undertakes unconditionally to pay a bank in the UK once the completed paperwork and documents have been accepted without any discrepancies. If the documentation is accurate, payment is guaranteed to be made on time.

Whilst letters of credit are used between exporters and importers, a credit risk to the bank only arises when an importer's bank grants a facility to an importer. For export customers, it is simply a secure method of payment with no credit risk liability attached.

For example, a UK business is exporting some goods to China; however, this is the first time they have dealt with the company, and they want to be sure they will be paid. The Chinese company will ask their bank to open a documentary credit and the Chinese bank, once satisfied as to the creditworthiness of their customer, will correspond with the UK bank that holds the account of the exporter.

The documentary credit will specify what documents the exporter has to provide and if the documents provided are error free, payment is guaranteed by the Chinese bank to the UK bank. Typically the documents would include a bill of lading, an invoice, a bill of exchange and maybe an insurance document.

When the goods are loaded to a ship (or freight plane if going by air), a bill of lading (or air waybill for air freight) will be issued. The exporter then simply presents the documents to their bank, and receives their funds (if that is the agreed payment method).

ACTIVITY 2.3

Speak to your international trade manager, and ask for examples of how they assist customers who import and export.

Documentary collections

An overseas bank, acting for the exporter's bank, will release the documents, allowing the importer to take the goods once the terms of the bill of exchange have been accepted.

There is a risk that the bill of exchange will not be accepted, in which case the exporter will retain ownership of the goods, although their goods will still be overseas. Even if the bill has not been accepted, there is still a risk to the exporter of non-payment unless the bill of exchange has been guaranteed by the importer's bank.

Open account trade

This is similar to offering credit to a UK customer. The seller invoices the overseas customer, stating when they expect to receive payment.

This option has the highest risk of non-payment. Open account trading should only be used where there is an established trading relationship and the seller is confident that the customer is able and willing to pay. That said, the majority of UK international trade operates on an open account basis.

Bills of lading

A bill of lading is used for goods that are moved by ship; it acts as receipt of shipment and gives title to the goods. The equivalent document for goods moved by air is known as an 'airway bill'.

The bill of lading is issued by a carrier to a shipper, acknowledging that the goods in transit have been received on board as cargo for transportation to a named place for delivery, which may be one port or a number of ports if the journey passes through more than one destination.

A clean bill of lading confirms that the goods have been received on board the vessel in apparently good condition, without defect, and stowed ready for transport.

Depending on what payment methods are used, banks may be able to assist their customers by advancing funds in anticipation of payment being received on the underlying contract.

Bill discounting/acceptance credits

Exporters in possession of an accepted bill of exchange may be able to get the bill 'discounted' by their bank and therefore receive immediate payment. The bank would advance a proportion of the funds due and be repaid when the importer settles the bill. This discounting process is also known as an acceptance credit.

The rate of discount, or amount advanced, and the fees charged for providing this service will be determined by the creditworthiness and standing of the importer or the importer's bank.

Forfaiting

Traditional bill discounting by an exporter's local bank may alleviate cash flow pressure, but it does not address the commercial, credit and political risks of the importing country.

Forfaiting is designed to assume all of these risks. It is essentially a form of bill discounting but is provided without recourse to the exporter in the event of non-payment at maturity. Forfaiting therefore enables exporters to convert a credit sale into a cash sale, and potentially pass on the financing costs to the importer. Forfaiting tends to be used for large, long-term capital projects.

Guarantees/avalization

Having accepted a bill of exchange, importers can also obtain a guarantee from their bank against a *lien* on the title documents for the goods. A lien is a weak form of security that allows the bank to retain possession of the goods until the loan is repaid.

The bank guarantees (avalizes) the importer's bill of exchange and adds its name to ensure that the bill will be paid at its due date. The importer can then sell the goods, receive the cash and have sufficient monies to pay the bill when it falls due.

Standby letters of credit

A standby letter of credit fulfils a different function from a documentary letter of credit. A bank may issue a standby letter of credit on behalf of a customer to provide assurances of its customer's ability to perform under the terms of a contract. Such a standby letter of credit assures the beneficiary of the performance of the customer's obligation.

The beneficiary is able to draw under the credit by presenting a draft (bill of exchange) and copies of invoices, together with evidence that the customer has *not* performed their obligation. The bank is obliged to make payment if the documents presented comply with the terms of the standby letter of credit. It is a contingent liability similar to a guarantee.

Bonds, indemnities and guarantees

When selling overseas, buyers commonly request bank guarantees or bonds from their suppliers. This provides a means of securing performance or other obligations under the terms of a contract.

Banks will act as guarantor for a seller and will unconditionally pay a buyer a specific sum on demand. The wording of this demand is included in the guarantee. In return, banks take a counter-indemnity from their customers for the full amount of the guarantee, together with any costs incurred.

A counter-indemnity is a legal agreement, under which a guarantor (the bank) agrees with its customer that the customer will reimburse the bank in the event that it has to pay any claims under the bond or guarantee it has issued on behalf of its customer.

ACTIVITY 2.4

Obtain a copy of your bank's standard counter-indemnity.

What obligations has the borrower agreed to do?

The most common forms of guarantee (or bond) used in both domestic and international trade include:

- customs guarantees (VAT duty deferment bonds);
- demand guarantees;
- tender guarantees (or bid bonds);
- performance guarantees (or bonds);
- advance payment guarantees;
- retention money guarantees;
- warranty guarantees;
- missing bills of lading guarantees (or indemnities).

Customs guarantees

One of the most common types of guarantee used by importers is a duty deferment bond, which is also known as a VAT bond or customs guarantee. These are issued by banks in favour of HM Revenue & Customs (HMRC), enabling goods to be imported into the UK from non-EU member states without the immediate payment of duties or taxes.

An importing customer has to pay VAT and import duty on goods imported to the UK from most non-EU countries. VAT and import duty must be paid before the importer can have access to their goods. However, the importer can request their bank to issue a guarantee in favour of HMRC covering deferment of import duty and VAT on their regular import business, thus allowing the payment to be deferred for 28 days. In effect, this allows a period of credit before VAT and import duty payments fall due, thereby improving the importer's cash flow.

Demand guarantees

Demand guarantees are issued by the bank on behalf of its customer in favour of a contractor to cover an event of default by the customer on their tender or contractual obligations. These guarantees are also known as 'contract guarantees'.

If called upon to do so (after formal demand by the contractor), the bank will make the payment to the contractor and then, in turn, demand repayment from its customer.

Tender guarantees (or bid bonds)

A tender guarantee is normally issued by a bank on behalf of its customer in favour of an importer to cover an event of default on the customer's tender or contractual obligations. Such bonds cover the following eventualities:

- withdrawal of the tender whilst the importer is considering to whom to award the contract;
- the exporter refusing to sign the contract once it has been awarded;
- the exporter failing to provide a performance guarantee once the contract has been awarded.

Performance guarantees (or bonds)

These are used to safeguard the importer against the financial consequences of an exporter failing to perform under the contract.

Advance payment guarantees

Sometimes a contractor will require an advance payment of some of the contract price. In this situation, a bank would guarantee to return the advance payment should the goods/services not be delivered. It does this to safeguard against the customer failing to perform the contract.

Retention money guarantees

Sometimes a contract will call for part of the contract value to be withheld until all aspects of the contract have been completed and accepted by the customer.

Warranty guarantees

Warranty guarantees are used to safeguard the contractor against the financial consequences of a buyer failing to perform under their warranty obligations. Examples of such a failure might include the failure to correct defects in the goods or services being provided.

Missing bills of lading guarantees

Bills of lading (which evidence title to the goods) need to be produced to a carrier at the port of discharge in order that the holder can take delivery of the goods.

Sometimes bills of lading might go through several hands, including banks, and arrive after the carrying vessel has shipped or they may even get lost in transit. An importer would want to avoid the goods being offloaded and incurring penalty storage charges (demurrage) but if the carrier released the goods to the importer without the bills of lading, it could face serious consequences. In these circumstances, the carrier would only be prepared to release the goods against an indemnity from the importer that has been 'joined into' by the importer's bank.

Foreign exchange risks

When dealing in foreign currencies there are three types of risk that companies encounter:

- transaction risk;
- translation risk;
- economic risk.

Transaction risk

Transaction risk is the risk of an exchange rate changing between the transaction date and the subsequent settlement date, which could lead to a gain or a loss arising on conversion. The most common area where transaction risk is experienced relates to imports and exports and managing transaction risk is by far the largest part of currency risk exposure.

Businesses can take action internally to reduce their foreign exchange currency risk. Internal hedging techniques include netting, matching, and leading and lagging.

Netting

Some companies have subsidiaries in different countries selling to other members of the group. Netting applies where the UK parent and its foreign subsidiaries offset intra-group currency flows.

The group finance director or finance team controls the netting of currency cash inflows and outflows across the group, leaving only the net balance exposed to risk which may need to be hedged.

Matching

Netting only applies to transfers within group companies. Matching can be used for intra-group transactions and those with third parties. The company attempts to match its currency inflows with its outflows in respect of amounts and timing. For example, a company with exports to the EU, expecting euro receipts, may try to import goods from the EU and match up the currency receipts and payments.

Leading and lagging

This involves speeding up or delaying payments when a change in the value of a currency is expected. Sometimes an exporter may offer a discount to its customer overseas to try to obtain immediate payment if the foreign currency is expected to fall against sterling.

Translation risk

Translation risk occurs where the reported performance of an overseas subsidiary in home-based currency terms changes in the Statement of Financial Position (balance sheet) because of movements in exchange rates. Values in the Statement of Financial Position can increase or decrease depending on currency movements between the periods of the financial statements.

Whereas transaction risk is concerned with cash flows, translation risk is concerned with values. As such it is an accounting risk rather than a cash-based one, and would not normally be hedged.

Examples of translation exposure can include:

- debts/loans in foreign currency;
- fixed assets, such as land and buildings, plant and machinery, etc, that are located overseas;
- shares in foreign companies (eg subsidiaries).

Economic risk

Economic risk is the variation in the value of the business (ie the present value of future cash flows) due to unexpected changes in exchange rates.

The basic rule of thumb is:

- if the GBP (sterling) *appreciates,* then imports to the UK become cheaper, but exports from the UK become more expensive;
- if the GBP (sterling) *depreciates,* then imports to the UK become more expensive, but exports from the UK become cheaper.

Ideally, a UK company should try to buy goods in currencies that are falling in value against sterling and sell in currencies that are rising against sterling. Changes in exchange rates result from changes in the demand for and supply of the currency. These changes may occur for a variety of reasons, and are often linked to economic factors.

The spot market

The spot market is where currency can be bought and sold *now* for immediate delivery. The spot market quotes buying and selling prices for foreign currencies. An example of how spot rates are quoted is:

	Buy	Sell
GBP/USD	1.3327 –	1.3257

The first figure is the rate at which the bank can buy dollars (from the customer); the second is the price at which it can sell dollars (to the customer). The bank would add an appropriate margin to either side of these rates, and that margin would be determined by the size of the trade.

Forward currency contracts

The forward market is where currency can be bought and sold at a fixed future date for a predetermined rate. A customer can access this market by entering into a forward currency contract.

Once a forward contract is entered into, it must be completed. If, for whatever reason, all or some of the forward contract is not used, then it will be closed out by the bank either buying or selling the foreign currency with the bank using the spot rate prevailing in the market at the maturity date.

Because forward contracts must be closed out, this represents a credit risk to the bank. As such, providing a forward contract to a customer is a lending request. Most banks would apply a risk margin to the transaction, and this is normally around 10 per cent of the contract value. For example, imagine an importer has agreed to buy some goods worth USD 60,000 from China, and agreed terms are 30 per cent on order, and 70 per cent on shipment. Let's assume the goods will be shipped six weeks after order, so the requirement for payment is:

On order: USD 18,000

In six weeks: USD 42,000

If the dollar rate today is 1.33, the first payment can be made for GBP £13,533.85. So far so good! The final payment is due to be made in six weeks' time, and if the rates are unchanged, a further GBP £31,578.94 will be paid at that time.

However, currency markets are volatile, and it is possible, likely even, that 1.33 will not be the rate in six weeks' time. If the rate changes, the importer will pay a different amount:

If the rate moves to 1.38, the importer will only have to pay GBP £30,434.78, a difference of £1,144.16 less to pay for the second tranche of dollars.

However, the rate could move the other way, and if it moves to 1.28, the importer will need to pay GBP £32,812.50 for the dollars – £1,233.56 *more* than it currently thinks.

A forward contract resolves the problem, as the importer says to the bank, 'I want to buy USD 42,000 in six weeks' time', and the bank offers them a rate which will be much closer to the current rate, let's say 1.3250. The importer knows that in six weeks' time they will pay precisely £31,698.11 for the dollars, which means they have removed the exchange rate risk from the transaction.

Forward currency options

A forward currency option is another type of contract that gives the buyer of the contract the right, but not the *obligation* to buy or sell a fixed amount of a particular currency at a specific exchange rate (known as the strike price), on or before a specified future date. This differs from a forward currency contract which creates an *obligation* under the contract.

The appeal of currency options is that the maximum loss is limited to the cost of the premium paid for the contract. The purchaser of the contract retains the upside potential, because there is no obligation to buy or sell.

Currency options permit both hedging against an unfavourable foreign exchange movement, and allow the holder to profit from a favourable currency movement.

Currency swaps

Currency swaps rely upon two different parties who have borrowings or cash flows in different currencies. Currency swaps require the matching up of two companies' mutual requirements in terms of type and amount of currency and the term of the financing.

Interest rate management

Interest rate hedging works on very similar principles to those of foreign exchange hedging. If a company is borrowing on a variable rate of interest and interest rates rise, then the business will have to pay a higher interest cost than it would have if rates had stayed the same. If borrowing is on a fixed rate basis and rates fall, they would not benefit from a fall in interest rates.

Fixed rate loans

One of the most common hedging products made available to business banking and commercial customers is a straightforward fixed rate loan. A fixed rate loan is a loan where the repayment of interest and capital does not fluctuate during the term of the fixed rate. This allows the borrower to know what their future repayments are, and to budget accordingly. Fixed rate loans protect the downside of rates increasing but not the upside if rates fall. Variable rate loans, by contrast, fluctuate in line with movements in base rates.

Fixed rate loans are most commonly provided to smaller, less sophisticated business customers, whereas the more complex derivative products tend to be used for larger, more complex businesses.

Caps, collars and floors

An interest rate cap is a contract that gives the purchaser the right to set a maximum level for the interest rate payable. It sets an *upper* limit on the interest to be paid, but allows the company to benefit from falling rates. Under the terms of the cap agreement, the bank promises to pay any interest charge above the agreed rate. A premium for this arrangement is charged rather like the premium paid for an insurance policy.

Similarly, an interest rate floor is a contract in which the buyer pays the bank at the end of each period in which the interest rate is *below* an agreed strike price.

A collar combines a cap and a floor. If a company enters into both a cap and a floor agreement it is known as a collar.

Forward rate agreements

Forward rate agreements (FRAs) are used to hedge future interest rate risk. They are arrangements whereby one party compensates another should interest rates differ from an agreed rate at some point in the future.

They are agreements about the future level of interest rates, enabling a business to lock into borrowing at a future date at an interest rate that is agreed now. FRAs are purchased from a bank.

Interest rate futures

Interest rate futures are exchange-based instruments traded on a regulated exchange; the buyer and the seller of a contract do not transact with each other directly, they do it through an exchange.

The buyer agrees to receive the interest on a particular sum of money on an agreed future date. The seller of the contract agrees to pay the interest on the sum of money on the agreed future date. The rate of interest is specified in the contract.

Using interest rate futures allows a business to effectively fix the rate of interest at which it borrows or deposits money.

Note these methods are not only used when borrowing, they apply to companies that have surplus funds and want to maximize their earnings potential. The buyer and seller will make profits or losses depending on how interest rates move during the period of the contract.

Interest rate swaps

Interest rate swaps are where an intermediary (a bank) matches two borrowers who wish to swap interest payments due on two separate loans. The swap is typically between a borrower paying a floating rate and a borrower paying a fixed rate.

The swap contract is set up so that the cash flows relating to interest payments are swapped for the period on a principal amount. The effect is that it allows a company that is paying a fixed rate of interest to pay a floating rate instead and vice versa.

Interest hedging products are complex products and need to be suited to each individual customer's needs. In 2013 the FCA undertook a review of the way some banks sold interest rate hedging products (IRHP) to SMEs. It does not make pleasant reading. In 2016 it published a report into the failings of some banks when selling IRHPs which led to the banks paying more than £2.2 billion to SME customers who were mis-sold IRHPs. We discuss this further in Chapter 3.

Product suitability

Whichever products or services you are providing to customers, they must be suitable and appropriate to meet the needs of the customer.

Consider the following:

- If a customer wanted funding to purchase a fixed asset, would you provide funding by way of overdraft or loan?
- If a local supermarket customer wanted help with their cash flow, which product would be more suitable: an overdraft or an invoice-discounting facility?
- If a customer wanted to hedge their foreign currency receipts and wished to protect themselves from an unfavourable movement in exchange rates, but wanted to profit from favourable currency movement, which would be more suitable: a forward currency contract or a forward currency option?

Usually, if a customer were looking to purchase a fixed asset, a loan would normally be more appropriate than an overdraft. However, there could be circumstances where it might be suitable to lend on overdraft.

If the asset to be purchased was going to be paid from the sale proceeds of another asset (such as a bridging loan), it might be quicker and easier to provide funding on overdraft. That is in effect what a bridging advance is.

Overdrafts and invoice-discounting facilities are both forms of working capital finance and are appropriate for funding cash flow. However, in this instance you would not provide an invoice-discounting facility to the retailer as they predominantly deal with cash receipts. They tend not to have debtors so an invoice-discounting facility would not be appropriate for this type of customer.

The customer who wanted to hedge foreign currency receipts would be more suited to a forward currency option as this gives the contract holder a right but not an obligation to buy or sell currency on or before a specified future date.

Product suitability is key in the fight against mis-selling.

Digitalization

Whilst we discuss digitalization in a later chapter, it is worth considering some of the digital products and services provided by banks and non-banking organizations here.

Technology is an important driver in the banking marketplace and this is evidenced by the emergence of non-banking disrupters such as **FinTechs, peer-to-peer** lenders and **crowdfunding**.

Financial technology (FinTech)   The development of new technology and innovation that aims to compete with traditional financial methods in the delivery of financial services. Those engaged in the industry develop new technologies to disrupt traditional financial markets.

Peer-to-peer (P2P) lending   Non-bank financial intermediaries that are able to lend money to individuals or businesses through online services that match lenders with borrowers. Sometimes known as 'crowd-lending'.

Crowdfunding   Enables individuals to contribute funds to a specific company or project via an online platform.

Whilst these new entrants are not replacing the traditional high-street banks, they are opening up new avenues for products and services.

Banking digital products

The more traditional high-street banks are not standing idly by waiting for these new entrants to take away their customers; they are investing heavily in technology all the time and banks are improving the digital services they offer to SMEs. This is evident by the various 'Going digital' transformation programmes in all banks.

Going digital means developing better levels of personalization, better access to finance online and more cost-efficient ways for SMEs to manage their banking needs.

The banks are also developing multichannel offerings, so that SME customers can access the same services on a smartphone, tablet or PC as they would by using a branch, whenever they choose.

Banks are also developing high-quality advisory services that can be delivered through digital channels. Customers can now speak with, for example, a mortgage advisor face-to-face or on screen using video meeting technology.

Digitalization also enables the banks to use real-time predictive analytics to anticipate customers' changing needs and send them relevant service reminders and alerts.

Banks that are successful in transforming the digital experience for their SMEs should benefit from improved operating efficiencies, lower costs and improved customer satisfaction and loyalty.

Non-banking digital products

Whilst traditional bank lending remains a dominant source of finance for SMEs in the UK there is evidence that things are changing.

Alternative finance

Many new start-ups are pioneering alternative financing as a way to capitalize their businesses and two types of alternative finance which are increasingly growing in popularity are peer-to-peer lending and crowdfunding. These both circumvent traditional bank lending.

Alternative finance can enable SMEs to raise finance in a relatively simple way without having to visit a high-street bank or having to make an appointment to see a lending manager; they simply go online to apply for funding. In this scenario they bypass the traditional banks completely, and as a relationship manager you wouldn't even know that one of your customers had taken on debt from elsewhere.

Whilst P2P and crowdfunding are not replacing the traditional high-street banks, they are opening up new avenues for products and services, such as digital and mobile wallets.

Digital wallets

A digital wallet is a digital version of the wallet you carry around with you. It stores payment information so that you can pay for goods and services. For businesses, it's another way to accept payments from their customers. A digital wallet can also be used to receive digital rewards, boarding passes, tickets, room keys and identification.

A mobile wallet is simply the mobile version of a digital wallet. A mobile wallet functions as a contactless mobile payment known as 'tap and go' at the point of sale.

An SME digital wallet can offer additional functionality that provides considerable value for the small-business owner in terms of expense reconciliation, receiving instant customer payments, and being in full control of cash flow and budget management. We discuss this further in Chapter 6.

Throughout this chapter we have looked at a number of products and services, some of which are quite similar, whether you work in the retail part of the bank or business, commercial or corporate.

Some products are fairly easy to understand, and you will probably use some of the products yourself. But some, especially relating to international trade or treasury products (currency and interest rate hedging) can be quite technical, complex and require specialist knowledge.

Each bank will have specialists you can call on to help you learn more, so use them to help your customers. But remember: they are the experts, you're not. All you need to have is a basic understanding of what products and services can do in order to help you identify customer needs and wants. Once you have identified opportunities to help you can then introduce your colleagues to help your customers.

As we started this chapter you were asked to score yourself (1–10) on your understanding of the bank's most common products and services for retail and business customers alike. How would you rate yourself now? Has your understanding changed? Are there any areas you need to review again or discuss further with a colleague or your line manager?

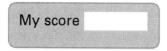

My score

Chapter summary

In this chapter we have explored:

- the different types of lending products and services made available to both personal and business customers;
- the features and benefits of products and services available to both personal and business customers;
- the products and services made available to business customers who import or export;

• the risks involved when trading outside of the UK and how you can help your customers to mitigate those risks.

Objective check

1 What are the benefits of the following personal banking products?
- basic bank account;
- features account;
- personal loan;
- credit card.

2 How would you align products and services to suit customer needs?

3 In what ways could a business's working capital needs be met?

4 What are the different lending facilities available to a business that is looking to invest in non-current assets?

5 Which products have been designed to meet the needs of importers and exporters?

6 What risks do businesses face when trading outside of the UK?

7 What impact is technology having on banking products and services?

Further reading

Hire Purchase/Leasing – ACCA website article [online]. Available at: http://www.accaglobal.com/uk/en/business-finance/types-finance/hire-purchase.html

Visit a major bank website and investigate the different products available for both personal and business customers

03

Reputational risk and ethics

This chapter begins by setting out what happened before, during and after the global financial crisis of 2007-09 that damaged many banks' reputations, and discusses how the banks restored their reputations and began to win back trust from the general public. There is still more work to do and you can play an important part in that.

LEARNING OBJECTIVES

By the end of this chapter you will be able to:

- assess the reasons for the global financial crisis;
- appraise the development of corporate governance in the UK, after the crisis;
- examine the concept of trust, and assess how banks have set out to rebuild trust with their customers;
- review whether banks' ethical behaviour and corporate social responsibility are restoring trust in the sector.

Introduction

Events in 2007–09 undermined the banking sector and threatened the UK economy. Following the crisis banks and bankers were vilified, whether their bank was culpable or not. The government and regulators stepped in to rehabilitate the banking sector and repair the economy.

Over time the banking sector itself has worked extremely hard to restore its reputation and win back trust. This can only be done through its people as it is people who earn trust by their skills, behaviours, competences and professionalism.

Before we start this chapter, how would you mark yourself, on a scale of 1–10, about your knowledge of the global financial crisis and how the banks can win back trust from the general population?

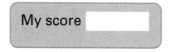

We'll come back to this at the end of the chapter, but for now let's examine what went wrong.

The global financial crisis

Between 2003 and 2007, economic growth in most of the world's major economies (including the UK) was booming, and the UK financial services sector grew more than twice as fast as the economy as a whole. Interest rates and inflation were relatively low and house prices were rising. This fuelled consumer spending and indebtedness, especially in relation to purchasing property.

With property prices increasing there was a diminished perception of risk, as it was assumed that low inflation would persist, thereby keeping interest rates and debt-servicing costs down. Strong economic growth and low unemployment meant that repossessions and losses to banks remained low.

Competition in the UK mortgage market had become increasingly intense since the deregulation and subsequent demutualization of many larger building societies, which led to margins on mortgage products being compressed.

Banks and building societies began to relax lending criteria such as salary multiples and loan-to-value limits, thereby agreeing more readily to lending, which by definition would be more difficult to service in the event of difficulties arising.

Other important trends in the pre-crisis years were the rapidly expanding role of global financial markets in the financial intermediation process, and the growth of the shadow banking system. Multinational companies, particularly in the United States, were increasingly able to access funds directly on the bond market, thereby reducing their need to use banks as intermediaries. This led banks to seek new sources of revenues.

Securitizing packages of loans and selling them on to wholesale investors quickly became an important and cheap way for banks to raise funds for new lending. Before securitization, banks operated the 'originate and hold' model. They originated the debt (granted a mortgage) and then held it until maturity, that is, until it was repaid. Then in the 1980s banks started to sell on some of their debts to investors. This is known as the 'originate and distribute' model. Banks and building societies began to securitize mortgages and commercial loans and sold them to other institutions and investors for cash to increase liquidity, using the cash to make further loans or for other purposes, such as taking long-term debt off their balance sheet.

With cheaper funding available from wholesale markets and senior bank management given significant financial incentives to meet return-on-equity (RoE) targets, banks began to increase their leverage by taking on more debt to lend on to customers.

Increased financial sophistication, innovation and the desire for enhanced yield, often through leverage, led to the development of more complex financial products aimed at meeting investor demands, such as structured credit and credit derivatives. Some of these financial products were so complicated and complex, senior managers lacked an understanding of the risks involved, a situation that would come back to haunt them.

A further trend in financial markets was the increased globalization of financial activity. UK financial services organizations were key participants, borrowing and lending heavily in global wholesale markets, with rapidly increasing levels of foreign borrowing helping to fuel the rapid expansion of credit in the United Kingdom. Many buyers of UK residential mortgage-backed securities were foreign institutions.

With a significant proportion of banks' funding coming from other financial institutions, chains of interdependencies created by complex financial products and linkages between financial institutions inevitably grew. The opacity of the system also grew and the ability of individual institutions and regulators to identify and assess the build-up of risks declined. This increased the risk that problems or concerns in one part of the global financial system could be rapidly transmitted to another part of the system, and then be transmitted on again, and again.

In 2007 two Bear Stearns hedge funds collapsed. This triggered a significant reduction of global interbank liquidity as investors grew concerned about banks' exposures to bad debts and to each other. As 2008 progressed, the functioning of financial markets deteriorated further and funding problems at many banks continued to grow. The failure of Lehman Brothers ended the confidence that major institutions were 'too big to fail': AIG (a US insurance conglomerate) was rescued; retail deposit runs led to bank failures.

In the UK, Lloyd's (after they rescued HBOS) and Royal Bank of Scotland (RBS) had to seek government and taxpayer support as they were both considered to be too big to fail.

Funding for some banks dried up, resulting in Northern Rock having to seek Emergency Liquidity Assistance (ELA) from the Bank of England; they experienced a **retail bank run,** the first UK banking run since 1866.

The bubble had burst.

> **Retail bank run** When a large number of customers withdraw their deposits simultaneously due to concerns about the bank. Having large numbers of customers withdrawing their funds means banks could run out of cash (liquidity).

In 2009 the Treasury Select Committee published a report entitled *Key Themes Emerging from the Experience of Banks and Building Societies.* The following are extracts from that report:

> The events of 2007–2009 demonstrated on a very large scale the vulnerabilities of banks whose business models depended heavily on uninterrupted access to secured financing. Many banks relied on excessive short-term financing of long-term, illiquid assets.
>
> Banks that were least affected by the crisis had the ability to resist short-term funding because they had access to other sources of funding such as deposits and other liquidity pools including central bank lending facilities.
>
> The crisis also identified weaknesses in governance, incentives and infrastructure which undermined the effectiveness of risk controls. These failures reflected four challenges in governance:
>
> 1 The unwillingness or inability of boards of directors and senior managers to articulate, measure and adhere to a level of risk acceptable to the bank.
>
> 2 Arrangements that favoured risk takers at the expense of independent risk managers and control personnel.
>
> 3 Compensation plans that conflicted with the control objectives of the bank.

4 An inadequate and often fragmented infrastructure that hindered effective risk identification and measurement.

A key weakness in **corporate governance** stemmed from what several banks admitted was a disparity between the risks that their banks took and those that their boards of directors perceived that their banks were actually taking.

Within some banks the stature and influence of revenue producers exceeded those of risk managers and control functions. There was an imbalance between risk and rewards in the approaches to remuneration.

The financial crisis also highlighted the inadequacy of many banks' IT infrastructures in supporting the board management of financial risk undertaken by the banks. This was in some cases a result of poor integration of data that had resulted from banks' multiple mergers and acquisitions.

SOURCE House of Commons Treasury Committee, *Banking Crisis: Dealing with the failure of UK banks*, 2009

Illiquid assets   Those assets held by a bank that cannot be turned into cash quickly.

Corporate governance   The framework of rules, practices, processes and procedures by which an organization is directed and controlled by the senior management of the organization.

Mis-selling

The problems facing banks after the global financial crisis continued with a series of scandals post-crisis. One prominent scandal that continues to impact banks' financial performance relates to mis-selling of payment protection insurance (PPI).

Payment protection insurance (PPI)

Payment protection insurance offers credit protection insurance or loan repayment insurance that enables borrowers to repay or partly repay their borrowings if the borrower dies, becomes ill, disabled and unable to work, or they become unemployed.

PPI is not in itself a flawed product; it was originally designed to ensure policyholders could receive payments to cover credit commitments in certain circumstances. The problem was how these policies were sold and to whom they were sold. Policies were sold by the banks to people who would not have been able to claim or who were told that a policy had to be taken out as a condition of the borrowing.

The root cause of mis-selling was seen to be endemic in the sales culture of some banks, allowing for aggressive selling techniques and sales targets linked to bonuses. The FCA estimated that more than 64 million PPI policies were sold between 1990 and 2010. UK banks have set aside more than £40 billion for consumer redress payments, and this figure is still growing. The payment of £415.8 million by banks in January 2018 took the total refunds and compensation actually paid to consumers to £30 billion (FCA, 2018a).

The lessons learned from PPI can be seen in most of the FCA's policy developments. Under the FCA's product governance and intervention requirements, firms are expected to design products for specific target markets and monitor how well these products perform for the market for which they had been designed. They are also expected to review sales staff incentives to ensure remuneration is not driving inappropriate sales.

The UK's experience with PPI has been used as the blueprint for a new European directive governing the sale and distribution of insurance policies, the Insurance Distribution Directive (IDD). The aims of IDD are:

- to improve regulation in the retail insurance market;
- to create more opportunities for cross-border business;
- to provide for fair competition between distributors of insurance products;
- to strengthen consumer protection.

The IDD introduces a new requirement for those staff that sell, advise on and transact insurance contracts for all types of insurance customers. In force from October 2018, the IDD requires all insurance distributors to act at all times in the best interests of customers.

Packaged bank accounts

Packaged bank accounts are current accounts that come with a 'package' of extra features such as mobile phone insurance, travel insurance or car breakdown services, all for a monthly fee. Again, it is not the products themselves that are flawed, but the way they were sold.

If a customer does not use all features of the packaged bank account that does not mean the bank was wrong to sell it to them. However, if the account was sold something they did not want, need or could not use then it may be considered to have been mis-sold.

ACTIVITY 3.1

Read the examples provided by the Financial Ombudsman Service case studies:

http://www.financial-ombudsman.org.uk/publications/technical_notes/packaged-bank-accounts-case-studies.html

Interest rate hedging products (IRHPs)

In 2013 the FCA undertook a review of the way some banks sold interest rate hedging products (IRHPs) to SMEs. In 2016 they published a report into the failings of some banks when selling these products. Here are some extracts of the report:

> In 2012, we identified failings in the way that some banks sold structured collars, swaps, simple collars and cap products, which we collectively refer to as IRHPs. The banks involved agreed to review their sales of IRHPs made to unsophisticated customers since 2001.
>
> The full review started in May 2013. Our final progress update shows that the banks have completed their sales reviews, and have fewer than 100 consequential loss claims still to assess. They have sent a redress determination letter to 18,200 businesses and paid £2.2 billion in redress, including more than £500 million to deal with consequential losses.
>
> SOURCE FCA, 2016a

ACTIVITY 3.2

Read the full report, *The FCA Review into Failings in the Way Some Banks Sold Interest Rate Hedging Products*, here:

https://www.fca.org.uk/consumers/interest-rate-hedging-products

LIBOR manipulation

The London Interbank Offered Rate, or LIBOR, was based on the average interest rate at which banks could borrow from one another and a large number of investments and trades were based on LIBOR.

In the lead up to and during the financial crisis some trading arms in the investment banking divisions of the banks colluded to keep the LIBOR rate artificially low. As LIBOR was used as an indicator of a bank's health the deliberate manipulation of the rates led to some banks appearing stronger and more profitable than they actually were. This was criminal activity and in 2012 the Serious Fraud Office (SFO) undertook an investigation. Charges were brought against 13 individuals with varying degrees of success. One guilty plea, made in October 2014, was the first criminal conviction for a LIBOR offence in the UK.

Following the scandal, the Financial Conduct Authority transferred the supervision of LIBOR to a new entity, the ICE Benchmark Administration (IBA). The IBA is an independent UK subsidiary of the private US-based exchange operator Intercontinental Exchange, or ICE (SFO, 2018).

In 2016 the FCA published a report entitled *Benchmark Enforcement,* which provided details of the fines imposed on the banks relating to manipulation in both the LIBOR market and the Gold and Foreign Exchange (FX) market.

ACTIVITY 3.3

Read the report here: https://www.fca.org.uk/markets/benchmarks/enforcement

Market abuse

In September 2015, the FCA and the Competition and Markets Authority published a report on market abuse entitled *Competition Law and Wholesale Markets.* You may wonder: what has market abuse got to do with banking? This report includes a number of case studies, where banks have been penalized for market abuse.

> **ACTIVITY 3.4**
>
> Read the full report on market abuse and all the case studies at:
> https://www.fca.org.uk/publication/other/comp-law-ws-markets.pdf

The FICC Markets Standards Board (FMSB)

The FICC Markets Standards Board (FMSB) was established in 2015 as a private-sector response to the conduct problems revealed in global whole-sale fixed income currencies and commodities (FICC) markets after the financial crisis. FMSB has only one ambition: to help raise standards of conduct in global wholesale markets and thereby make those markets more transparent, fair and effective.

The FMSB is not a regulator, and has no statutory or regulatory author-ity. Instead, it is a body made up of members from within the industry, and its outputs are voluntary standards and guidance designed for market participants to have access to what is acceptable practice in areas where there is uncertainty. Its board meetings are attended by representatives of the Bank of England and the FCA (FMSB, 2016).

RBS's Global Restructuring Group (GRG)

Before the global financial crisis RBS had built a significant share in the SME market, predominantly though real-estate lending often relying on increas-ing property values rather than analysing the quality of the borrower and cash flows. When the crisis occurred and property values fell, RBS expe-rienced a sharp increase in non-performing loans. At its peak, GRG took control of approximately 16,000 SME customers with £65 billion of assets.

In 2013 Lawrence Tomlinson, who was the Entrepreneur in Residence at the Department for Business, Innovation and Skills, published a report that focused on evidence he had received from RBS's business customers about GRG. Lawrence called for further investigation into RBS's and GRG's behaviour by the authorities to stop what he determined to be unscrupulous and unfair treatment of customers in GRG.

The FCA undertook an investigation and in 2016 and completed its review, albeit this was not released in the public domain until March 2018. The report concluded that there was evidence of widespread and inappropriate treatment of SME customers by RBS; however, there was no evidence of RBS forcing businesses into default for its own benefit. The report's authors found that 16 per cent of business they analysed were still viable when they entered GRG and were likely to have suffered 'material financial distress' due to its treatment of them.

Whilst RBS did not set out to engineer financial difficulty, the bank had a 'conflict of interest', with staff encouraged to prioritize the extraction of additional fees and interest margins to boost revenues, rather than looking after the needs of the customers. The report also concluded that GRG's management was aware, or should have been aware, of these issues and it was clear that the senior management in RBS were aware, at least in part, of some of these failures but chose not to prioritize action to overcome them.

RBS responded by saying that it was 'deeply sorry' that customers had not been treated well by staff in GRG during and after the financial crisis. The bank said: 'The culture, structure and way RBS operates today have all changed fundamentally since the period under review and we have made significant changes to deal with the issues of the past, including how we treat customers in financial distress' (UK Parliament, 2018).

Clearly mis-selling, market manipulation and abuse demonstrated severe failures in corporate governance.

Corporate governance

The development of corporate governance in the UK has its roots in a series of corporate collapses and scandals in the late 1980s and early 1990s. This led to the setting up in 1991 of a committee chaired by Sir Adrian Cadbury which issued a series of recommendations, known as the Cadbury Report (1992). The Cadbury Report addressed issues such as the relationship between the chairman and chief executive, the role of non-executive directors, and reporting on internal control and on the company's overall financial position.

The recommendations in the Cadbury Report have been added to at regular intervals since 1992. In 1995 a separate report set out recommendations on the remuneration of directors, and in 1998 the two reports were brought together in a single code (known initially as the Combined Code and now known as the UK Corporate Governance Code). In 1999 separate guidance was issued to directors on how to develop risk management and internal control systems.

In 2003 the code was updated to incorporate recommendations from reports on the role of non-executive directors and the role of the audit committee. Whilst the code does not carry legal force, it is a requirement under the Listing Rules of the London Stock Exchange that all listed companies either *comply* with its recommendations or *explain* to the shareholders the reasons for non-compliance.

The main principles of the code are set out in five sections:

1 leadership;

2 effectiveness;

3 accountability;

4 remuneration;

5 relations with shareholders.

Leadership

Every company should be led by an effective board, collectively responsible for the long-term success of the company. There should be clear division of responsibility between those responsible for the direction of the company (the board) and those responsible for day-to-day operations (the executive). No individual should have unfettered powers of decision. The code stresses that the role of the chairman is to lead the board of directors and ensure its effectiveness. It also highlights the duty of non-executive directors in constructively challenging and helping to develop proposals on strategy.

Board effectiveness

The board of directors should be made up of an appropriate number of persons with an appropriate balance of skills, experience, independence and knowledge to enable them to discharge their duties effectively. The procedures for the appointment of new directors should be formal, rigorous and transparent. On joining the board, new directors should receive induction. They should also update their knowledge and skills on a regular basis. To discharge their duties effectively, directors should be supplied with timely and good-quality information. The board should undertake a formal, rigorous evaluation of its performance, and that of its standing committees, on an annual basis.

Accountability

The board should present a balanced and understandable assessment of the company's position and prospects. This commitment relates to the information that the company provides to its shareholders and other stakeholders. The board must decide the nature and extent of the significant risks it will take in pursuing its objectives. To this end, it must maintain appropriate risk management and internal control systems.

Remuneration

Remuneration offered and paid to directors should be sufficient to attract, retain and motivate directors of the quality required to run the company successfully, but they should not be paid too much. A significant proportion of executive directors' remuneration should be performance-related in order to align the long-term interests of the company with the recipient. There should be a formal and transparent procedure for developing policy on remuneration and for setting the remuneration of individual directors. Consistent with best practices, no individual should be able to decide his or her own remuneration.

Relations with shareholders

It is the collective responsibility of the board to encourage dialogue with shareholders based on mutual understanding of objectives. The board should use the annual general meeting to communicate with investors and encourage their participation.

UK Corporate Governance Code (2016)

The UK Corporate Governance Code was updated in 2016 and applies to accounting periods beginning on or after 17 June 2016. It is designed to comply with new EU regulations on statutory audit. The code updates its guidance on ethical standards, audit committees and auditing standards.

One of the key roles for the board includes establishing the culture, values and ethics of the organization. The directors should lead by example and ensure that good standards of behaviour permeate throughout all levels of the organization. This is intended to help prevent misconduct, unethical practices and support the delivery of long-term success.

In February 2017, the FRC announced plans for a comprehensive review of the UK Corporate Governance Code. A public consultation, including a draft revised code, was issued in December 2017 and closed on 28 February 2018.

REGULATION
The UK Corporate Governance Code (2016)

www

For further information and updates visit:
https://www.frc.org.uk/consultation-list/2017/consulting-on-a-revised-uk-corporate-governance-co

---

It is anticipated that a new 2019 code will become effective for all companies with a premium listing of equity shares, whether they are incorporated in the UK or elsewhere and will be applied for accounting periods beginning on or after 1 January 2019.

As a relationship manager, especially if you have responsibility for lending, you will inevitably look to see how your businesses apply corporate governance within their organizations. Lenders will often benchmark customers in the five corporate governance sections.

Leadership

This looks at how strategy is communicated, accepted and implemented by the board and employees. You will need to understand who actually drives the strategy and how capable they are.

Effectiveness

It is not unusual in small SME owner-managed businesses to find that one or two people undertake a number of roles, and that some roles are combined. For example, a managing director of an owner-managed business may control both the day-to-day running of the business and the day-to-day finances.

Larger organizations are likely to have more clearly defined structures than smaller businesses. Whatever their size, businesses need to ensure that they have the most appropriate structure for their size and the markets in which they operate.

It is not uncommon for smaller or young companies to have gaps in their skills or knowledge base. This may not always be an impediment, as long as the gaps are recognized and understood. For example, a young business may not have the resources to produce forecasts and budgets, so it may use its auditors or accountants to help with this task. Things to look out for include:

- Do managers hesitate to make decisions or delegate difficult decisions upward?

- Do they spend too much time on minor matters and therefore overlook the major ones that can severely impact the organization?

Accountability

Here you will be trying to establish that the management team has the right balance of skills. To determine how well the team works together, a lender should consider experience, breadth, depth and integrity. Considering each of these in turn:

- Experience – this relates not only to the length of time members of the management team have spent in the business but also the level of abilities. Many smaller businesses can survive well during the good times, but do not have sufficient experience, skills or expertise when things start to go wrong. Inexperienced management teams that have not been through several business cycles may present a greater risk than those that have; the risk becomes greater when market conditions worsen.

- Breadth – this relates to identifying gaps in knowledge or skill. Where there are gaps, how are these filled? Does the management team bring in outside experience or skills? If they do, do they listen and act upon the advice given?

- Depth – if the performance of the business is reliant upon the efforts of one or two key individuals, you should be concerned with the risk if those people were to leave or become unable to carry out their duties. Does the business have a succession plan?

- Integrity – can the people who run the company be trusted? Integrity also relates to the management team's reliability, openness and willingness to share information (good or bad), and a readiness to honour all the obligations they make.

Risk management and financial acumen are also important areas to consider:

- Do the members of the management team know what risks they face now and in the future?
- Do they plan for risk or do they react only when risk emerges unannounced?
- Do they use management information to identify or anticipate risk?

Producing high-quality management information (MI) is not just about the ability to identify what can be measured, but also what needs to be measured to control risk. The best management information systems (MIS) should provide accurate data to the right people at the right time and it needs to be acted upon on a timely basis. High-quality MI is good evidence that the management team know what is going on; poor-quality MI provided infrequently or irregularly suggests that they do not.

The financial acumen of the management team is also of prime importance to lenders:

- Have managers got a firm hand on the finances?
- How well do they anticipate their funding needs?
- What information do they need, provide or use to support their funding requirements?
- Do they produce financial accounts and are these adequate for the business?
- How good are they at achieving their forecasts?

Remuneration

Do they pay too little or too much? Some small businesses are lifestyle businesses where the owner–manager uses the business to fund their own personal lifestyle. Do they take too much out of the business?

Relationships with shareholders

Who are the shareholders? Are they the same as the owners?

Assessing management is a big task, it takes time and involves raising a number of searching questions, the answers to which will provide you with evidence of the management team's capabilities and the effectiveness of their corporate governance.

CASE STUDY
Bradford & Bingley

Bradford & Bingley plc had a history stretching back to 1851, the year in which both the Bradford Equitable Building Society and the Bingley Building Society were established. The two societies merged in 1964 and operated as the Bradford & Bingley Building Society until the year 2000 when Bradford & Bingley's members voted to demutualize the society and form a public limited company.

Bradford & Bingley's Annual Report in the year prior to demutualization in 1999 reported that Bradford & Bingley had a loan book of £18.4 billion and retail savings balances amounting to £15.5 billion. By June 2008, Bradford & Bingley's residential loan book stood at £41.3 billion whilst customer deposits amounted to £24.5 billion.

Bradford & Bingley's expansion was aided by a number of acquisitions that began prior to demutualization, which included the acquisition of Mortgage Express in 1997. Mortgage Express was a specialist mortgage lender focusing on lending to the self-employed using self-certification mortgages. After that acquisition, Bradford & Bingley began rapidly to expand this area of its business, using its Mortgage Express arm to focus on self-certification, buy-to-let properties and providing 100 per cent plus (loan-to-value) mortgages. Upon acquisition, Mortgage Express accounted for 4 per cent of total Bradford & Bingley lending; after just a year, in 1998, this figure had risen to 15 per cent of new loans; by 2000 it was 40 per cent.

A second element to Bradford & Bingley's growth was a series of deals with the US company General Motors Acceptance Corporation (GMAC). The first of these, in 2002, committed Bradford & Bingley to acquiring a mixed loan portfolio of £650 million of buy-to-let, self-certified and standard loans from GMAC. This deal was followed by a flurry of loan acquisitions in 2003: £470 million was taken on from GMAC in March; £106 million in October; £450 million in November; and a three-year agreement covering £1.4 billion of loans was signed in December 2003.

A second three-year agreement was signed in 2006. Bradford & Bingley continued to implement this agreement after it moved into public ownership. The last tranche of loans was handed over from GMAC to Bradford & Bingley in public ownership on 27 February 2009. This committed Bradford & Bingley to purchasing a minimum of £350 million of UK mortgage assets per quarter for three years. In total,

Bradford & Bingley had taken on £6.5 billion of self-certified and buy-to-let UK mortgages from GMAC by the time it was nationalized.

The chairman, Richard Pym, admitted that, 'with the benefit of hindsight, the inflexibility that was built in to the GMAC contract did not allow us the flexibility that we would otherwise have liked as the market deteriorated'. He identified the principal problem as the fact that 'the underwriting criteria that were written into the contract in December 2006, meant that when credit conditions deteriorated there was no ability to change the underwriting criteria for the loans' (House of Commons Treasury Committee, 2009).

In 2008, Bradford and Bingley's business was 60 per cent buy-to-let and 20 per cent self-certified, and the value of buy-to-let mortgages on Bradford & Bingley's books was £24 billion, a figure which represented 20 per cent of the entire UK buy-to-let market.

Bradford & Bingley argued that its downfall was caused by difficulties in obtaining both wholesale and retail funding. The gap in the size of the increase in retail deposits (59 per cent) relative to that in loans (124 per cent) suggests that Bradford & Bingley, in common with many other financial institutions, funded much of this growth via the wholesale markets.

The availability of wholesale funding declined and the cost of both retail and wholesale funding increased. The market value of some of the bank's treasury assets reduced. Mortgage arrears increased and customers found it more difficult to secure mortgages elsewhere, increasing Bradford & Bingley's funding needs. Through June and July 2008 Bradford & Bingley had its credit rating cut by the major ratings agencies, which led to withdrawals of wholesale and retail deposits.

When the collapse came for Bradford & Bingley it was sudden and dramatic. In the week commencing Monday 22 September 2008, in a single 24-hour period, the company had £90 million withdrawn from its branches. The position on Wednesday was that the bank had an outflow of funds from the branches and from online of £12 million. On Thursday, they lost a further £26 million. On Friday, following further media reporting, they lost around £90 million and by lunchtime on Saturday had an outflow of around £200 million from branches and online. It was that which forced the regulators to act.

On 27 September 2008, the regulators determined that Bradford & Bingley was unable or likely to be unable to satisfy claims against it and as a result no longer met its threshold conditions to operate as a deposit-taker under the Financial Services and Markets Act 2000. This was because the bank was heavily reliant on buy-to-let and self-certified mortgages which proved particularly vulnerable to a sharp rise in the rate of arrears during the economic downturn.

The government transferred Bradford & Bingley's retail deposit business along with its branch network to Abbey National plc whilst the remainder of Bradford & Bingley assets and liabilities, comprising its mortgage book, personal loan book, headquarters and relevant staff, and treasury assets and wholesale liabilities, was taken into public ownership with the intention of winding down operations.

After 149 years as a mutual, Bradford & Bingley's life as a plc lasted a little over eight years, ending on 29 September 2008.

Summarize why Bradford and Bingley failed. Once you have completed your analysis, compare your answer to the one provided in Appendix 3.1.

Ethical behaviour

In 2017 Mark Carney, the governor of the Bank of England, gave a speech to the Banking Standards Board. In his opening remarks the governor reviewed the main elements of the Bank of England's work to lift ethical standards in the financial services industry, and he spoke of how codes of conduct such as the Senior Managers Conduct Regime (SMCR) could improve culture within the industry. (Note: the aim of the SMCR, introduced in 2016, was to reduce harm to consumers and strengthen market integrity by making individuals more accountable for their conduct and competence. SMCR is covered in more detail in Chapter 4.)

ACTIVITY 3.5

Follow the link given in the Further Reading section at the end of this chapter, and read the speech given by Mark Carney, the governor of the Bank of England entitled 'Worthy of trust? Law, ethics and culture in banking' (Carney, 2017).

His speech concludes that: 'Senior managers are increasingly focusing on building cultures of risk awareness, openness and ethical behaviour...'. The governor of the Bank of England makes a direct connection between SMCR and ethics.

Ethics

Ethics is concerned with morally correct behaviour. However, people may have different views about what is considered to be morally correct.

Question

You find a £1 coin in the street. What do you do? Pocket it (finders keepers) and move on? Put it in the nearest charity collection box? Take it to the police station and report you have just found it?

Would your answer be any different if instead of a £1 coin you found £2,000 in notes?

Morally correct behaviour is in the eyes of the beholder and is unique to an individual. It will be determined by your upbringing, personal values, the law and the view of others. Ethics has an element of judgment to it. Laws are based on what people feel are the acceptable and the ethical standards of society. All cultures have systems of ethics and what may be ethical in one culture may not be in another.

But ethics is not only about compliance with the law; ethics extends beyond this. Some people may equate ethical behaviour with legal behaviour, disregarding the fact that even though an action may not be illegal, it still may not be ethical. Yet some contend that the only requirement is to obey the law. They ignore the spirit of the law by only following the letter of the law. Consider tax evasion: this is illegal, whereas tax avoidance is not. However, deliberate attempts to exploit the tax system for personal gain are, in most people's eyes, considered to be both unethical and immoral.

Critics have argued that these traits were evident before, during and after the financial crisis. Consider the subsequent mis-selling incidents that have emerged such as the accusations of LIBOR fixing, foreign exchange market manipulations, interest rate hedging products, PPI, etc. Some of these products were designed to help customers, and many did, so it was not the products that were wrong. It was how they were sold that was called into question.

The responsibility to act ethically lies with both the individual (mis-selling a product for personal gain in order to achieve sales targets, bonuses or enhanced status) and the bank (instructing the individual to do so). Where customers have been mis-sold products, there must be joint culpability. People and organizations who took advantage of customers did not consider whether it was right or wrong, or even if it was the best outcome for the customer. They seemed more concerned with whether it was legal and profitable, not morally correct and in the best interests of the customer.

Consider a scenario where a commercial line manager is addressing front-line relationship managers. The line manager extols the virtue of a new, cheap but profitable insurance product recently launched for SME custom-ers. The policy provides cover if the policyholder becomes absent from the business due to ill health or death. In this event, the proceeds of the policy would repay the outstanding balance on the loan. The line manager explains that part of any relationship manager's role is that of being a risk manager, and what better way to mitigate risk for the customer (and the bank) if they sold a policy each time they lent? Does this sound ethical? Is it legal? Would you be surprised if some relationship managers began to make the purchase of a policy conditional for providing a lending facility?

Insurance policies are regulated products and any suggestion of forc-ing a borrower to take a policy out as a precondition of the borrowing is undoubtedly illegal, but recommending such a policy is not, as long as the customer makes their own informed choice. The question is whether this is an informed choice or whether there is an implied assertion that if the customer wants or needs the borrowing, they will have to take out a policy. Whatever the circumstances, it may or may not be legal, but it does appear to be unethical and could lead to a breakdown in trust between the customer and the bank.

Trust is slow to build and is much easier to damage than create, and noth-ing is more likely to lead to a breakdown of trust with customers than if they feel they have been misled. In Governor Carney's speech, he cites that 'in a system where trust is fundamental it ought to be of grave concern that only 20 per cent of UK citizens now think that banks are well run, down from 90 per cent in the late 1980s'.

This lack of trust has resulted from the perception that the interests of the customer have been disregarded in the pursuit of profit and aggressive sales cultures that have been prevalent over many years. Remember: Bradford & Bingley took 157 years to build trust, but this was destroyed in a matter of days.

Sustainability of financial services

The ability of financial markets to keep going is based on confidence and trust; if confidence and trust are undermined, the system fails. A financial system where there is a chance that it might fail is not sustainable.

Sustainability of financial services is vital for the population. If banks and other financial institutions were to fail, it would damage the monetary system and the economy as a whole. The economy could collapse if banks were unable to operate payment systems. The public could not receive or pay for goods and services unless they dealt in cash. But without access to ATMs they would not be able to access cash. They couldn't pay and they wouldn't be paid.

Without sustainable financial services, the entire population would be open to a high degree of uncertainty; and uncertainty can bring down an economic system. The effective functioning of an economy depends on banks ensuring the supply of credit and liquidity throughout the business cycle and in all market conditions. Banks are therefore a critical infrastructure component in an economy.

If a bank came close to failure, the authorities and regulators would initiate resolution powers to avert the collapse in order to restore trust in the whole financial system. This is what occurred during the global financial crisis. Banks are not like other corporate entities; compared to many other sectors banking affects a large number and a great variety of people, so banks have an implied social responsibility to the rest of the population. Banks and many other organizations are realizing that there is more to maximization of profitability or returns on investment; if they deal with the population, social and environmental impacts must be considered.

Corporate social responsibility (CSR)

Social responsibility is a form of corporate self-regulation integrated into a business model. It functions as a built-in, self-regulating mechanism whereby an organization monitors and ensures its compliance with the spirit of the law, ethical standards and international norms. It is also concerned with giving something back into the community.

When practising social responsibility, the overarching goal for an organization is to maximize its contribution to sustainability to ensure it meets the needs of the present without compromising the ability of future generations to meet their own needs. CSR promotes sustainability.

CSR in banking models

Social responsibility equates to providing fair and transparent financial services. Customers expect secure products and appropriate information or advice.

Responsible lending is also a requirement and banks need to consider the moral obligations of providing credit to organizations that pollute the environment, supply unsafe products or violate human rights. Responsible lending also means acting in the customer's best interests, ensuring affordability, transparency of terms and conditions and supporting a borrower if they experience financial repayment difficulties.

Banks are expected to provide jobs, and are legally required to provide appropriate working conditions and equal opportunities in the workplace that is free from discrimination. Banks are also required to obey the spirit of the law as well as the actual law. Because something is legal it does not mean it's ethical.

The perception of a lack of ethical culture within banks was a major contributing factor in the lack of trust in the banking sector. So a culture of ethics and integrity within the banking sector needed to be re-established. It is not enough to come up with ethical principles; they must also be implemented. Ethics is an ongoing project to help restore trust in the banking sector.

Banks are legally required to help combat areas that can damage society such as corruption, bribery and money-laundering activities that can finance crime and terrorism. Banks are also expected to improve financial capability such as financial literacy, awareness and financial education.

Banks are expected to contribute to social issues such as providing banking services to disadvantaged or socially excluded citizens such as those who are unable to afford financial products and services, or helping customers with special needs and protecting vulnerable customers.

Customer vulnerability

The FCA defines a vulnerable customer as someone who, due to their personal circumstances, is susceptible to detriment, particularly when a firm is not acting with appropriate levels of care (FCA, 2015).

Much consumer protection legislation is underpinned by the notion of the average or typical consumer, and what they might expect, understand or how they might behave. Consumers in vulnerable circumstances, however, may be significantly less able to represent their own interests, and are more likely to suffer harm than the average consumer.

> Would you consider RBS customers in GRG to be vulnerable?

Many of the SME customers transferred to GRG were not financially sophisticated and their financial distress may have added to their vulnerability. In addition, being inside such a unit would have been a new experience for many, and some of the concepts and terms used would not have been well understood.

Many banks have additional questions they ask customers around their vulnerability prior to lending, and have set up separate units to deal with customers who are experiencing financial difficulty.

Social responsibility and sustainability are evident in the way banks are recovering after the global financial crisis. These issues are important to the way banks are looking to restore trust and faith in the sector. There is a genuine commitment at board level to create customer-centric banks and a recognition that good conduct must link directly to ethics, social responsibility, personal morality and integrity.

> **Social responsibility**   An ethical framework that acts for the benefit of the society in which an organization operates.

Product governance

Delivering the right outcome for customers is critical and that means replacing the 'product push' sales approach of the past with a much more thoughtful and transparent 'product life cycle' approach. In the context of achieving the right long-term outcome for customers, banks need to move from a product push to a product life cycle approach.

Regulators in the UK have already been emphasizing the importance of the product life cycle approach. To achieve an approach focused on customer outcome banks need to access and make use of all the right data about customers to make an informed sales decision.

The following are extracts from the regulator's (FSA/FCA) Retail Product Development and Governance Review (2012):

The key finding from our review is that, whilst firms had taken on board many of our messages on treating customers fairly, there were still weaknesses in product governance arrangements. Overall, firms still focus too much on their commercial position, potentially at the expense of consumer outcomes. At the governance level, we found a basic weakness in firms' identification of the target market(s) for their products. We believe this reflects a strategic failure to consider:

- 'What do consumers need and want? How can we make it?'

rather than:

- 'What can we make? How can we persuade consumers to buy them?'

Both banks and regulators will continue to focus on product suitability and evolve methods to measure customer outcomes rather than just the traditional customer satisfaction measures. Banks will have to fundamentally rethink their product strategies on which products they sell, to whom they sell and which geographies they should concentrate on aligned with a clear focus on the customer needs and outcome.

In March 2018 the FCA completed its review into product governance in small to medium-sized retail banks. It examined how well banks consider customers' needs when they design and sell products and provide after-sales services. The review looked at two-year fixed rate savings products from a sample of small to medium-sized banks. The FCA focused on how firms' product governance frameworks help them identify and manage the ongoing conduct risks of their products.

They found that all firms had appropriate product-focused committees and that senior management were involved throughout the decision-making process and the life cycle of the products. Whilst product design processes were embedded and established, more needed to be done to review those processes once products had gone on sale.

They found examples of good practice and room for improvement in some areas. Some firms needed to strengthen their product review processes to ensure they act on any identified lessons or risks, for example, recording the outcome of product reviews more clearly. All firms gave clear and concise information in their letters to customers. However, some firms need to be clearer in their terms and conditions and other product information about whether customers can withdraw funds before the term ends without penalty.

SOURCE FCA, 2018b

Rebuilding trust and reputation

The Banking Standards Board (BSB) was established in April 2015 to promote high standards of ethical behaviour and competence across UK banks and building societies. It states:

> The UK economy needs a strong, stable banking sector that serves the best interests of its customers. For the sector to contribute fully to the economy and society it needs to be trusted; not only by its customers, but also by its staff, potential employees, regulators and by policymakers.

The BSB is a private-sector body funded by membership subscriptions and open to all banks and building societies operating in the UK. It is neither a regulator nor a trade association; it has no statutory powers, and it will not speak or lobby for the industry. It will, instead, provide challenge, support and scrutiny for banks committed to rebuilding the sector's reputation, and it will provide impartial and objective assessments of the industry's progress.

An industry response

One leading industry initiative is the Chartered Banker Professional Standards Board (CB:PSB), which is a voluntary joint initiative by eight leading banks in the UK and the Chartered Institute. It was established in 2011 and was set up to:

- develop a series of professional standards to support the ethical awareness, customer focus and competence of those working in the banking industry;
- facilitate industry and public awareness and recognition of the standards;
- establish mechanisms for the implementation, monitoring and enforcement of the standards;
- help build, over time, greater public confidence and trust in individuals, institutions and the banking industry overall, and enhance pride in the banking profession.

The Board's overall aim is to restore public confidence and trust in the industry, and promote a culture of professionalism amongst individual bankers, creating industry-wide standards for professional knowledge, skills and competences.

The Chartered Banker Code of Professional Conduct

The Chartered Banker Institute's Code of Professional Conduct sets out the ethical and professional values, attitudes and behaviour expected of all professional bankers. All members of the Institute are bound to comply with the code of conduct (Chartered Banker, 2016).

The code sets out how individuals should follow best practice and demonstrate their personal commitment to professionalism in banking, by:

- treating all customers, colleagues and counterparties with respect and acting with integrity;
- developing and maintaining their professional knowledge and acting with due skill, care and diligence, considering the risks and implications of their actions and advice, and holding themselves accountable for them and their impact;
- being open and cooperative with the regulators;
- complying with all current regulatory and legal requirements;
- paying due regard to the interests of customers and treating them fairly;
- observing and demonstrating proper standards of market conduct at all times;
- acting in an honest and trustworthy manner, being alert to and managing potential conflicts of interest;
- treating information with appropriate confidentiality and sensitivity.

To be able to properly recognize and apply the values, attitudes and behaviours set out in the code in their daily professional activities, individuals must have gained the requisite levels of competence relevant to their role.

To help members maintain these high standards the Institute's Code of Professional Standards identifies key attitudes and behaviours expected of members and provides guidance to help members recognize and develop appropriate behaviours. Failure to meet the high standards expected may result in suspension or expulsion from the Institute.

Doing the right thing and making the right decisions: questions to ask yourself

The following six questions form a good model for asking yourself the right questions when making decisions:

1 *Is it legal?* If the answer is no, talk to your line manager immediately or to another trusted senior manager.

2 *Does it go against any bank policies or procedures?* If the answer is yes, talk to your line manager immediately or to another trusted subject matter expert.

3 *Does it go against the bank's values?* If the answer is yes, it is probably not something that will enhance the bank's reputation and could even damage it. If you are unsure, talk to your line manager or to another trusted senior manager or subject matter expert.

4 *Can you justify taking this action to your colleagues, manager and family?* If it would be hard to justify and would make you feel embarrassed or uncomfortable, then it's probably not the right thing to do.

5 *Does it set a good example to other colleagues or people you know?* If the answer is no, think about the consequences of colleagues or other people you know doing this. If it's not right for them, it's probably not right for you

6 *Would you be happy if other people knew about the action you have taken?* If the answer is no, this probably puts the bank's reputation at risk so *do not do it* – talk to your line manager.

Generally speaking, when making a decision, if you can answer yes to Question 6 it's probably all right to do it, but you can always ask someone else for advice.

What would you do if you saw or heard a colleague doing something you thought was unethical or even illegal?
What if the person in question was more senior than you?
What should you do if you have done something wrong?

Raising concerns

What should you do if you suspect something you have seen or heard about is unsafe, unethical, unlawful or not in line with policies or procedures? You should always speak up if you have suspicions of inappropriate behaviour or conduct so that it can be investigated as soon as possible. You cannot wait for something to go wrong before acting. There should be no negative consequences for you even if your concerns turn out to be unfounded.

All banks have support mechanisms (internal and/or external) in place to address these kinds of problems and most provide an anonymous hotline to help.

Whistleblowing

The Financial Conduct Authority (FCA), alongside the Prudential Regulation Authority (PRA), has published rules in relation to whistleblowing. The FCA's report examines the impact of whistleblowing for firms regulated by the FCA, whilst the PRA's approach is more aligned to the individual whistleblower.

These changes follow recommendations in 2013 by the Parliamentary Commission on Banking Standards (PCBS) that banks should put in place mechanisms to allow their employees to raise concerns internally (ie to 'blow the whistle') and appoint a senior person to take responsibility for the effectiveness of these arrangements.

Individuals working for financial institutions may be reluctant to speak out about wrongdoing for fear of suffering personally as a consequence. Mechanisms within firms to encourage people to voice concerns by, for example, offering confidentiality to those speaking up can provide comfort to whistleblowers. It is, however, important that individuals also have the confidence to approach their employers.

The FCA has published a package of rules designed to build on and formalize the good practice already widespread in the financial services industry. These rules aim to encourage a culture where individuals feel able to raise concerns and challenge poor practice and behaviour (FCA, 2016b).

ACTIVITY 3.6

Full details of the whistleblowing rules can be found on the FCA's website – follow this link to find out more: https://www.fca.org.uk/news/press-releases/fca-introduces-new-rules-whistleblowing

Now read the following FCA report paying particular attention to the case studies which illustrate the range of issues whistleblowers have reported to the FCA: *How We Handle Disclosures from Whistleblowers* (February 2015): https://www.fca.org.uk/publication/corporate/how-we-handle-disclosures-from-whistleblowers.pdf

As stated above, the PRA's approach to whistleblowing is more aligned to individuals who 'blow the whistle'. Their policy is to guide firms to set up internal procedures which will encourage workers to come forward, but further allows for direct contact should the whistleblower suspect their employer:

- will cover it up;
- would treat them unfairly if they complained;
- hasn't sorted it out despite having already been told.

The PRA website offers guidance around who should blow the whistle, and how they should do so, and goes on to discuss what will happen once the issue has been reported (Bank of England, 2018).

This subject is taken very seriously by the regulators. Barclays' CEO James ('Jes') Staley has been involved in an incident recently relating to an alleged attempt to unmask a whistleblower from within his organization.

ACTIVITY 3.7

Investigate the circumstances of the Jes Staley case by reading the FCA report here: https://www.fca.org.uk/news/press-releases/ fca-and-pra-jointly-fine-mr-james-staley-announce-special-requirements

What is your analysis? What impact would this have on whistleblowing within Barclays?

Your contribution

One of the roles and responsibilities of a relationship manager is to restore trust and confidence in your own bank and the banking sector generally. Trust is built around knowledge and experience, and being able to articulate this to customers and prospects. One way to achieve this is by developing nurturing and collaborative relationships with customers. History teaches us that effective communication lies at the heart of good relationships as a means of building trust and nurturing long-term relationships.

Communication is a two-way process that helps you to understand your customers and helps the customer to understand the bank's methods and processes. A good relationship manager is someone who, from the customer's perspective, does what he or she says they will do and within the timeframe expected or agreed.

You need a number of personal skills to build trust and confidence and this includes being an effective communicator, which also means you have to be a good listener. The relationship manager will want to put their views across in a way that is acceptable to the customer, taking enough time to discuss all their concerns. They treat their customers as they would like to be treated, with decency and respect. The best banking relationships are based on openness and honesty; there should be no nasty surprises, either from the bank or the customer.

It is your duty to help improve the bank's reputation by dealing effectively and professionally with customers; above all, the customer wants to feel he or she is being treated fairly by you and the bank. Your ability to achieve this will give you and your bank a competitive advantage in the marketplace.

ACTIVITY 3.8

Consider a colleague who does the same job function as yourself, and who you consider to be an exemplar in the role.

Ask yourself:

- *What makes them so special?*
- *What attributes do they possess that others don't?*
- *How would their customers describe them and why?*
- *What qualities do you need to develop to become like your role model?*
- *What do you need to change to become more like them?*

The role model you chose in Activity 3.8 will have certain qualities that make them stand out, such as:

- they act in a professional and ethical way at all times;
- they consider the risks and implications of their actions and are accountable for them;
- they treat everyone with respect;
- they lead by example and are a role model for others;
- they continuously develop and maintain their technical and professional knowledge, skills and competences;

- they uphold the name and reputation of the bank, the banking profession and the financial services industry as a whole;
- their customers admire, respect and trust them;
- they really enjoy their job.

As we started this chapter you were asked to score yourself about the knowledge you had on the crisis and how the banking sector is working to restore its reputation. How would you score yourself now?

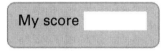

How have your views changed? Are there any areas you need to review or revisit or discuss further with a colleague or with your line manager?

The global financial crisis, mis-selling and market abuse and manipulation have undoubtedly damaged the reputation of the banking sector, including those banks and bankers who were not culpable or guilty of any wrongdoing. Indeed, before, during and after the global financial crisis the vast majority of relationship managers remained well-balanced professional individuals who exhibited and continue to exhibit all the right ethical and professional behaviours. They achieved this by holding on to their principles and values and focusing on their customers throughout what was a very challenging and difficult period.

There are many lessons to be learned from the events of 2008–09 including the reasons why things went so disastrously wrong, and how the sector has recovered and continues to do so. Regulation, corporate governance, risk management and conduct regimes have all played their part, as have the banks. It is now your turn.

Chapter summary

In this chapter we have explored:

- the events leading up to the global financial crisis;
- a number of mis-selling and market abuse incidents;
- the development of corporate governance in the UK;
- trust, and how the banks have set out to rebuild trust with their customers;
- what is meant by ethical behaviours;
- the sustainability of the financial sector.

Objective check

1 What do you assess to be the core reasons for the global financial crisis?

2 How has corporate governance changed in the years since the crisis?

3 What actions have banks taken in their attempts to rebuild trust with their customers?

4 Do you believe these actions have been successful? What else should be done?

Further reading

Bank of England (June 2015) *Fair and Effective Markets Review* [online]. Available at: http://www.bankofengland.co.uk/markets/Pages/fmreview.aspx [accessed 9 September 2017]

British Bankers Association (2015) *Good Returns: What banks are putting back into communities* [online]. Available at: https://www.bba.org.uk/publication/bba-reports/good-returns-what-banks-are-putting-back-into-communities-2/ [accessed 3 November 2017]

Carroll, AB (1991) The pyramid of corporate social responsibility: Toward the moral management of organizational stakeholders, *Business Horizons*, 34 (4), pp 39–48

Financial Reporting Council (October 2010) *The UK Approach to Corporate Governance* [online]. Available at: https://www.governance.co.uk/resources/item/257-the-uk-approach-to-corporate-governance [accessed 9 September 2017]

FSA (2012) *Retail Product Development and Governance: Structured product review* [pdf]. Available at: https://www.fca.org.uk/publication/finalised-guidance/fg12-09.pdf [accessed 9 February 2018]

HM Treasury (July 2009) *Reforming Financial Markets* [pdf]. Available at: https://www.gov.uk/government/publications/reforming-financial-markets [accessed 9 September 2017]

HM Treasury (March 2012) *Review of HM Treasury's Management Response to the Financial Crisis* [pdf]. Available at: https://www.gov.uk/government/publications/review-of-hm-treasurys-response-to-the-financial-crisis-2007-09 [accessed 9 September 2017]

House of Commons Treasury Committee (2008) *Financial Stability and Transparency: Sixth report of session 2007-08* [pdf]. Available at: https://publications.parliament.uk/pa/cm200708/cmselect/cmtreasy/371/371.pdf [accessed 9 September 2017]

International Organization for Standardization (2016) *ISO 26000: Social responsibility* [online]. Available at: https://www.iso.org/iso-26000-social-responsibility.html [accessed 9 September 2017]

Senior Supervisors Group (2008) *Observations on Risk Management Practices during the Recent Market Turbulence* [pdf]. Available at: https://www.sec.gov/news/press/2008/report030608.pdf [accessed 9 September 2017]

UK Parliament (2009) *The Banking Crisis: Dealing with the failure of the UK banks* (7th edn) [pdf]. Available at: https://publications.parliament.uk/pa/cm200809/cmselect/cmtreasy/416/416.pdf [Accessed 9 September 2017]

Walker, D (2009) *A review of corporate governance in UK banks and other financial industry entities: Final recommendations* [online]. Available at: http://webarchive.nationalarchives.gov.uk/+/http:/www.hm-treasury.gov.uk/d/walker_review_261109.pdf

References

Bank of England (2018) *Whistleblowing and the Bank of England* [online]. Available at: https://www.fca.org.uk/publication/corporate/how-we-handle-disclosures-from-whistleblowers.pdf [accessed 27 April 2018]

Carney, M (2017) 'Worthy of trust? Law, ethics and culture in banking', Speech by Mark Carney, Governor of the Bank of England, 21 March 2017. Available at: https://www.bankofengland.co.uk/-/media/boe/files/speech/2017/banking-standards-board-worthy-of-trust-law-ethics-and-culture-in-banking.pdf?la=en&hash=140DB30905F90F73DD6A1BADFF3E13BF931AB8E8

Chartered Banker (2016) *Professional Standards Board* [online]. Available at: https://www.cbpsb.org/ [accessed 9 September 2017]

FCA (2015) *Occasional Paper No. 8: Consumer Vulnerability 2015* [pdf]. Available at: https://www.fca.org.uk/publication/occasional-papers/occasional-paper-8.pdf [accessed 24 May 2018]

FCA (2016a) *Interest rate hedging products (IRHP)* [online]. Available at: https://www.fca.org.uk/consumers/interest-rate-hedging-products [accessed 27 April 2018]

FCA (2016b) *FCA introduces new rules on whistleblowing* [online]. Available at: https://www.fca.org.uk/news/press-releases/fca-introduces-new-rules-whistle-blowing [accessed 27 April 2018]

FCA (2018a) *Monthly PPI refunds and compensation* [online]. Available at: https://www.fca.org.uk/news/ppi-monthly-refunds-compensation [accessed 27 April 2018]

FCA (2018b) *Retail banking: Product governance review* [online]. Available at: https://www.fca.org.uk/publications/multi-firm-reviews/retail-banking-product-governance-review [accessed 27 April 2018]

FMSB (2016) *FICC Market Standards Board* [online]. Available at: www.fmsb.com [accessed 27 April 2018]

House of Commons Treasury Committee (2009) *Banking Crisis: Dealing with the failure of UK banks* [pdf]. Available at: https://publications.parliament.uk/pa/cm200809/cmselect/cmtreasy/416/416.pdf

SFO (2018) *LIBOR* [online]. Available at: https://www.sfo.gov.uk/cases/libor-landing/ [accessed 27 April 2018]

UK Parliament (2018) *Treasury Committee publishes RBS-GRG report* [online]. Available at: https://www.parliament.uk/business/committees/committees-a-z/commons-select/treasury-committee/news-parliament-2017/rbs-global-restructuring-group-s166-report-17-19/ [accessed 27 April 2018]

Appendix 3.1

Bradford & Bingley

Lessons learned:

- the rapid expansion of the business;
- strategic risk to become the UK's market leader in the high-risk buy-to-let and self-certified market;
- poor risk assessment;
- a business model that provided 100 per cent plus mortgages (assumed property prices will continue to increase and not fall);
- poor credit assessment;
- inadequate due diligence on the GMAC mortgage business contract;
- inflexibility of the GMAC contract which committed the business to take on more mortgage business despite a downturn in the property market;
- inability to change the underwriting criteria for the GMAC contract;
- an unbalanced funding structure and overreliance on the wholesale markets;
- the loss of customer confidence, leading to a run on the bank, precipitating a liquidity crisis.

04

The changing nature of banking

In this chapter we look at the changing nature of banking as banks embrace new technology.

LEARNING OBJECTIVES

By the end of this chapter, you will be able to:

- analyse the benefits for banks of undertaking big data analytics;
- assess how artificial intelligence is supporting customer relationships;
- analyse the impact that open banking might have on the bank/ customer relationship;
- assess how mobile channels are changing the way customers do their banking;
- assess the differences between an omnichannel experience and a multichannel approach;
- explain the different types of CRM systems used in banking.

Introduction

In this chapter we discuss how banks are innovating new technologies to better serve their customers and how this is helping banks to move from a multichannel approach to an omnichannel experience. We also examine how CRM technology plays its part in relationship and marketing strategies and how this may impact on you in your role as a relationship manager.

But before we start, how would you mark yourself, on a scale of 1–10, about your knowledge of the impact technology has on banking?

My score

We don't expect you to know all the answers yet, but we hope you will do so after you have had chance to read this chapter. We'll come back to this at the end of the chapter, but for now let's examine how banks are changing by adapting new technology.

Customer data and information

Banks have a vast amount of data on their customers. For many banks their technology systems possess some of the richest data available. But data on its own is worthless unless it can be transformed into information. When it does, it becomes very valuable.

A problem with large established banks is that they can become data rich, but information poor. This is largely due to the legacy computer systems they operate. Over the last 30 years many banks have grown organically and by mergers and acquisitions. This has resulted in some banks ending up with a number of different and disparate computer platforms and systems. These systems may operate well for their original intended purpose, but are now often stand-alone and, because of segmentation, many are operated on organizational or departmental lines. The danger is that these systems don't talk to each other. Legacy systems may have more data, but less information.

Legacy systems all need to service the customer but these systems may not necessarily connect to each other. For instance, the retail part of the bank may have its own independent computer platform and the business or corporate side of the bank another. This lack of connectivity does not provide a single or complete view of the customer. If it could, managing data and information would provide a bank with a genuine source of competitive advantage. This can be seen through the emergence of technology-driven challenger banks and FinTechs.

Big data

'Big data' involves the collection and analysis of vast amounts of data. For many years, organizations held traditional structured data, which could be neatly stored and organized in databases. However, the development of the internet has led to a vast increase in structured and unstructured data generated by all different forms of digital content such as texts, e-mails, posts, tweets and video. This has resulted in increasingly large and complex data sets, which can become harder to analyse.

Once data is stored, **data analytics** is used to analyse the data to identify trends, relationships, patterns and other correlations to better understand customer needs and to help organizations to focus their resources more effectively and efficiently. Data is only as good as the intelligence we can glean from it, and that entails effective data analytics and a whole lot of computing power to cope with the exponential increase in volume.

> **Data analytics**   A process of inspecting, transforming and modelling data with the aim of discovering useful information and knowledge. Big data analytics brings benefits of speed and efficiency.

Many of the techniques and processes of data analytics have been automated into mechanical processes and algorithms that examine raw data to gather information which can then be used to optimize processes to increase the overall efficiency of a business or system. Data can also be extracted and categorized to identify and analyse behavioural data, such as purchasing trends and patterns of behaviour.

There are a number of potential benefits to organizations undertaking big data analytics. Big data analytics:

- can examine vast quantities of data quickly and efficiently;
- allows for large quantities of data to be examined to identify trends and correlations, eg customers' purchasing habits;
- can help management to take advantage of current social trends by introducing new products to meet customers' needs;
- provides a greater focus on the individual customer;
- improves organizational decision-making;
- reduces costs.

Banks have the analytical capabilities to find hidden patterns from their big data which will help them to spot opportunities to save money or sell more because the data might reveal previously unnoticed patterns in the way people buy certain products. It could identify inefficiencies in the way the rest of the business operates. Banks are investing a lot in the technology and skills required to store and analyse their ever-increasing data sets, to discover these potentially valuable hidden patterns.

Banks can use big data analytics to understand a customer's financial intentions and needs before they act on them, and send relevant marketing material ahead of time. For example, a bank could determine that a customer is considering buying a house and send information on specific mortgages the customer is likely to be approved for.

Banks also have an opportunity to personalize their online banking offerings to each individual, using big data insights. Bank websites will become more dynamic and may change according to the personal preferences and interests of the user. The layout and marketing material on websites will change in real time to reflect what the customer has looked at previously, or the user's other activities over the internet.

Big data can give banks a much deeper insight into customer spending habits and patterns. By using **artificial intelligence** (AI) banks are able to track and trace each and every customer transaction. The benefit of this is that it allows banks to better target their clients with relatable marketing campaigns that are tailored to cater to the customer's own personal requirements.

> **Artificial intelligence (AI)** A term for 'simulated intelligence processes' in machines and computer systems. These machines can be programmed to think like a human and mimic the way a person acts.

Such machines and computer systems are, in theory, able to perform tasks normally requiring human intelligence, such as visual perception, speech recognition and decision-making. AI technology is also used to predict, detect and deter security intrusions in the fight against cybercrime. Bank customers will be most familiar with AI being used in fraud detection.

Have you ever had an occasion where a card transaction has been declined, followed by an almost instantaneous automated call or message from the bank to discuss irregular activity on your account? When fraud has been correctly detected this process is extremely satisfying. Even if the bank has misunderstood and blocked a safe transaction, customers should still feel reassured that their bank is keeping a close eye on security to protect them. That is AI in action. AI can also be used in credit assessment, to enable banks to identify or predict potential customer financial problems before they arise.

Barclays is developing an AI system not too dissimilar to Apple's iPhone personal assistant, Siri, to let customers talk to a device and get information they need for the most common transactions.

Metro Bank is planning to offer its customers a money management service that uses AI technology. In the summer of 2018 the bank plans to launch a service, known as Insights, that will use AI technology from Personics to help customers manage their finances. Available through Metro Bank's banking app, Insights will use predictive analytics and AI to monitor transaction data and patterns in real time to identify trends in customers' spending habits. It can also provide personalized prompts to help them control their spending. Prompts might include information about subscriptions, alerts to unusual spending, helping customers avoid additional fees, and alerting them to large or duplicated transactions. The service will also provide spending analysis, and more features are planned.

Challenger banks

Challenger banks can have a considerable advantage over long-established banks that still operate with legacy systems. This new breed of younger banks has better technological systems and processes that enable them to deliver information and not just data. These new entrants become data and information rich because their customer base is smaller. They can also be more selective about the data they collect. These newer systems are able to provide a more seamless route to good-quality information.

One of the biggest problems banks face with their digital channels is hidden defection. Purchasing a new banking product from competing banks or FinTechs is taking place everywhere (see the next section for more on FinTechs). Direct (branchless) banks and FinTechs are taking a substantial share of new purchases on the strength of their relatively simple product lines and streamlined operations which appeal to many consumers. They appear to be well-positioned to continue expanding their share. Interestingly these direct banks tend to lead in **net promoter scores** in most countries.

Net promoter score   An index-based system showing the willingness of customers to recommend a company's products or services to others.

FinTechs

Over recent years technology companies and new start-ups (FinTechs) have rapidly expanded their activities into financial services, innovating and competing or collaborating with banks and other financial institutions in a number of segments of the financial services market.

Far from being under threat from the technology industry, banks work hand-in-hand with technology companies and have invested heavily in these disrupters. By becoming closer to technologists, banks are able to ensure that their customers acquire the next banking technology solutions as quickly as possible and are providing banks with the opportunity to explore new growth opportunities. As such, these new technologies are essential to the future health of the banking sector.

Open banking

In 2016, the Competition and Markets Authority (CMA) published a report on the UK's retail banking market which concluded that there was insufficient competition between the larger, more established banks and smaller, newer challenger banks and FinTech companies who were finding it difficult to grow and access the banking markets. This coincided with the Second Payment Services Directive (PSD2), a directive from the European Union. PSD2 enabled regulated third-party providers, with a customer's consent, to access a customer's bank account information and/or request payments.

In 2016 the Open Banking Implementation Entity (OBIE) was established by the CMA to create software standards and industry guidelines to drive competition and innovation in UK retail banking. It was introduced to enable customers and SMEs to share their current account information securely with other third-party providers. OBIE works with the UK's largest banks and building societies as well as challenger banks, FinTechs, third-party providers and consumer groups. Its role is to:

- design the specifications for the application programme interfaces (APIs) that banks and building societies use to securely provide open banking;
- support regulated third-party providers and banks and building societies to use the open banking standards;

- create security and messaging standards;
- manage the open banking directory which allows regulated participants like banks, building societies and third-party providers to enrol in open banking;
- produce guidelines for participants in the open banking ecosystem;
- set out the process for managing disputes and complaints.

It also aims to attract new providers and technology companies to enter the market and create more innovative services for customers.

Open banking went live in January 2018. It opens the way to new products and services that could help give customers and small to medium-sized businesses more control over their finances. It could give customers more detailed understanding of all their bank accounts. For example, customers could allow a provider to display all their bank account information, even if they are multibanked, in one secure place, providing better oversight and transparency of all their finances, whichever banks they use, at any time.

Open banking can also help customers to budget, shop around for better deals and find the best products and services that suit their needs. Customers can also choose to give a regulated app or website secure access to their current account information and to make payments directly from a bank or building society.

New data sharing will also see an overhaul of the credit ratings system and availability of information and data. It will make financial administration easier and provide SMEs with access to credit, allowing them to negotiate better commercial terms by being able to demonstrate their creditworthiness. Customers are able to decide for how long the providers can access their data and can withdraw their permission at any time.

Every provider that uses open banking to offer products and services is regulated by the FCA or European equivalent and must be named on the FCA's Open Banking Register. At the moment, the nine biggest banks and building societies are all enrolled on the Open Banking Implementation Entity's (OBIE) Open Banking Directory.

Alternative finance and the government bank referral scheme

In August 2017 the UK government published a report stating that over the previous nine months, 230 small businesses that had been rejected for loans by some of the UK's biggest banks, had secured £3.8 million from alternative lenders. The government-backed bank referral scheme, launched in November 2016, requires nine of the UK's biggest banks to pass on the details of small businesses they have turned down for loans to four finance platforms: Funding Xchange, Business Finance Compared, Funding Options and Alternative Funding. These platforms then share their details with alternative finance providers and go on to facilitate a conversation between the business and any provider who expresses an interest in supplying finance to them. Loans resulting from this scheme ranged from £200 to £500,000, with an average size of £16,000. A number of sectors have benefited, including construction, retail, technology and science.

As highlighted in the 2017 Small Business Finance Markets report, the most common response from smaller businesses when they do not get the full amount of finance applied for is to give up or cancel their plans. This can mean businesses missing potential expansion opportunities, with a knock-on effect on UK economic growth. It is therefore heartening to see the positive start made by the bank referral scheme.

Research shows that 71 per cent of businesses seeking finance only ask one lender and, if rejected for finance, many simply give up on investment rather than seek alternative options. In 2016, 220,000 small and medium-sized businesses sought a loan or overdraft; 25 per cent of these were initially declined by their bank and only 7 per cent of those declined were referred to other sources of help (UK Government, 2017).

Customer expectations

The banking landscape is changing and technological innovation is driving new levels of customer expectations. The emergence of new technologies is leading to more efficient banking services, generating many new opportunities for banks and better products and services for their customers. Digital platforms, mobile banking, smartphones and tablets are revolutionizing the way customers buy products, both in the retail and corporate segments.

Omnichannel experience

The digitalization of the banking sector is witnessing a transformation from a multichannel approach to an omnichannel experience. A multichannel approach focuses on maximizing the performance of each individual channel, such as telephone, web, mobile and tablets, whereas an omnichannel approach puts the customer at the centre and promotes the use of all channels simultaneously.

Omnichannel means that, whichever channels the customer decides to use, they are linked to one platform with integrated devices, providing a seamless banking experience. It allows a customer to move seamlessly across the channel of their choice, enabling them to continue or complete an action without having to start all over again. Omnichannel facilitates sharing customer information without the customer having to repeat themselves at each separate handover.

The omnichannel experience requires integrated systems and channels that facilitate transparency and data sharing so that each customer's buying habits and needs are known and can be addressed bank-wide. It removes silos and breaks down the walls that separate many functions and processes. The omnichannel approach is not just about technology; technology is simply its enabler.

Digital channels

Mobile channels have become the new way for busy customers to do their banking. Transactions on smartphones and tablets continue to displace those on desktop and laptop computers, with nearly all banks showing more mobile than online transactions. By accelerating the migration of customers from high-cost branches and contact centres to self-service mobile and online channels, banks could:

- generate greater customer loyalty by developing simple, digital channels that customers embrace;
- reduce the levels of routine or avoidable transactions in branches and call centres as the customers will do it themselves;
- reduce the number of high-cost branches and call centres;
- generate cost-saving benefits by reducing or redeploying staff into higher-value activities.

Banks will need to become more enterprising and thoughtful about guiding customers to mobile self-service.

Mobile adoption has been highest among the youngest consumers. Many older consumers require active guidance and information from banks about using mobile apps. Sometimes, banks can overlook this group, and neglect to give older consumers guidance or information about the benefits of using mobile apps. Consumers who do not use bank mobile apps report several reasons for this, notably habit, but also lack of knowledge and access issues. In addition, older users are slightly more dissuaded by habit and security concerns.

Many banks, however, actively support elderly people and non-digital customers who find it difficult, for whatever reason, to embrace new digital banking services. For instance, they have trained employees on hand who provide free advice and digital financial education programmes for those less digitally inclined. This might not be the case for some of the 'digital-only' new entrants to the market.

Younger people present a separate challenge, mostly involving the basics of banking. They are still navigating how to pay bills, deposit cheques, transfer money and generally resolve issues with their accounts. In a report by PwC entitled *Millennials and Financial Literacy: The struggle with personal finance,* it was reported that most millennials have inadequate financial knowledge. When tested on financial concepts, only 24 per cent demonstrated basic financial knowledge. It also reports that millennials are heavy users of alternative financial services (AFS). In the five years to 2015, 42 per cent of millennials used an AFS product, such as payday loans, pawnshops, auto title loans, tax refund advances, and rent-to-own products (PwC, 2015).

New designed branches

The products and services of the banks have traditionally been delivered through their branch networks but these networks have been contracting for many years. The impact of the financial crisis and the new regulatory costs bearing down on profits, coupled to the digitalization of the banking sector, have made banks look again at the viability of their branch networks. There are a number of reasons for doing this, including:

- the desire to cut costs and improve efficiencies;
- mergers within the industry (duplication of branches on the same high street);
- competitive pressures from new entrants;
- changes in the way people want to bank (digital);
- availability of alternative means of accessing financial services (FinTechs).

The effects of branch closures on customers, banking staff and the local community, especially in rural areas, is often controversial. This has led to accusations that banks are exacerbating financial exclusion rather than enabling financial inclusion. But not all banks are closing branches, and some of the newer challenger banks are committed to having branch structures.

Today's modern branches have been designed and equipped with self-service areas, tablets and new digital technologies, but also with private areas to provide immediate personalized advice to those customers who need it. This may be for life cycle changes, personalized financial advice, complex transactions or life-changing decisions where the customer feels human interaction is necessary.

Some banks are also providing access to customers by means of pop-up stores that can be flexibly set up in shopping centres, markets or remote rural places. This direct access represents value for customers when compared to digital-only technology companies that sometimes limit access by providing just a switchboard number or direct access only via the internet.

Social media and banking

The emergence of social media has also changed modern-day communications. Many banks still struggle with social media and some have failed so far to build an integrated and strategic approach to it. The dilemma banks have is that customers want and expect it and the danger of not embracing this medium is that competitors will. Understanding bank customers and what they are looking for is an area where social media can be hugely beneficial.

While social media (Twitter, Facebook, etc) is packed full of opinions, wishes and comments, a lot of this noise can be irrelevant. However, if the data can be distilled, it could have the potential to give banks a vital insight and better understanding of their customers.

Question

How does your bank collate and manage information from social media?

Cyber-security

Financial institutions are one of the primary targets for cyber-attacks. As a result, the industry is committing considerable amounts of money towards protective measures for customers in order to maintain trust and confidence in its systems and operations. After wave upon wave of increasingly sophisticated cyber-attacks the banking sector is facing attackers who are streamlining and upgrading their techniques rapidly. The banking sector is trying to fight back at the same speed.

These repeated attacks can affect customers' finances, their confidence and can have severe economic and reputational consequences for the bank. Banks invest heavily in IT systems aiming at the highest possible security levels, but cybercriminals exploit any vulnerability to penetrate a bank's systems. In some respect the banks are always playing catch-up.

ACTIVITY 4.1

Read the following report by *Information Age* entitled *Cybercrime and the Banking Sector: Top threats and secure banking of the future.* Then answer the following questions in writing before referring to the answers in Appendix 4.1. You will find the report at: http://www.information-age.com/cyber-crime-banking-sector-123464602/

---

1 Why are banks such a lucrative target for cybercrime?

2 What is one of the biggest threat banks face?

3 In what ways do cybercriminals obtain sensitive data on bank customers?

Customer relationship management (CRM) systems

Technology is not just about channel strategy; it is also prevalent in relationship and marketing strategies. Customer relationship management (CRM) unites the potential of new technologies and marketing to deliver long-term profitable relationships. The most important aspect of CRM is that it only works well where cross-functional integration of people, operations, strategies, processes and technology are all aligned and united behind the common goal of customer-centricity. Customer-centricity puts the customer at the heart of everything.

In his book *The Handbook of CRM*, Payne (2006) notes that the emergence of CRM as a strategic management approach is a consequence of a number of important trends. These include the:

- shift in business focus from transactional marketing to relationship marketing;

- realization that customers are a business asset and not simply a commercial audience;
- transition from organizational structures based on functions to those based on processes;
- recognition of the benefits of using information proactively rather than reactively;
- greater use of technology in managing and maximizing the value of information;
- acceptance that there is a trade-off between delivering and extracting customer value;
- development of one-to-one marketing approaches.

Different types of CRM

There are a number of different types of CRM: operational, analytical and collaborative CRM.

Operational CRM

This is concerned with the automation of various business processes involving front-office customer contact points which could include salesforce automation, marketing automation and customer service automation, such as call centres.

Analytical CRM

This involves the capture, storage, organization, analysis, interpretation and use of data derived from the operational side of the organization (systems that talk to each other).

Collaborative CRM

This involves the use of collaborative services and infrastructures to make interaction between an organization and its multiple channels possible.

Marketing automation

Marketing automation covers customer personalization, profiling, telemarketing, e-mail marketing and campaign management. These activities are designed to get the appropriate mix of products and services in front of the chosen customers at the right time. It involves understanding customer behaviours as well as their needs and wants. This does not mean that technology is able to identify a customer's needs and wants, but it can flag up occasions where human involvement can take place. For example, the bank's computer system might flag that a foreign currency payment has been received into a business customer's account for the first time. The relationship manager receives notification and is then able to contact the customer to find out if it is a one-off payment or whether they are now exporting for the first time. If they are exporting for the first time, the relationship manager may then have a conversation with the customer about the products or services that could help them, such as currency hedging techniques that can help to mitigate the currency risks.

Bank systems can also automatically diarize events to ensure the bank can intervene well in advance of, say, a renewal date, giving the relationship manager sufficient time to discuss renewal with them before they can talk to a competitor.

Salesforce automation

This includes territory planning as well as portfolio and lead-prospecting management systems. Frequently this involves laptop or mobile applications that have the ability to upload and download information. It can also provide up-to-date real-time banking information that can be shared with customers.

Service fulfilment

Service fulfilment encompasses the ability of an organization to serve the customers it already has. Initiatives here could be in the area of e-mail response management or telephony management such as:

- automatic call distribution;
- computer telephony integration;
- queue or workflow management;
- interactive voice response and predictive dialling.

Some CRM systems can also provide electronic capabilities that can be triggered by the customer, such as:

- self-searching capabilities (products and services);
- interactive chat;
- e-mail;
- multimedia sessions;

- browser;
- application sharing.

Sharing information

Customers will probably have an expectation that anyone who deals with them will know them and that they will be fully aware and up to date concerning their relationship with the bank. This can be compromised if there are certain aspects of information that are only stored in the relationship manager's head. This is information that has not been committed to a permanent, tangible record.

Unless this information is recorded somewhere problems can arise, particularly if the manager moves on. Information needs to be shared in a systematic way and is best recorded and made accessible via computerized records such as an electronic customer contact report. This may also include 'soft data' such as the customer's likes and dislikes, positive feedback or complaints. Recording complaints is important, particularly if it relates to some sort of service failure that may affect subsequent dealings with the customer.

> Question
>
> How does your bank use CRM?

Relationship management digital tools

The drive to digital, in its quest for efficiency and increased availability, could result in less genuine engagement between a bank and its business customers. The danger is that business customer interactions may become more transactional rather than advisory, and therefore less valuable to them.

The best relationship managers understand their customers. They know their customers' strengths and weaknesses and where potential opportunities or threats may lie. This is valuable information for a small business. The solution lies in using the intelligence generated by digital tools that would allow banks to re-engage with business customers. Digital tools can help provide valuable insight and guidance to help businesses succeed.

Banks can offer access to a variety of business planning tools that will enable someone thinking of starting or growing their business to validate their ideas and understand the process needed to get up and running. The same tool would allow a business looking for funding to produce a business plan, including forecast profit and loss statements, balance sheets and cash flow forecasts.

This means that banks can provide guidance and engage with their small business customers at the earliest stages in the business life cycle. As the business grows, more tools can be introduced to help them through later stages of the life cycle. For example, if a business customer spots an opportunity to operate in a new geographical area, the bank could help them to better understand new potential markets, local laws and regulations as well as looking after their foreign exchange requirements and options.

Banks are also developing tools that can check the financial health of a business customer's suppliers and buyers and/or new prospects. Banks undertake financial health checks on their borrowing customers, why not on the borrower's buyers and suppliers? It can add real value and improve the customer's own credit management, if they knew whether they were likely to get paid on time.

These sorts of tools do not require a great deal of time investment from banks or their relationship managers, but will be invaluable for any business customer. Giving business customers access to such tools and guidance they need to succeed is the first step on the path to a relationship which benefits both the business customer and the bank. These tools not only help businesses to grow and develop but they provide relationship managers with the insight needed to better serve and engage with their customers.

The development of technology and the wider digitalization of banking have lowered the cost of new entry into the banking market, facilitating digital-only new entrants as well as new product and service innovations such as contactless payment technology and mobile payment systems.

Digital banking has also had a significant impact on customer behaviour, in particular on the use of branches and how customers engage with their bank(s).

The pace of technological change in banking is speeding up. Mobile banking tools have been rapidly adopted, and a growing financial technology sector is developing and applying new tools to compete with the more traditional banks.

There is a now a wide variety of business lending available, including general purpose business loans, overdrafts, business mortgages, credit cards, asset and invoice finance as well as alternative lending platforms (peer-to-peer and crowdfunding).

Before open banking, there was a lack of tools to help SMEs make price comparisons and there was a potential risk to SMEs' credit ratings from searching. Open banking now provides a mechanism for 'soft' searching, so that SMEs can be confident that they can shop around for credit and obtain indicative price quotes without adversely affecting their credit rating. It opens the door for the alternative finance sector. Regulations under the SBEE Act which came into force in June 2016 require providers to share SME data, through CRAs, with alternative providers.

As we started this chapter you were asked to score yourself about the knowledge you had about the changing face of banking and the impact technology has had on the sector. Having read this chapter, how would you score yourself now?

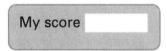

How have your views changed? Are there any areas that you need to revisit or review?

Chapter summary

In this chapter we have explored:

- the changing face of banking as new technologies take hold;
- the impact of big data analytics and AI on the banking sector;
- the competition offered by challenger banks and FinTech companies and how traditional banks are responding;
- the omnichannel experience versus the multichannel approach;
- the CRM systems and relationship management tools employed in banking.

Objective check

1 What are the benefits of undertaking big data analytics?

2 How is AI being used to support customer relationships?

3 What impact is open banking likely to have on the bank/customer relationship?

4 How are mobile channels changing the way some customers bank?

5 How does an omnichannel experience differ from a multichannel approach?

6 What are the different types of CRM?

Further reading

For further information and updates refer to the open banking website that can be found at: https://www.openbanking.org.uk/about-us/

References

Payne, A (2006) *Handbook of CRM: Achieving excellence through customer management*, Routledge, Abingdon

PwC (2015) *Millennials and Financial Literacy: The struggle with personal finance* [pdf]. Available at: https://www.pwc.com/us/en/about-us/corporate-responsibility/assets/pwc-millennials-and-financial-literacy.pdf [accessed 5 July 2019]

UK Government (2017) Matchmaking scheme helps businesses find £4 million of finance [online]. Available at: https://www.gov.uk/government/news/matchmaking-scheme-helps-businesses-find-4-million-of-finance

Appendix 4.1

Answers to question on cyber-security

1. Why are banks such a lucrative target for cybercrime?

The answer is simple: cybercriminals go where the money is, and banks have more money than most other organizations.

2. What is one of the biggest threat banks face?

One of the biggest threats, and often one of the hardest to detect, is that of malicious, careless and compromised users. These employees, contractors and partners are already inside the bank's secure perimeter and have legitimate access to its sensitive data and IT systems.

3. In what ways do cybercriminals obtain sensitive data on bank customers?

Criminals can send phishing e-mails or set up fake websites that dupe consumers into giving away sensitive financial data. They can also leverage information from social media sites to socially engineer their way into accounts via customer service.

05

The changing nature of regulation and legislation

In this chapter we examine the legislation and regulation with which banks and financial services organizations must comply.

Banks and building societies are regulated under both UK and European legislation. European laws will continue to apply as they will be transposed into UK law and will not be automatically repealed on the UK leaving the EU.

A number of European and international bodies also regulate UK banks and building societies. These include the European Banking Authority, which ensures effective and consistent prudential regulation and supervision across the EU banking sector, and the Basel Committee on Banking Supervision, which issues the Basel Accords setting out the prudential capital requirements for banks globally.

LEARNING OBJECTIVES

By the end of this chapter, you will be able to:

- assess the UK regulatory environment in which financial services operate;

- analyse the roles of the various bodies and organizations responsible for regulating the UK financial services industry;
- evaluate the effect of regulation and legislation on banks in the UK;
- evaluate the role of industry codes such as the Banking Conduct Regimes, the Lending Code and the Standards of Lending Practice.

Introduction

In this chapter we look at the regulatory and legal environment in which banks operate and consider the level of, and reasons for, the high levels of regulation in the sector.

As a relationship manager you need to be aware of, and act in accordance with, the requirements of regulators and be able to explain these to customers. A relationship manager who has a good knowledge of banking will be able to explain clearly why banks do what they need to do to be compliant with the law and with the spirit of the law. This chapter will enable you to accomplish that.

But before we start, how would you mark yourself, on a scale of 1–10, about your knowledge of the main regulations and legislation that banks have to comply with?

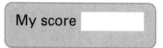

My score

We don't expect you to know all the answers yet, but we hope you will do after you have read this chapter. We'll come back to your score at the end of the chapter, but for now let's examine the regulation and legislation that affect banks and other financial services organizations.

Regulation

The fast-changing nature of the financial services industry, and in particular the banking sector following the financial crisis, has necessitated a complete rethink of how the industry is governed and regulated. The financial services industry is one of the most heavily regulated industries in the UK.

A considerable amount of legislation and regulation impacts on banks so in this chapter we will look more closely at the changing face of legislation and regulation.

Background

Before the global banking crisis of 2007–09, and until 2013, banking regulation was provided by the Financial Services Authority (FSA), the Bank of England and the Treasury. In the aftermath of the crisis, the FSA was highly criticized for providing 'light touch' regulation. Because the crisis was seen, amongst other things, as a failure of regulation, a new regime was born, and it is this regime that forms the basis of regulation for the banking sector in the UK today.

Post-crisis UK financial services regulation

In response to the aftermath of the crisis the Financial Services (Banking Reform) Bill was introduced to Parliament in 2013. The Bill focused on changing the structure and delivery of regulation within the financial services sector. Figure 5.1 shows the relationship between the different bodies.

Figure 5.1 UK financial services regulatory authorities

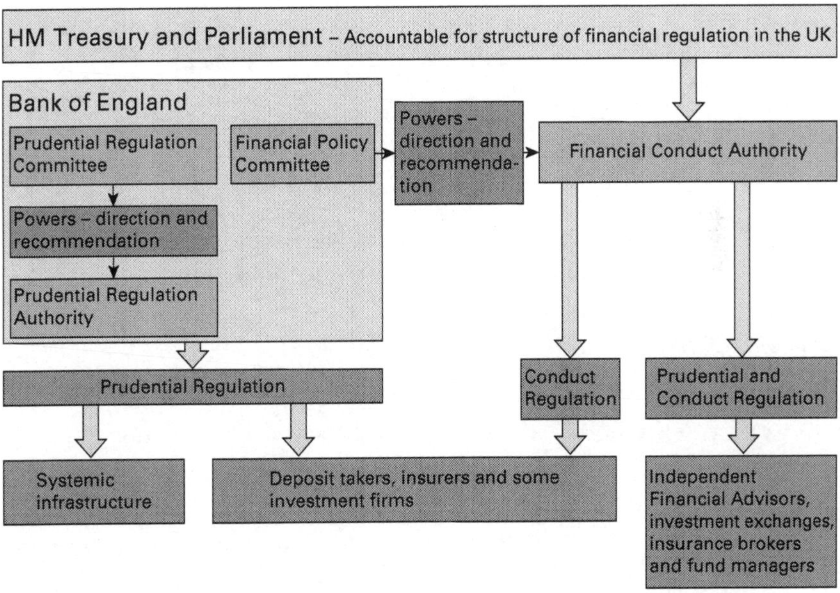

SOURCE Adapted from Bank of England

The UK regulatory regime

The UK approach to financial regulation has developed since the financial crisis, and now involves the following bodies, each of which has its own objectives, duties and responsibilities:

- HM Treasury;
- Bank of England;
- Prudential Regulation Committee;
- Prudential Regulation Authority;
- Financial Policy Committee;
- Financial Conduct Authority.

The overall structure of how these various bodies interact with each other is complex, but can be summarized below.

HM Treasury

HM Treasury is the economic and finance ministry of the government and is responsible for all aspects of public spending. The direction of the UK's economic policy aims to achieve strong and sustainable growth for the UK.
It has three objectives (UK Government, 2017):

1 To place public finances onto a sustainable footing.
2 To ensure the stability of the macro-economic environment and financial system, enabling strong, sustainable and balanced growth.
3 To increase employment and productivity, and ensure strong growth and competitiveness across all regions of the UK through a comprehensive package of structural reforms.

As part of objective 2, it is responsible for financial services policy, which includes the banking and financial services regulation referred to above.

Bank of England

The Bank of England is the central bank of the United Kingdom, and has statutory responsibility for financial stability and for the regulation of banks and insurance companies. Ensuring the financial system operated within the UK is safe rests with the Bank, and it has policymaking committees which consider issues and make decisions on how it will meet its statutory responsibilities. In respect of financial regulation, the Bank has two important committees: the Prudential Regulation Committee and the Financial Policy Committee (Bank of England, 2017).

Prudential Regulation Committee (PRC)

Prudential regulation rules mean that the Bank of England will ensure that more than 1,500 financial firms such as banks, building societies, credit unions, insurers and major investment firms are managed prudently. They must all have sufficient capital and good risk controls in place.

The PRC is a group of 12 people, chaired by the governor of the Bank of England, who make the most important decisions of the Prudential Regulation Authority, the body responsible for enforcing the prudential regulation rules.

Prudential Regulation Authority (PRA)

The PRA has three statutory objectives:

1 To promote the safety and soundness of firms regulated.

2 To contribute to securing an appropriate degree of protection for insurance policyholders.

3 To facilitate effective competition between firms.

The PRA will regulate and supervise firms to ensure they do not cause harm to financial stability in the UK. Their goal is *not* to prevent any firm failing, but rather to ensure that any firm which does fail, does not cause significant disruption to critical financial services.

The regulating of firms is achieved by setting standards and policies for firms to follow. Assessing whether firms are meeting those standards and policies provides the supervision element of the PRA's role.

The PRA has stated its intention to focus on the firms and issues that pose the greatest threat to the stability of the UK financial system. They will consider not only current issues and risks, but also those that might arise in the future. They will aim to intervene at an early stage where they judge it necessary. Finally, their approach is judgement-based, that is to say the PRA will use their judgement to determine whether firms are safe and sound.

Financial Policy Committee (FPC)

The FPC's role is to identify, monitor and take action to remove or reduce **systemic risks** to the UK financial system. It receives a letter from the chancellor of the exchequer each year outlining its remit, and sends a formal response to the chancellor.

> **Systemic risk**   The risk of collapse of an entire financial system or entire market.

A report is published twice annually by the FPC, and this provides a view of risks to stability, and an assessment of the preparedness of the financial system to withstand those risks. The FPC works closely with the PRC to produce the design of stress-testing frameworks, which will assess whether banks have sufficient capital to withstand any shock which materializes.

Two sets of powers are available to the FPC: powers of direction to regulators; and powers of recommendation to anyone, to reduce risks to financial stability. The committee is made up of 13 members, and meets four times a year.

Financial Conduct Authority (FCA)

The FCA is the regulator whose vision is to make markets work well so that consumers get a fair deal. It is responsible for requiring financial services organizations to put the well-being of their customers at the heart of how they run their business, promoting effective competition and ensuring that the markets operate with integrity.

The FCA is a separate institution and is independent of the Bank of England, being ultimately accountable to Parliament through the Treasury. The FCA operates the prudential regulation of those financial services organizations not supervised by the PRA, such as asset managers and independent financial advisors.

The FCA has considerable power over the financial services industry. The main powers that have been granted to the FCA include:

- approving persons in the industry to perform certain controlled functions, eg approving the senior board management of banks;
- imposing penalties for market abuse;
- taking disciplinary action;
- authorizing unit trust schemes and recognizing collective investment schemes;
- recognizing investment exchanges;
- keeping under review the desirability of regulating Lloyd's insurance market and designated professional bodies;

- making rules;
- demanding information from authorized persons;
- conducting investigations with HM Treasury;
- instituting criminal proceedings where necessary;
- maintaining a public record of authorized persons, schemes, prohibited individuals and approved persons;
- initiating or participating in banks' insolvency proceedings;
- cooperating with other regulators.

Senior Managers and Certification Regime (SMCR)

The financial crisis in 2007–09 and subsequent malpractice events (PPI, LIBOR and markets manipulation, etc) have highlighted concerns about the performance and behaviour of some of the individuals working in the financial services industry. Following its reforms to the regulatory system in the Financial Services Act 2012, the government brought forward reforms to the way individuals who work in the financial services sector are regulated (Financial Conduct Authority, 2017c).

Before SMCR the main way individuals who worked in the financial services industry were regulated was through the Approved Persons Regime (APR). Under APR, financial services firms could not employ a person to perform a 'controlled function', unless that person had been approved by the PRA or the FCA.

The SMCR introduced a new regulatory framework for individual accountability which replaced the Approved Persons Regime (APR) for banks from 7 March 2016. The new framework has four components:

1 Senior Managers Regime (SMR).

2 Certification Regime (CR).

3 Rules of Conduct (RoC).

The Senior Managers Regime replaced the APR in its application to persons performing the senior roles in a bank. These roles, known as Senior Management Functions (SMFs), have been specified in rules made by the PRA and FCA.

Those individuals performing a senior management function (SMF), whether based in the UK or offshore, are specified as:

- chairman;
- chief executive officer (CEO);
- chief finance officer (CFO);
- chief risk officer (CRO);
- head of internal audit;
- risk committee chair;
- audit committee chair;
- remuneration committee chair;
- executive directors;
- non-executive directors;
- money laundering reporting officer (MLRO;)
- compliance oversight functions;
- significant responsibility senior managers (performing a key role and most likely reporting to the board and/or a board member).

SMR imposes greater disciplinary action should governance controls be lacking in the business area for which they are responsible. The action that could be taken is criminal prosecution that could lead to a fine and/or imprisonment, in the event that a bank fails as a result of an act or omission by senior managers. (This new offence does not apply to credit unions or foreign banks with branches in the UK.)

There is a criminal penalty of up to seven years' imprisonment and/or an unlimited fine in circumstances where it can be proved beyond reasonable doubt that deliberate and reckless professional misconduct occurred which subsequently resulted in a bank failing.

Certification Regime (CR)

The Certification Regime applies to individuals who are not carrying out SMFs but whose roles are deemed by the regulators to be capable of causing significant harm to the bank or its customers. The regime requires banks themselves to assess the fitness and propriety of persons performing other key roles, and to formally certify this at least annually.

Those affected by the Certification Regime are:

- material risk takers;
- those in customer-facing roles via qualification such as financial advisors and mortgage advisors;

- managers of certified persons;
- significant influence function roles.

Individuals included in the Certification Regime do not require FCA and/or PRA approval, but it is the responsibility of senior managers who have certified the individuals to conduct the initial and ongoing annual assessment.

Rules of Conduct (RoC)

Under SMCR, the regulators have the power to make Rules of Conduct which apply to senior managers, certified persons and other employees. SMCR therefore gives the regulators flexibility to ensure a more effective, better targeted regulation of individuals working in the banking sector.

Individual Conduct Rules (ICR)

The accountability conduct rules are a formal framework by which the FCA and PRA hold individuals to account for the actions that they take in their banking institution. These rules provide a uniform benchmark for what is and is not acceptable across the UK banking profession.

The Individual Conduct Rules automatically apply to all those that fall into the Senior Managers Regime and the Certification Regime and also all employees of the banking institution except for job roles that are ancillary in nature (eg cleaners, reception, security, catering). The banking institution is mandated to appropriately train all applicable staff on how the new accountability rules affect them and also how the rules may be applied to their day-to-day roles.

Fitness and Proprietary Rules (FPR)

All institutions must ensure that those individuals subject to the SMCR are verified as being fit and proper to exercise their duties. The check on fitness will involve the following:

- criminal record checks of the relevant individuals;
- financial credit checks of the individuals;
- employment references for the last five years.
- records must be kept for five years; checks are renewable annually to ensure ongoing fitness and proprietary compliance.

It is senior managers' responsibility to certify individuals and ensure that they meet the FCA's 'fit and proper' assessment requirements.

The conduct rules state that all UK financial services firms' employees (apart from ancillary staff) should act:

- with integrity;
- with due skill, care and diligence;
- in an open and cooperative manner with any regulators;
- in the interests of customers and the fair treatment of customers;
- so that market conduct standards are observed.

Firms must make sure the application has been completed by the firm and the candidate, and accurately records and discloses all information. A copy of the application, signed by the candidate and firm must be retained by the firm and provided to the FCA on request.

As part of the fitness and propriety test regime, the FCA insists that firms should establish their own criteria before submitting an application to them. They do however offer guidance to firms around the checks they should make, and this guidance includes regulatory references, checking qualification certificates, credit checks, directorship checks and criminal records checks (Financial Conduct Authority, 2017d). These checks are made via the government's Disclosure and Barring Service (DBS). There are three checks that can be made via DBS, but financial services organizations are only allowed to complete standard checks, which show spent and unspent convictions, cautions, reprimands and final warnings (UK Government, 2018).

Cast your mind back to Chapter 3 where we discussed Mark Carney's speech to the Banking Standards Board. He spoke of the Bank of England's work to lift ethical standards throughout the financial services sector. Mr Carney spoke of how the codes of conduct, such as that developed by SMCR, could improve the culture within the industry. He also made a direct connection between SMCR and ethics.

Independent Commission on Banking (ICB)

The ICB was a UK government inquiry into how the banking crisis happened, and its aim was to make the UK banking system safer. Its report was published in September 2011 and became known as the Vickers Report, after Sir John Vickers, who was chair of the Commission (National Archive, 2012).

The main recommendation of the report was that banks should manage their retail banking and their higher-risk investment bank business as separate operations. The terminology used in the report was 'ring-fencing' which means separating the retail bank, corporate and commercial arms of the bank from the more high-risk activities of the investment banking arm. This is to be implemented in 2019. At the time of writing, the final preparations for this ring-fencing are taking place within all of the affected banks and it is likely to have a significant impact on how business and corporate customers are managed.

ACTIVITY 5.1

Find out how your bank is implementing ring-fencing.

How are business and corporate customers being segmented into the retail and investment operations?

Financial Services (Banking Reform) Act 2013

This act received Royal Assent in December 2013, and essentially legislated the core recommendations of the ICB (www.legislation.gov.uk, 2013). The government stated (UK Government, 2013) that it had acted to transform the banking industry across four key areas:

1 Structure: implementing into law the ring-fencing of retail and investment activities.

2 Supervision: restoring the Bank of England to the centre of the supervisory regime, and extending its powers to deal with systemic risks.

3 Culture: imposing higher conduct standards on the banking sector.

4 Competition: empowering consumers by giving them greater choice.

Payment Services Regulator (PSR)

The UK has adopted regulations to implement the first EU Payment Services Directive, which came into force in November 2009.

The payments system industry in the UK is enormous. It makes payments totalling £81 trillion per annum. The PSR's objective is to ensure the payment systems are operated in a way that considers and promotes the interests of businesses and consumers that use them. Its aim is to promote competition and the development of, and innovation in, payment systems and to make cross-border payments easier.

In addition to its responsibilities as conduct regulator, the FCA also has the Payment Services Regulator which is a subsidiary of the FCA.

The Second Payment Services Directive (PSD2)

A second Payment Services Directive came into force in January 2016 and was implemented on the statute books on 13 January 2018. As its name implies, it is a follow-up to the first Payment Services Directive.

A new trade association was formed in 2017 known as Payments UK, which takes on most of the activities formerly falling under the remit of the British Bankers Association, Council of Mortgage Lenders, Financial Fraud Action UK and the UK Cards Association. It has 300 member firms, including all the major banks and payment providers in the banking and finance services industry (Payments UK, 2018).

PSD2 will update the current framework on payment services, extending its scope to payment services providers that were previously unregulated, and improving the transparency and security of payment services. PSD2 reflects the changes in mobile and internet payments and allows better comparison of deals for consumers. Other key changes involve consumer protection, risk management and incident reporting, extension of scope to include all currencies, and requirements for strong customer authentication and secure communications.

PSD2 extends the requirements on banks to provide certain information to their customers including information on charges and interest as well as rules to enable customers to allow third-party providers to access their accounts (as in open banking, discussed in Chapter 4).

EU Payment Accounts Directive (PAD)

The UK has also adopted regulations to implement the EU Payment Accounts Directive, which came into force in September 2016. Several aspects of the regulations were already in place including Current Account Switch Service (CASS) and the requirement on banks to provide basic bank accounts. This directive sets common regulatory standards that EU member states are required to meet in order to:

- improve the transparency and comparability of fees related to payment accounts that are used for day-to-day payment transactions;
- facilitate switching of those accounts;
- ensure access to bank accounts with basic features.

Current Account Switch Service (CASS)

CASS provides a standardized current account switching service across all participating banks and building societies. CASS applies where the customer wants a trouble-free service that automatically transfers all payment arrangements to their new bank and closes their existing account.

CASS may only be used for the transfer of personal, small business, charity and trust current accounts and it comes with a guarantee. It guarantees that all payments associated with the customer's old account will be switched to the new account and ready for use with effect from a pre-agreed switch date. All customers using the service are protected by the guarantee. Any payments that continue to be made into, or collected from the old account, will be automatically redirected to the customer's new account.

To switch, the customer must complete a Current Account Switch Agreement and a Current Account Closure Instruction, provided by the bank or building society, before the switch can go ahead. The transfer is guaranteed to take place within seven working days.

CASS also provides a Partial Switch Service. The Partial Switch Service provides selected features of the Current Account Switch Service, but does not involve the customer closing their existing account or automatically transferring all of their payment arrangements. The service is not limited in terms of time and is not covered by the Current Account Switch Service Guarantee.

Financial Ombudsman Service (FOS)

The FOS is an independent public body which was set up to resolve disputes between consumers and firms regulated by the FCA. If a regulated firm is unable to resolve a customer's complaint, it must advise the customer to refer their complaint to the FSO. As an independent arbitrator, the FSO's decision, including the extent to which a customer should be compensated, is binding upon the firm.

Financial Services Compensation Scheme (FSCS)

The FSCS is an independent public body which has been set up to ensure that consumers are compensated in the event of failure of an authorized financial services firm. The FSCS is funded by the financial services industry, with every authorized firm paying an annual levy. Customer's deposits are covered up to a maximum of £85,000 per person and it has been calculated that 96 per cent of UK savings and current account deposits are protected by the scheme.

European Banking Authority (EBA)

The European Banking Authority (EBA) is an independent EU authority which works to ensure effective and consistent prudential regulation and supervision across the European banking sector. Its overall objectives are to maintain financial stability in the EU and to safeguard the integrity, efficiency and orderly functioning of the banking sector.

The main task of the EBA is to contribute to the creation of the European Single Rulebook whose objective is to provide a single set of harmonized prudential rules for financial institutions throughout the EU. The EBA also plays an important role in promoting convergence of supervisory practices and is mandated to assess risks and vulnerabilities in the EU banking sector.

Basel Committee on Banking Supervision (BCBS)

In 1974, central bankers from a group of 10 nations, which includes the UK, formed the Basel Committee on Banking Supervision. Its 45 members comprise central banks and bank supervisors from 28 jurisdictions. The committee was formed to create policy guidelines and statements of best practice for the supervision of banks. Their policy recommendations, known as the Basel Accords, provide the basis for measuring minimum **capital requirements** within their own countries and beyond.

> **Capital requirement** (also known **capital adequacy**)   The amount of capital a bank or other financial institution has to hold as required by its financial regulator.

The first of the Basel Accords, implemented in 1992, was known as Basel I, and was a way of measuring the credit risk of individual banks. The methodology attempted to calculate minimum levels of capital which would be required during times of financial stress, and was based on a calculation of risk-based assets.

The second accord, Basel II, which improved the calculation methodology, was in the process of being implemented when the global financial crisis of 2007–09 occurred. This gave the committee the opportunity to reassess the validity of the proposed capital requirements, and the committee found some serious mis-calculations of risk.

These mis-calculations led to a third accord, known as Basel III. It was originally intended to be implemented in 2015, but at the time of writing in 2018 there is still some contention around some of the requirements. One of these relates to how individual banks' assessment of risk differs from that of the regulators. It is now expected the accord will become fully operational by 1 January 2019.

There is no disagreement that banks must hold more capital against their assets, and the Basel III proposals can be summarized as:

- An increase in the minimum amount of equity as a percentage of assets from 2 per cent to 4.5 per cent.

- An additional requirement of 2.5 per cent of equity as a capital conservation buffer, taking the total equity required to 7 per cent. The buffer can be used during times of financial stress to encourage banks to lend; however, any banks that do this may not be able to pay dividends to its shareholders.

- In boom times, regulators can also introduce a counter-cyclical buffer requiring an additional 2.5 per cent of equity, taking the requirement to 9.5 per cent. This would have the effect of slowing down bank lending.

It is expected that banks will try to exceed these capital requirements, as there would be significant benefits to being seen as a safer bank, with cheaper capital costs and higher stock market valuations.

All banks are subject to regular **bank stress tests** by their country's central bank, to maintain stability during times of financial stress. In the case of the UK, this is the Bank of England, and in the November 2017 test, all the major UK banks passed the stress-testing requirements.

The purpose of the Basel III Accord is to reduce the ability of the banks to damage the economy by taking on too much risk when borrowing. Time will judge its success.

> **A bank stress test**   An analysis conducted under unfavourable economic scenarios designed to determine whether a bank has enough capital to withstand the impact of adverse developments.

Banking Conduct Regime

As part of its overall Handbook (Financial Conduct Authority, 2017a), the FCA produces a number of sourcebooks which contain rules and guidance. There are sourcebooks for banking, and for mortgages and home finance. There are also separate sourcebooks for insurance, market conduct and client assets and specialist sourcebooks which relate to particular activities, such as credit unions, investment funds and consumer credit.

Firms involved in the activities covered by the sourcebooks must abide by the high-level Principles for Businesses (PRIN). These state that a firm must:

- conduct its business with integrity;
- conduct its business with due skill, care and diligence;
- take reasonable care to organize and control its affairs responsibly and effectively, with adequate risk management systems;
- pay due regard to the interests of its customers, and treat them fairly;
- pay due regard to the information needs of its clients, and communicate information to them in a way which is clear, fair and not misleading;
- take reasonable care to ensure the suitability of its advice and decisions for any customer who is entitled to rely upon its judgement;
- arrange adequate protection for clients' assets when it is responsible for them;
- deal with its regulators in an open and cooperative way, and disclose to the appropriate regulator anything relating to the firm of which the regulator would reasonably expect to be notified (Financial Conduct Authority, 2017b).

Banking Conduct of Business Sourcebook (BCOBS)

This sourcebook applies to any firm which accepts deposits within the UK. It applies to banking customers, defined within BCOBS as:

- consumers;
- micro-enterprises;
- charities with an annual income of less than £1 million.

The definition of a micro-enterprise follows the EU definition, which is an enterprise employing fewer than 10 people *and* with a turnover or balance sheet value of less than €2 million.

BCOBS sets out the rules and guidance for firms to follow, including:

- Communications: firms need to ensure they are clear, fair and not misleading, and cover communications made via telephone, internet or by e-mail. Such communications include marketing activities and promotional literature.
- Information: firms must provide information in good time and in a language or medium that can be understood.
- Notifications: firms must provide reasonable advance notification of any material changes to interest rates, or of any introductory or bonus rates coming to an end.
- Financial difficulty: firms must deal with customers who are experiencing financial difficulty in a positive and sympathetic manner.
- Switching customers' accounts to new providers.
- Dealing with customers' accounts that have become dormant or lost.
- Unauthorized payments: made from customers' accounts, including liability for them. This section also applies to incorrectly executed payments.
- How interest rates are calculated and applied to accounts.
- Cancellation rights and the effects of cancelling.

You may note the absence of specific timeframes or actions; that is because the FCA set out their guidance in a way that achieves a customer outcome. Firms are free to interpret the guidance in whichever way they want, but they must nevertheless still meet the outcomes.

Mortgages and Home Finance Conduct of Business Sourcebook (MCOBS)

This sourcebook applies to every firm carrying on a home finance activity, or who communicates or approves a financial promotion of:

- regulated mortgage contracts;
- equity release (including lifetime mortgages and home reversion plans);
- home purchase plans;
- regulated sale-and-rent-back agreements;

There is further guidance available for any firm who outsources any of these regulated activities. As with BCOBS, the MCOBS rules and guidance for firms to follow include:

- Communications: firms need to ensure they are clear, fair and not misleading, and cover communications made via telephone, internet or by e-mail. Such communications include marketing activities and promotional literature.
- Information: firms must provide information in good time and in a language or medium that can be understood.
- Notifications: firms must provide reasonable advance notification of any material changes to interest rates, or of any introductory or bonus rates coming to an end.
- Financial difficulty: firms must deal with customers who are experiencing financial difficulty in a positive and sympathetic manner.
- Switching customers' accounts to new providers.
- Dealing with customers' accounts which have become dormant, or lost.
- Unauthorized payments made from customers' accounts, including liability for them. This section also applies to incorrectly executed payments.
- How interest rates are calculated and applied to accounts.
- Cancellation rights and the effects of cancelling.

Consumer Credit Sourcebook (CONC)

This sourcebook is a specialist sourcebook for any regulated activities relating to credit. It applies to all regulated firms who provide any credit-related products, and it sets out the obligations which specifically relate to credit activities.

Further guidance is available in the following areas which apply to customers:

- customers experiencing financial difficulties;
- financial promotions and communications with customers;
- pre- and post-contractual requirements;
- responsible lending;
- cost caps for high-cost short-term credit (eg payday loans);
- arrears, default and recovery (including repossessions);
- debt advice;
- cancellation.

Fair treatment of customers

Firms are required to demonstrate that:

- they are delivering fair outcomes to customers on a consistent basis;
- senior managers are ensuring that all staff understand what the fair treatment of customers means, setting expectations, identifying and correcting errors;
- they measure performance on customer fairness issues, and act upon the results;
- they are delivering fair outcomes to customers;
- they have no serious failings.

Regulated firms need to demonstrate outcomes are achieved, which can only be done by showing that policies, procedures and training are in place, and that customers feel they are being fairly treated.

Lending Standards Board (LSB)

The Lending Standards Board was set up in 2010. Its primary focus was to transition from the then Lending Code to the present-day Standards of Lending Practice (SLP). It is funded by registered firms who pay an annual fee dependent upon the size and complexity of their lending business.

The LSB launched the SLP for personal customers in 2016 and for business customers in 2017, and aims to demonstrate how self-regulation can deliver good customer outcomes, thereby complementing the work of the FCA. Its remit is to promote fair lending, and to make sure borrowers receive a fair deal from their lender. The LSB is also responsible for ensuring compliance with the SLP.

Standards of Lending Practice (SLP)

The Standards of Lending Practice is a voluntary code of practice covering lending to small business customers. Firms have to register and once they do, are expected to deal with their customers in line with the good lending practices outlined in the SLP.

There are two separate Standards, for personal and for business customers. The Standards apply to lending undertaken across all delivery channels in the UK. Registered firms must also ensure that the Standards apply to any third party or agent acting on their behalf and ensure those acting on its behalf comply with the Standards.

SLP for personal customers

The Standards apply throughout the life cycle of lending products, from the initial offering through to repayment, and include dealing with customers who are experiencing financial difficulties. They cover lending by credit cards, charge cards, overdrafts and loans, although it is expected a wider range of consumer lending products will be covered in the future.

> **REGULATION**
> The Standards of Lending Practice (SLP)
>
> Find out the latest updates to the Standards of Lending Practice at:
> https://www.lendingstandardsboard.org.uk

The six Standards and expected outcomes are (Lending Standards Board, 2018a):

1 Financial promotions and communication: must be clear, fair and not misleading, such that the customer understands the features, risks and pricing of the product.

2 Product sale: customers will only be provided with a product that is affordable and meets their needs.

3 Account maintenance and servicing: customer requests will be dealt with in a timely, secure and accurate manner. Information provided will be clear and detail any action required by the customer.

4 Money management: customers will be helped to manage their finances through proactive and reactive measures designed to identify signs of financial stress and help avoid financial difficulties.

5 Financial difficulty: customers in financial difficulty will receive appropriate support and fair treatment.

6 Consumer vulnerability: firms are expected to provide inclusive products and services that take account of the broad range of customers and are flexible enough to meet the needs of customers who are classed as being vulnerable. It requires registered firms to have a vulnerable person's strategy.

As mentioned in Chapter 3, the FCA defines a vulnerable consumer as a person who, due to their personal circumstances, is especially susceptible to detriment, particularly when a firm is not acting with appropriate levels of care (Financial Conduct Authority, 2015).

SLP for business customers

The standards define business customers as those with less than £6.5 million of turnover (excluding VAT) and which are not complex, do not have multilayered or multiple ownership structures and are UK-based. As with the personal standards, the products covered are credit cards, charge cards, overdrafts and loans, but again it is expected that future releases may include other types of lending such as asset-based lending (invoice discounting, factoring, HP and leasing).

The eight standards and expected outcomes are (Lending Standards Board, 2018b):

1 Product information: it must be clear, fair and not misleading and enable the customer to understand the features, risks and pricing of the product.

2 Product sale: customers will only be provided with a product that is affordable and meets the needs of the business.

3 Declined applications: customers have the right to appeal declined decisions and be made aware of alternative sources of finance available.

4 Product execution: information provided to business customers will be clear in terms of the action they need to take, and their requests will be dealt with in a timely, secure and accurate manner.

5 Credit monitoring: customers will be supported by measures designed to identify signs of financial stress. These measures will be both proactive and reactive.

6 Financial difficulty: business customers in financial difficulty, or in early stages of recovery procedures, will receive appropriate support and fair treatment, so that they may deal with their debts in the most suitable way (remember RBS GRG).

7 Portfolio management: customers whose debts are sold on will be treated fairly, and all communications regarding the sale and what this means for the customer will be provided in good time. Debts of customers who are suffering from mental or critical illness will not have their debts sold.

8 Vulnerability: products and services will be inclusive, and contain appropriate flexibility to meet the needs of customers who are in a vulnerable situation.

Legislation

In addition to regulation, voluntary or otherwise, there is legislation that applies to banks. This section details the main areas of legislation impacting banks and their staff, which of course includes you, if you are a relationship manager.

As a member of the European Union, the UK is bound to act according to the regulations and directives of the EU.

Anti-money laundering

In 2015 the European Union Fourth Anti-Money Laundering Directive came into force, requiring member states to update their **money laundering** legislation by the middle of 2017.

Money laundering The process by which proceeds of crime are converted into assets that seem to have a legitimate origin.

For the UK, the appropriate legislation (the Proceeds of Crime Act of 2002) was updated via the Crime and Courts Act 2013, the Serious Crime Act of 2015 and the Money Laundering (Amendment) Regulations of 2012.

This legislation imposes significant and extensive obligations on banks and other financial institutions. Those obligations extend to individuals, for example, for failing to report knowledge or suspicion of money laundering activity, which is punishable by a prison sentence of between 5 and 14 years.

All banks train relevant staff extensively and in some cases on a quarterly basis on how to identify potential money laundering cases. Any suspicious activity should be reported via a suspicious activity report (SAR) to an appointed money laundering reporting officer (MLRO).

It is extremely important that any suspicions a staff member has are not communicated to the customer making the transaction. This is known as 'tipping off' and it is a criminal offence to tip off a customer on completion of an SAR, or to notify them that any investigation into money laundering is taking place. The penalty for tipping off can be an unlimited fine, and up to five years in prison.

The MLRO is responsible for ensuring any suspicious activity is disclosed to the relevant authorities. Regulated firms may permit the MLRO to delegate these duties, although this can only be to a suitably qualified individual within the firm.

ACTIVITY 5.2

Obtain a copy of your organization's SAR form and identify what information is required.

On-boarding new customers

Concerns around money laundering also impact the on-boarding of new customers to the bank to prevent financial crime. These are known as **customer due diligence** checks (CDDs). Banks are required to **know your customer** (KYC) and the requirements include identity and address verification for every key party to the account.

> **Customer due diligence (CDD)** Requires banks to identify customers. These checks include identity and address verification for every key party to the account.
>
> **Know your customer (KYC)** A legal requirement to verify all bank customers during and after the account-opening process.

'Know your business' (KYB) applies to business accounts and addresses the risks of money laundering by taking account of the structure of business, country risk, sources of wealth, the initial source of funds paid into the account and expected account activity.

Banks are also required to conduct ongoing monitoring, which essentially means scrutinizing transactions to ensure they are consistent with what they know about the customer. This process is known as **ongoing know your customer** (OKYC).

> **Ongoing know your customer (OKYC)** A process of ongoing monitoring, involving scrutiny of transactions to ensure they are consistent with what is known about the customer.

Bribery Act 2010

The Bribery Act of 2010 came into force in July of 2011. It states that an organization could be liable for failing to prevent a person from bribing or allowing you to be bribed, on its behalf.

You need to be aware of this law as you may be involved in hospitality with customers either by providing or receiving hospitality. Whilst the Act specifically states that normal, proportionate hospitality is not likely to be caught under the Act, it is nonetheless important that all staff, especially relationship managers, are aware of the implications. Your own bank will have set limits at a level where you need to report the value to your line manager. If you are in any doubt, discuss it with your line manager.

An organization can defend itself from an action if it can demonstrate it has adequate procedures in place to prevent bribery, which includes staff training (Ministry of Justice, nd).

Question

Consider these two hypothetical scenarios. As a lending manager your customer has offered you tickets to see:

- Leyton Orient FC playing Oldham Athletic AFC in the Carabao cup.

- Barcelona playing Real Madrid in the Champions League cup final for you and three of your friends.

Your customer is willing to fly you out on their private jet on an all-expenses trip. Which, if either, could be considered to be a bribe?
   Write down your thoughts before referring to the answer which is provided at the end of the chapter (Appendix 5.1).

Data protection

Data protection in the UK was previously determined by the Data Protection Act of 1998. Its aim is to ensure that businesses and government handle personal data correctly. The Act legislates that handling personal information must comply with eight principles. Personal data must be:

1 fairly and lawfully processed;

2 processed for limited purposes;

3 adequate, relevant and not excessive;

4 accurate and up to date;

5 not kept for longer than is necessary;

6 processed in line with the data subject's rights;

7 secured in a safe location;

8 not transferred to countries outside the European Economic Authority unless that country ensures an equivalent level of protection for personal data.

Essentially, the Data Protection Act renders personal data as confidential. Compliance is managed by the Information Commissioner, an independent supervisory authority within the UK.

The General Data Protection Regulation (GDPR)

The General Data Protection Regulation (GDPR) (EU) 2016/679 is an EU regulation on data protection and privacy for all individuals within the European Union. It aims to create identical data privacy laws throughout the European Union. The UK adopted GDPR on 27 April 2016. It became enforceable from 25 May 2018 and replaces the Data Protection Act 1998.

Under GDPR, organizations will not be allowed to collect personal information or data without the owner's prior consent. It requires organizations to inform individuals about why they are collecting their personal data, how it is going to be used and with whom it is going to be shared. Individuals can also ask for their personal information or data to be deleted at any time. This is known as the 'right to be forgotten'. The Data Protection Bill will:

- make it simpler to withdraw consent for the use of personal data;
- allow people to ask for their personal data held by companies to be erased;
- enable parents and guardians to give consent for their child's data to be used;
- require explicit consent to be necessary for processing sensitive personal data;
- expand the definition of personal data to include IP addresses, internet cookies and DNA;
- update and strengthen data protection law to reflect the changing nature and scope of the digital economy;
- make it easier and free for individuals to require an organization to disclose the personal data it holds on them;
- make it easier for customers to move data between service providers.

Organizations with more than 250 employees must document all the data they are processing. Smaller organizations (SMEs) need only to document data on a regular basis. The new law will make the consequences of failing to protect personal data for banks and other organizations far more serious.

Organizations will also have to review their systems, especially around technical security issues such as encryption and security patches/updates. Fines can be issued for misusing data, or failing to process data correctly. A failure to ensure that all devices (laptops, memory sticks, etc) are encrypted can also expose organizations to a fine; and these fines can be very substantial. The Information Commissioner's Office (ICO) has the power to issue fines for any serious data breaches. The ICO can issue fines of up to €20 million or 4 per cent of global turnover, whichever is greater.

Most organizations that monitor and track data and behaviours must appoint a Data Protection Officer (DPO) who is responsible for monitoring compliance with the law, training staff and conducting internal audits. The DPO will be the first point of contact for supervisory authorities and regulators and for individuals whose data is processed, including customers and employees. It will be mandatory to report any data security breaches to the Information Commissioner within 72 hours of any breach.

REGULATION
The European Union Data Protection Regulation

Find out the latest updates to the EU Data Protection Regulation at:
https://www.eugdpr.org

How do you think GDPR could impact you as a relationship manager?

GDPR is still relatively new and its full impact will only be felt over time. However, it will impact you in many ways:

1 Personal data can be a name, e-mail, address, date of birth, personal interests, etc. Typically, this is the kind of data you store in your CRM systems. GDPR and CRM are about building deeper customer trust and loyalty and both require professional handling of personal customer data.

2 Basic data such as names, addresses and phone numbers are classed as general data and can be open to all employees within your bank. On the other hand, more sensitive data such as account balances and limits, agreements and contracts require more security and relevant user access.

3 The conditions for obtaining consent are stricter and consent will not be valid unless separate consents are obtained for different processing activities. This means you have to be able to prove that the customer has agreed to certain actions.

4 All banks will have to review business processes, applications and forms to be compliant with GDPR and this would include e-mail or newsletter marketing practices. In order to sign up for communications, prospects will have to provide their prior explicit consent. If you use a database to store prospect or customer information, then you cannot ignore GDPR. If your bank purchases marketing lists, you are still responsible for getting the proper consent information, even if a vendor or outsourced partner was initially responsible for gathering the data.

5 Adhering to GDPR requires the collection of vast amounts of customer data, which is then collated and used for various activities such as KYC, KYB, OKYC and customer on-boarding. All these processes will have to be GDPR compliant.

Open banking, GDPR and CASS

Open banking, discussed in Chapter 4, is intended to create more competition, provide new products and services and innovation in the banking sector. It involves encouraging customers to give third parties access to their data to enable them to offer new services in ways that their existing banks do not. GDPR sets out to protect the handling of customer's data. So the two go 'hand in hand'. But will it stimulate customers to take up these new products or services? It's too early to tell yet, as both only came in to force in early 2018.

CASS, on the other hand, has been around since 2016 and whilst it does work well, the expected volumes of customers switching banks have not materialized. Customers appear to be still reluctant to move banks. Account switching is still a minority activity, reflecting ingrained habits and customer apathy. Furthermore, the majority of CASS switchers have not moved to the new challenger banks or FinTechs, but instead have switched to other large traditional banks.

So whilst there are many potential opportunities for new challengers and FinTechs it seems that these new disrupters are being perceived as secondary banks, with most customers retaining their existing providers as their primary bank. Why? Because the large traditional banks have scale, and scale provides significant profit opportunities. The larger banks have the largest numbers of customers and vastly more resources.

However, these banks are still operating with old legacy systems, and most of the large banks have had occasions where their systems have failed, with customers unable to access their bank accounts and payments. Yet, despite the inconvenience caused by these failures, the majority of customers still don't move banks.

So whilst the new challengers and FinTechs might be meaner, leaner and more innovative, they lack the scale advantages that their larger competitors enjoy. As open banking becomes a reality then the most successful operators will be the ones that have scale and for the moment that advantage lies with the incumbent banks. So the new challengers and FinTechs may find it difficult in the short term to gain sufficient scale themselves to get appropriate returns on their investment. Perhaps this is why some disrupters, particularly the FinTechs, have formed strategic partnerships with their larger banking competitors to improve the digital offerings to secure 'customer delight'.

However, there are much larger disrupters on the horizon, such as huge technology organizations that have more scale than even the largest banks. Imagine if Facebook, PayPal, Google, Amazon or Apple were able to obtain banking licences? Now that would severely disrupt the banking market and pose the greatest threat to the large, traditional banks. These large technology giants have begun to provide quasi-banking services.

PayPal currently offers banking services and credit to SMEs. Apple has leasing arrangements for its latest phones and Amazon has launched 'Pay Monthly' which offers loans against purchases that can be repaid in regular instalments. Open banking, CASS and GDPR have helped to open the door.

Consumer protection

The Consumer Credit Act of 1974 (amended in 2006), the Financial Services and Markets Act of 2000 and various European regulations are the cornerstones of consumer protection in credit-related matters in the UK.

The legislation covers:

- information requirements of consumers before entering into a credit agreement;
- the content and form of agreements;
- how annual percentage rates are calculated;
- procedures in the event of default, termination and early settlement;
- advertising of credit;
- additional protection for credit card purchases between £100 and £30,000 (s.75 Consumer Credit Act).

This is the legislation that supports the FCA Sourcebook on Consumer Credit.

Markets in Financial Instruments Directive II (MiFID II)

This second directive regulates firms who provide customers with services relating to financial instruments, such as shares, bonds and derivatives. MiFID II took effect in January 2018, and replaced the first directive which had been in operation since November 2007.

This directive is a direct result of the financial crisis, and its aim is to strengthen investor protection by extending requirements of MiFID I across areas such as product governance, transparency and market structure.

Small Business, Enterprise and Employment Act 2015 (SBEEA)

SBEEA aims to help make the UK the most attractive place to start, finance and grow a business. It is expected to open up new opportunities for small businesses to:

- compete;
- get finance to create jobs;
- grow;
- innovate;
- export.

The Act has a number of implications for banks:

1 The Act requires banks to provide information about SMEs to credit reference agencies (CRAs) and places a duty on CRAs to provide information about SMEs to lenders.

2 The Act introduced measures to improve access to finance for small businesses. Banks will be under a duty to forward details of SMEs they decline for finance to designated platforms to help SMEs link to alternative lending opportunities (subject to consent from the SME).

3 The Act aims to speed up cheque payments and reduce red tape whilst increasing the quality of information on the public register (Companies House).

4 The Act will increase transparency of ownership and control of UK businesses, making it more difficult for businesses incorporated in the UK to be used as a cover for criminal activities, thereby ensuring the UK is seen as a trusted and fair place to do business.

The provisions introduced are being implemented in a phased approach. The majority of the implementation has taken place but a small number of provisions are yet to come into force. Changes with the highest impact are being delivered in the later stages to allow companies more time to prepare.

Bank levy

Introduced in 2011, the UK government wanted to ensure banks and building societies made a fair contribution, beyond taxation, to recognize the part played by the financial services industry in the financial crisis. The levy is paid in the form of a Corporation Tax surcharge on a phased reduction up until 2021 (UK Government, 2015).

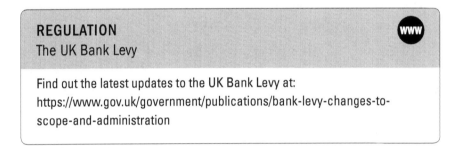

REGULATION
The UK Bank Levy

Find out the latest updates to the UK Bank Levy at:
https://www.gov.uk/government/publications/bank-levy-changes-to-scope-and-administration

As we started this chapter you were asked to score yourself about your knowledge of regulation and legislation. Having read this chapter, how would you score yourself now?

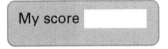

My score

How have your views changed? Are there any areas that you need to revisit or review?

As bankers we always have to comply with regulation and legislation, so how comfortable would you be in explaining this to customers, if you had to?

The nature of banking is changing at a considerable pace, driven in part by technological advances. The nature of regulation and legislation is also moving at a considerable pace as legislators and regulators play catch-up with changing events.

You need to keep abreast of the changes and you can achieve this by visiting the websites given in the Regulation features throughout the chapter.

Finally, as we write, the UK has not yet left the EU so Brexit is an unknown, but whatever your own thoughts on the matter banks will continue to have their activities closely monitored by the regulators both at home and abroad to make sure they are compliant with any jurisdictions that affect the banking sector. Be prepared.

Chapter summary

In this chapter we have explored:

- the regulatory structure of the financial services industry and the implications for banks;
- a number of the FCA sourcebooks;
- the Senior Managers Conduct Regime (SMCR);
- the legislation that impacts on banks and bankers.

Objective check

1 Outline the UK regulatory environment in which financial services operate.

2 Who is responsible for ensuring compliance with the Standards of Lending Practice?

3 What effect does regulation and legislation have on banks in the UK?

4 What are the roles of Banking Conduct Regimes, the Lending Code and the Standards of Lending Practice?

Further reading

Financial Conduct Authority (2017) *FCA: About us* [online]. Available at:
   https://www.fca.org.uk/about [accessed 24 December 2017]
Find out what other protections the FSCS makes available for products other than savings and current accounts by visiting the FSCS website at https://protected.fscs.org.uk/
Implementation of the revised EU Payment Services Directive (PSD II). Available at: www.gov.uk/government/consultations/implementation-of-the-revised-eu-payment-services-directive-psdii

References

Bank of England (2017) *The Bank of England* [online]. Available at: https://www.bankofengland.co.uk/ [accessed 24 December 2017]

Financial Conduct Authority (2015) *Occasional Paper No. 8: Consumer Vulnerability 2015* [pdf]. Available at: https://www.fca.org.uk/publication/occasional-papers/occasional-paper-8.pdf [accessed 24 May 2018]

Financial Conduct Authority (2017a) *FCA Handbook* [online]. Available at: https://www.handbook.fca.org.uk/handbook [accessed 26 December 2017]

Financial Conduct Authority (2017b) *PRIN 1.1 Application and Purpose* [online]. Available at: https://www.handbook.fca.org.uk/handbook/PRIN/1/?view=chapter [accessed 26 December 2017]

Financial Conduct Authority (2017c) *Senior Managers and Certification Regime* [online]. Available at: https://www.fca.org.uk/firms/senior-managers-certification-regime/banking [accessed 3 January 2018]

Financial Conduct Authority (2017d) *Fitness and Propriety* [online]. Available at: https://www.fca.org.uk/firms/approved-persons/fitness-propriety [accessed 13 February 2018]

Lending Standards Board (2018a) *The Standards for Personal Customers* [online]. Available at: https://www.lendingstandardsboard.org.uk/the-standards-for-personal-customers/ [accessed 2 January 2018]

Lending Standards Board (2018b) *The Standards for Business Customers* [online]. Available at: https://www.lendingstandardsboard.org.uk/the-standards-for-business-customers/ [accessed 2 January 2018]

Ministry of Justice (nd) *The Bribery Act 2010* [pdf]. Available at: https://www.gov.uk/government/uploads/system/uploads/attachment_data/file/181764/bribery-act-2010-quick-start-guide.pdf [accessed 2 January 2018]

National Archive (2012) *The Independent Commission on Banking: Final Report* [pdf]. Available at: http://webarchive.nationalarchives.gov.uk/20120827143059/http://bankingcommission.independent.gov.uk/ [accessed 24 December 2017]

Payments UK (2018) *The Second Payment Services Directive (PSD2)* [online]. Available at: https://www.paymentsuk.org.uk/policy/european-and-uk-developments/second-payment-services-directive-psd2 [accessed 2 January 2018]

UK Government (2013) *Banking Reform Act becomes law* [online]. Available at: https://www.gov.uk/government/news/banking-reform-act-becomes-law [accessed 24 December 2017]

UK Government (2015) *Bank Levy: Rate reduction* [online]. Available at: www.gov.uk/government/publications/bank-levy-rate-reduction/bank-levy-rate-reduction [accessed 3 January 2018]

UK Government (2017) *HM Treasury: About us* [online]. Available at: https://www.gov.uk/government/organisations/hm-treasury/about [accessed 24 December 2017]

UK Government (2018) *Apply to Check Someone Else's Criminal Record* [online]. Available at: https://www.gov.uk/dbs-check-applicant-criminal-record [accessed 13 February 2018]

www.legislation.gov.uk (2013) *Financial Services (Banking Reform) Act 2013* [online]. Available at: www.legislation.gov.uk/ukpga/2013/33/contents [accessed 24 December 2017]

Appendix 5.1

Answer to bribery question

Both could be a bribe or not. It depends on the motives and to some extent values. 'Please' and 'thank you' come to mind.

If the customer offered you tickets as a 'please' ('Please sanction my lending facilities and I'll take you to see Leyton play Oldham' or 'Please agree my lending request and I'll fly you and three of your friends out on an all-expenses trip to the Champions League Cup Final') then both would be considered to be bribes because the customer is trying to influence the outcome of the lending request.

On the other hand, if the customer was offering you the trips as a 'thank you' it would be less likely that tickets to the Carabao cup would be considered to be a bribe. It largely depends on their value. However, the cost of an all-expenses trip to the Champions League Cup Final for you and your friends would not stand up to much scrutiny. The cost would be well outside the realms of hospitality and there are moral as well as ethical implications for you personally if you were inclined to accept such an offer. In the latter case, I would decline the offer and report it to my line manager.

06

The role of the relationship manager

This chapter reviews what is meant by the term 'relationship management' and how this is applied to retail and business customers. We will examine the attributes a relationship manager needs to have when meeting customer needs and expectations.

LEARNING OBJECTIVES

By the end of this chapter you will be able to:

- analyse the differences between a salesperson and a relationship manager;
- evaluate the impact of technology on the relationship management role;
- describe the life cycle stages of both retail banking customers and business customers;
- evaluate the differences between skills and competences;
- assess the benefits of working as a team.

Introduction

Relationship management in banking is of prime importance, not only for the banks but for their customers. Relationship managers' performance in the role can create competitive advantage for the bank and for themselves. It needs special qualities to undertake the role effectively. Whichever part of the bank you work in, all successful relationship managers demonstrate common attributes and traits with which they routinely add value to the customer and the bank. Whether you work with retail customers, business customers or wealth customers, the skills required may be different but being competent in the role extends far beyond skill sets. It is your own personal attributes, values, attitudes and behaviours which will set you apart.

Before we start, how would you mark yourself on a scale of 1–10 about your understanding of what relationship management is?

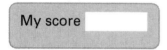

My score

We'll come back to this at the end of the chapter, but for now let's start by looking at what relationship management is not.

Salesperson versus relationship manager

Selling is an important part of relationship management but there is a distinct difference between a salesperson and a relationship manager.

Question

What do you think are the differences between a salesperson and a relationship manager? Write down your thoughts before reading on.

Selling is executing a transaction between a seller and a prospective buyer (or buyers) where money is exchanged for goods or services. Consider the following example.

I want to buy a newspaper so I go to the nearest shop and purchase one. The choices involved in this decision are the location (where's the nearest shop?) and opening times (will it be open or closed?). I have determined the need and sourced the supply. I wasn't persuaded to buy a newspaper; I just did.

This is a different type of sale than if I decided to purchase a new car. This is likely to involve persuasion. The initial persuasion may come from advertising (marketing). I choose which brand I want. I visit the car show-room and a salesperson approaches me, probes my needs and persuades (directs) me to a model that will best suit my needs and my price range. After considering it I decide it meets my requirements better than any other alternative, so I purchase the car and the transaction is completed. The sales-person closes the transaction.

A salesperson is primarily focused on closing the sale; they are not neces-sarily looking to develop a long-term relationship, although there may be an ongoing relationship with the dealership for servicing and maintenance. In this event, the salesperson hands over the relationship to another part of the channel. While developing a long-term relationship may be beneficial, it is only a secondary consideration; for the salesperson, closing the sale is the first.

Question

Think about how the scenario described above is different from relationship management. Write down your thoughts before reading on.

A relationship manager is concerned primarily with developing a long-term relationship in order to meet the customer's (or prospective customer's) immediate and future needs for the duration of the relationship. This is a different sales cycle than just executing a transaction.

A relationship manager also differs from a typical salesperson due to the difference in power structure. With a salesperson/customer relationship almost all of the power is with the buyer. A relationship manager, on the other hand, provides a valuable service because of their familiarity with the customer's historical needs and their desire to meet the customer's immedi-ate and future needs. This causes the power structure to be more balanced and more of a partnership.

Retail customers

There are many types of roles in retail banking that are involved with serv-ing retail banking customers. They may have different roles and different titles, but they all have one common denominator: helping to meet and fulfil customer needs. So in this context we will adopt the term 'relationship manager' because whichever role you are in, if you interact with customers either directly or indirectly, then you are helping to manage the customer relationship.

The changing nature of relationship management

Banking is more than just a utility; it is a relationship business. In today's banking environment it is key to rediscover the art of customer relationship management and adapt it to a virtual and hyper-competitive world. So how do you as a relationship manager rediscover the art? You start by engaging customers and prospects.

Emotional engagement

To engage with customers you need to develop an emotional relationship with them. Every customer's financial situation is unique to them and customers need to feel like their personal needs are being addressed and met. While digital and mobile banking is easy, quick and convenient and can delight customers, it does not engage them. Customers want banks that will make their financial lives better and simpler. Trust and security are also important considerations. Customers want to believe that somebody is taking care of them and their loved ones. This means that you must have a deep understanding and knowledge of their needs, interests and personal situations.

Customer engagement requires a shift in thinking from 'what makes me happy?' to 'what makes the customer happy?' You have to be focused on their well-being rather than your own. Customers want their relationship manager to be an advocate for them. If this is done well, they can then become advocates for you and your bank. However, there's no point engaging with customers if you don't provide value.

Creating value

Customer relationships need to grow and it takes a lot of time and effort. By applying that effort you need to create value at every customer encounter. So you need to focus on the quality of engagement measured through the day-to-day value you add.

Advice

Complex personal and financial relationships need a relationship manager to guide them through the minefields of life so there will always be a place for face-to-face advice, whether in person or by video link, particularly in higher-margin, more complex financial and investment products. You therefore need to be reaching out to customers more frequently with relevant information and advice that adds value. Selling is obviously important, but if that's the only reason you are talking to customers you don't really have an advisory relationship with them, and that opens the door to competitors. If you want to engage with customers and build loyalty, then you need to add value that is clearly centred on the customer. There is no 'one size fits all' advice. How you align the bank's products and services with your customers' own financial goals and well-being is critical.

For example, you may notice that a customer is building up surplus cash balances in their current account each month. They could be saving up for something. You ask them and they say no. So you suggest they consider using some of these surplus funds to make additional payments on their mortgage. These extra payments could result in the mortgage being paid off that much earlier thereby saving them money over the life of the original mortgage.

Small bits of advice can go a long way in creating trust and loyalty. Don't forget: if you don't provide advice, some other bank or FinTech might. In today's environment, if a customer is looking for a loan they would be just as likely to turn to the internet (comparison websites, P2P or crowdfunding) as they would to their bank and you wouldn't even know about it. This means a potential service gap has emerged, creating opportunities and conditions for other competitors to sneak in and steal customers away, unannounced. Technology and rapid advancements in data analytics provide the perfect platform for this to occur.

Technology

While technology is important, relationship management requires more than technology. Most life-changing financial decisions have emotional ties that artificial intelligence and data analytics can only go so far to uncover. In addition to harnessing technology and data analytics, you must not overlook the power of the physical connection. Humans are, after all, social animals.

Branches

Branch reduction programmes, together with a shift towards customer call centres (onshore or offshore) and the move towards online and mobile banking, have been considered by some commentators to be just cost-cutting exercises by banks to improve profitability. But that detracts from the importance of branches in the community. The banks don't want to get rid of their high-street branch networks; they are responding to what customers want.

Personalized face-to-face contact and customer care from specialized branches and advisors is what customers want and need. Compared with digital channels, future branches will offer added value both for banks and for customers to justify their existence.

Local SME customers still need in-branch servicing, particularly those that use cash (notes and coin), such as local retailers. Branches provide a number of specialized products and services to accommodate business customers' needs, such as:

- automated deposit units where business customers can quickly deposit notes, coins and cheques;
- coin machines that allow business customers to pay in large volumes of coin;
- night safes where business customers can safely pay in out of hours.

To resist the threat from digital channels, to differentiate and to add value, branches are experiencing a radical change in their look and feel. Branches should make customers feel comfortable by offering personal advice and support, in addition to mobile and online offerings, as this is important for building and maintaining trustworthy emotional relationships.

Banks should make their branches inviting and welcoming places and give customers both a reason and an opportunity to enter the branch. Successful banks will focus on the environments that customers prefer rather than expect. This will give branches a reason to exist in a world where digitization and changing customer behaviours open up the field for new competitors (bank and non-bank). Branches should be positioned as 'portals of knowledge' and tomorrow's banks will be all about educating customers, informing them, building financial literacy and customer understanding.

Retail customer life cycle stages

People's financial requirements change over the course of their lifetime. At each stage of the **customer life cycle** there are certain common characteristics customers may have. Banks align their products and services to customers' changing needs throughout the life cycle.

For example:

Life stage	Products/services
Birth	Young saver
School/student	Student loans/overdraft
Young professional	Mortgages, insurances, pensions
Married or single	Mortgages, insurances, pensions, financial planning
Parenthood	Mortgages, insurances, pensions, financial planning, budgeting
Pre-retirement	Financial planning, pensions, investments
Post-retirement	Pensions, savings, spending, estate planning, health planning, downsizing, long-term care planning

Customer life cycle   Used to map the different stages a customer goes through throughout their lifetime. It enables banks to market their products and services to customers as they move through each of the life cycle stages.

Financial capability

Financial capability is the ability to manage your financial affairs. It focuses on developing people's financial skills and knowledge, and improving their financial well-being. It means being able to manage your finances on a daily basis and through significant, unplanned, life events.

Such life events could include:

- redundancy;
- ill health;
- physical or mental incapacity;
- divorce.

Changes of circumstances of this magnitude can represent a significant financial challenge for the unprepared. To be financially capable, people need to be able to select products or services that meet their needs now and in the future and to be able to access them via the most convenient channels (branch, telephone, internet or mobile banking). Financially capable customers find and use information and know when and where to seek advice. They are then able to understand and act on this advice.

Vulnerable persons

The financial services industry has a duty to ensure the fair treatment of customers, including society's most vulnerable. Ensuring that customers in vulnerable circumstances are treated not only fairly but with empathy and sensitivity to their circumstances is a priority for the financial services industry.

It is important to recognize that no two vulnerable customers are the same. Vulnerability is a dynamic state, which is affected by personal factors, life events and wider circumstances or relationships, including those between customers and their bank or other financial service providers. It is not always easy to detect the signs of vulnerability, and people do not always feel comfortable talking about their personal circumstances.

The FCA's occasional paper *Consumer Vulnerability* (FCA, 2015), published in February 2015, emphasized the need for a holistic approach towards consumer vulnerability, embedded across organizations:

- When customers seek help and support, firms should treat them sensitively and flexibly and be responsive to their needs.

- Customers should be able to access practical, jargon-free information and help through the range of communication channels that each firm provides. They should also be informed about other external sources of help relevant to their situation.

- Customers should not need to tell firms about their particular circumstances or characteristics more than once.

- Customers should have access to specialist support to help make informed choices in light of their individual situation. Where customers require regular or ongoing assistance in such circumstances, firms should consider opportunities to provide dedicated points of contact to support them.

- At a customer's request, firms should make it easy for a friend or family member to help manage their money.

- Customers particularly at risk of being scammed or financially abused need to be (and feel) protected by their financial service provider.

- Evaluation and monitoring procedures should centre on obtaining a positive outcome for the customer.

Needs and wants

People buy to satisfy both needs and wants: needs are the essential things you need to survive such as a roof over your head, or food on the table; wants are non-essential, for example, buying a newspaper or a new car.

As incomes rise, needs tend to be satisfied so the importance of wants increases in relation to needs. But consider this: you or someone you care about has a heart attack. They have an immediate *need* and require urgent medical assistance from a paramedic, doctor or nurse. They may *want* a consultant cardiologist to look after them, but they need to wait until one becomes available.

When selecting products or services customers will also consider risk and reward. In general, the greater the risk, the greater the reward. Customers' attitudes to risk may influence the choices they make.

All financial products have risk attached. If you take up a loan, can you continue to make repayments, particularly if a significant life event occurs? Even savings accounts have risk attached. In the current economic environment savings accounts pay little interest to savers, but at least it is safer than keeping cash under the bed.

Stages in the life cycle can also affect your attitude to risk. Younger people tend to take greater risks because they can rebuild their financial resources later, whereas older people have less time left to rebuild theirs.

Therefore, when dealing with customers you need to understand:

- what it is the customer needs or wants;
- why they want it;
- when they want it by;
- what are the risks; and
- what it is the customer expects from the bank.

A good relationship manager will be able to ask relevant questions about the customers' circumstances to enable him or her to understand their needs and wants in order to help them make the right choices.

Retail banking relationship managers

Before the global financial crisis, many bank business models were based on growth. The primary focus was on customer acquisition rather than customer retention. By obtaining more customers they could sell more products and services to them. Selling became a byword in banking, as did cross-selling, up-selling, sales targets and bonuses. Sales became product-based, not necessarily needs-based, and customers do not like to be sold to.

Today bank business models have altered, with the primary focus now on **customer retention**. The theory is, the longer you keep the customer (and meet their needs), the deeper the relationship becomes, generating a greater share of the customer's wallet. This requires a different culture and skill set for relationship managers. Furthermore, anyone who deals with the customer can strengthen or destroy the relationship, so relationship management is only as strong as its weakest link. Therefore, all bank personnel who serve the customer must take a stake in managing the relationship.

> **Customer retention**   The ability of an organization to retain its customers over the duration of the relationship.

Done correctly, it will generate trust which underpins long-term partnerships with the customer. This shifts power from the bank towards the customer. In this context customers see trust as something to value, especially if the person delivering that value is open, honest, transparent, and has a track record of delivering on the promises they make. So relationship managers need to be committed to developing high-quality relationships with their customers.

Premium banking

Premium bank accounts are provided to mass-affluent customers. They provide a sampling of private banking services but at a much lower price point than private banking. The accounts do not generate as much revenue as traditional private banking, but given the large number of customers that use them they amount to sizeable revenues for the bank.

In essence, it is wealth management but at a much smaller scale. These accounts are at a lower cost and lower level of service than private banking clients, who generally are at a higher cost and receive a higher level of service.

Private banking

Most private banks define their value proposition along one or two dimensions, and meet the basic needs across others. The value propositions of a private bank are:

- parent brand;
- one-bank approach;
- unbiased advice;
- strong research and advisory team;
- a unified platform.

Many banks leverage the parent brand to gain a client's trust and confidence. These banks have a strong presence across the globe and present private bank offerings as a part of the parent group.

A 'one-bank' approach is where private banks offer an integrated proposition to meet clients' own personal needs, the needs of family members and their business needs. A private banking manager will manage the whole relationship including that of the business needs. Private banking managers can structure solutions including lending solutions that are unique to the client's circumstances. They use their expertise with alternative securities and are able to work across geographical borders and jurisdictions. They can arrange credit secured against most asset types, whether the client needs a mortgage, a personal loan or wants to borrow against an investment portfolio. Many private banking clients use specialized lending services to invest in property abroad, which is something normally outside the remit of a traditional bank branch.

Private banking requires a deep understanding a client's need and risk appetite, providing unbiased advice and tailoring their solutions accordingly. Most modern private banks follow an **open architecture** product platform or a **closed architecture** product platform.

Open architecture   Product platform where a private bank distributes all the third-party products and is not restricted to selling only its proprietary products.

Closed architecture   A product platform where the bank sells only its proprietary products and does not entertain any third-party product.

These days the needs of the clients are so diverse that it is practically impossible for a bank to cater to those needs by its proprietary products alone. Clients today demand best-of-breed products and most banks follow an open architecture product platform where they distribute products of other financial services organizations to their clients in return for commission.

Wealth management

A wealth management advisor sits down one-on-one with each client and discusses goals, comfort levels with risk, and any other stipulations or restrictions the client may have in regard to the investment of their assets. The wealth management advisor then composes an investment strategy that incorporates all information gained from the client to help the client achieve their goals. The advisor continues to manage the client's money and uses investment products that meet with the client's stipulations.

Wealth management advisors cannot open banking accounts for clients, but they can assist them in determining the right kind of accounts to open at the bank of the client's choosing.

Wealth management services

Question

What services would you expect wealth management organizations to provide to these customers? Write down your thoughts before reading on.

Services provided to wealth management clients include the following:

- Access to a suitably qualified, named relationship manager, experienced in delivering bespoke financial solutions. The relationship manager will be contactable and will conduct regular meetings to ensure that the service meets the current and future needs of each individual client.

- Retirement planning is a crucial area. A wealth relationship manager will review the client's affairs, and recommend an approach to investments which will ensure a financially healthy retirement. This will inevitably include advice on investments/pensions.

- Estate planning helps customers to understand what will happen to their wealth in the event of their death. This service ensures a client's assets are treated in exactly the way the customer would want.

- Tax is a complex area for the wealthy and is therefore a vital element of the wealth management offering. Advice will include managing current tax liabilities, such as income tax and capital gains tax, and future potential tax liabilities, such as inheritance tax.

- Investment planning will ensure that individuals are making the most of their wealth. Clients will be advised around matters such as portfolio balance, growth strategies and risks to capital.

- Wealth relationship managers provide regular investment updates which allow clients to keep a high-level view of performance of the investment funds they participate in.

Wealth relationship managers will begin by understanding what their client's needs and wants are, and get a good understanding of their current financial position and their goals for the future. Based on their findings, they will introduce their clients to a range of specialists who can fulfil their needs at a particular point in time. These specialists will often be experts and highly qualified in their particular field, such as investment management, where their colleagues will build and recommend investments directly to their clients.

The wealth relationship manager will complete a detailed **fact find** document which includes an understanding of the client's attitude to risk. Estate planners, tax planners and international banking experts might all be part of a team to deliver this service.

> **Fact find**   An information-gathering form that enables wealth managers to provide the most appropriate advice to their clients.

ACTIVITY 6.1

Obtain a copy of a completed 'fact find' form from one of your wealth management colleagues. Then examine it to identify the areas that were discussed with the customer. Ask your colleague to explain why the information is considered necessary and how they used this information to identify customer needs and wants.

The wealth relationship manager will have a detailed knowledge and understanding of their client, and will conduct regular reviews of their finances, suggesting changes based on performance and the goals as their needs change. The aim of the relationship manager will be to grow their portfolio of clients, and maintain lifetime relationships between the bank and client.

Wealth and investment managers are considered to be Approved Persons under SMCR and are subject to the FCA's Client Asset Sourcebook (CASS) which contains the operational obligations imposed on investment firms, including asset managers. (Note: the FCA's CASS should not be confused with Current Account Switch Service.) The CASS rules are aimed at ensuring that under property, trust and insolvency law, the client's money is protected in the event of the failure of an investment firm.

Wealth management versus private banking

Private banking and wealth management are terms that overlap, but they are different. Private banking differs from wealth management in that it does not involve investing the client's assets. Although they advise the client on possible investment options, private banking managers do not make the actual investments.

Wealth management staff advise their clients on the best possible investments and help them in investing assets. They do not provide the clients with private banking facilities such as account management. A wealth management advisor will sit down with clients to discuss their financial goals and any reservations in the type of investments they can invest in.

In general, private banking can often be thought of as a subset of wealth management but wealth management firms cannot provide clients with private banking facility services. For access to advice from private banking or wealth management advisors clients usually need at least £250,000 in savings, investments and/or personal pensions and/or a sole annual income of at least £250,000.

Business customers

As we learned in Chapter 1, customers come in all shapes and sizes. From micro-businesses, to small and medium-sized (SMEs). Remember how SMEs are defined? By employee headcount and turnover or balance sheet value. We also discussed just how important SMEs are to the UK economy. So, it doesn't matter if you are dealing with micro-, small or medium-sized companies, they will all have a need for your bank's products and services at some point in the relationship.

At the centre of relationship management is understanding the customer's business, no matter what size. Only by understanding your business customers can you, as a relationship manager, begin to understand their needs and then fulfil these needs with appropriate products and services that add value to the customer. Business customers can have complex needs and in some circumstances the customer may not even be aware they have a need.

Consider a business customer who is looking to export their products or services abroad for the first time and who will have to accept the sales proceeds in a different currency. They realize they will need to convert the sales proceeds into their home currency or operate a new currency account. What they may not realize is that by the time the sales proceeds are received the exchange rate may have moved and changes in the exchange rate can provide unexpected gains or losses. The exporter may be willing to take this risk and even accept a loss as a cost of doing business, without realizing there are many ways to mitigate this risk. This is an example of where the relationship manager can add value, explain the risks and help the exporter eradicate or mitigate it.

In this example the relationship manager has:

- anticipated and identified the need(s);
- provided a solution (advice – exchange rate risk mitigation);
- addressed a need the customer didn't know they had;
- completed a sale (foreign exchange currency options, potentially a currency account);
- developed a trust partnership with the customer to meet their immediate requirements, and longer-term needs.

Long-term banker/customer relationships are based on professionalism and trust and the relationship must be mutually beneficial for both parties. The degree of professionalism and trust will determine how the relationship is perceived by the customer and this will determine the level of commitment the customer is willing to invest in the relationship. It requires trust on both sides.

Business customer life cycle stages

Similar to retail customers, business customers also have their own life cycles that, over time, go through various different life stages, from birth to, ultimately, closure. Business customers do not always go through the life cycle stage by stage; some may start and then fail very quickly. Others may decide to remain in a particular stage, for example, to avoid expansion beyond a certain level for fear of loss of control or outside influence.

Movement through the different stages is determined by desire, expertise, strategic choices and available resources. Each stage has different characteristics and challenges.

Stage One: birth and introduction

At this stage, the business begins as an idea. An entrepreneur is motivated to start a new enterprise because they believe they have an idea that the market wants and they can profit from the venture.

During this stage, good planning is essential as many things can go wrong. This is the most difficult stage to survive.

Needs

- good advice, usually from family or friends – it could and should also be from the bank because bankers have valuable experience of all different types of customer across a whole range of industries and sectors moving through the different stages of the life cycle;
- financial (seed capital) commonly comes from the owner's own resources and/or from family, friends – bank finance is also available from the start-up stage and beyond.

Challenges

- limited human resources;
- obtaining sufficient financial resources;
- high start-up costs;
- a weak position in the supply chain (initially).

Skills

- creativity and innovation;
- flexibility;
- research and development;
- marketing;
- business planning.

Sales

- demand has to be created and customers encouraged to use the products/ services, so sales can be low or non-existent at this early stage;
- little or no profit is made;
- cash is consumed.

Stage Two: development and growth

The second stage is the development/growth period. As the product/service becomes accepted in the marketplace sales begin to build. During this stage, a business will record negative profits (losses) until breakeven is achieved. How the business is managed and how it is able to compete in the marketplace will determine whether it will survive. Many young businesses fail at this stage as cash becomes difficult to manage.

Needs

- good business planning;
- market knowledge;
- market access;
- marketing and promotion;
- the ability to track and conserve cash.

Challenges

- good business planning (the bank can help here);
- business acumen (how to run the business as it expands);
- financial acumen (how to manage financial resources as it expands);
- underestimating financial resources;
- managing cash flow to avoid 'cash burn' (running out of cash);
- underestimating the time it takes to become established in the marketplace.

Skills

- educating buyers;
- product quality;
- fast error correction;
- strong after-sales service (for gaining customer feedback).

Sales

- sales volumes begin to grow;
- costs of production reduce if the business is able to gain benefits from economies of scale (as production expands it becomes cheaper to produce);
- profitability increases.

Stage Three: growth and expansion

This is the point where the business is able to generate sufficient revenues and is able to expand. However, not all businesses want to expand to a point where the owner loses control. With many lifestyle businesses, the owner's raison d'être may be simply to build the business to a position where it is able to fund their own personal lifestyle.

For those wanting to expand, expansion may require recruiting new employees or increasing or improving its assets (new/larger premises, equipment, etc).

Needs

- good accounting and management systems;
- staff recruitment;
- product quality;
- securing additional finance.

Challenges

- increased competition and potential retaliation from competitors;
- moving into new products/markets;
- the entrepreneur may need to delegate some responsibility as they cannot do everything themselves (letting go of the reins);
- succession planning.

Skills

- delegation;
- brand management;
- securing distribution channels;
- engineering or re-engineering the product/services as consensus emerges on the features that buyers value.

Sales

- sales growth rates increase;
- profits increase;
- cash starts to be generated as long as it does not get consumed by the pace of growth (overtrading risk) or the owner taking too much out of the business to fund their lifestyle.

Stage Four: maturity

At this stage, the product is fully established in the marketplace, the business is stable and able to generate strong cash resources for ongoing investment.

This is the stage where the owner might begin to explore an exit strategy. Should they wish to sell the business at some future time it is the most appropriate time to put plans in place as the value of the business will be at its highest; if they leave it too late and it enters the next stage, the value of the business will deteriorate.

Needs

- brand differentiation;
- talent retention;
- cost structure optimization.

Challenges

- the danger of complacency;
- aggressive new entrants may enter the marketplace, attracted by the profit margins available;
- succession planning.

Skills

- brand defence;
- operational efficiencies;
- new product development or product rejuvenation.

Sales

- sales peak as market saturation is achieved;
- eventually, towards the end of this stage, sales begin to slow down;
- profitability peaks;
- cash generation peaks.

Stage Five: decline and closure

Changes in the economy or society, changes in taste, lifestyle and/or deteriorating market conditions can all be catalysts for decline and ultimately closure. This is the easiest stage to reach for any business because it is the point where a business begins to fail:

- negative cash flow becomes a feature and the business is unable to survive without cash;

- many owners will then try to divest themselves of the business, but it is usually too late – the time to consider divesture was at the previous stage.

Interestingly, there are many more business births in the UK than closures and this is a continuing trend. The Department for Business, Energy and Industrial Strategy (BEIS, 2016) reported that there were 383,000 business births and 252,000 business deaths (closures) in 2015. Business births outnumbered business closures by 131,000

The role of the business relationship manager is to help businesses through the stages by helping to identify the risks at each stage and provide appropriate advice throughout the journey. Appropriate advice can be important areas to add value, particularly where the smaller business has limited knowledge or experience. Providing smaller businesses with access to trusted, unbiased information about their finance options is essential. But advice is not just about finance options; it should be on wider business issues including risk management, ie the risks their business might face.

Large corporate/global multinational corporations (MNCs)

Large corporates and multinational corporations, and even some companies operating at the higher end of the SME range, have very different banking needs from smaller business customers. These larger players may be multibanked and need access to financial products and services that remain outside of the remit of the traditional SME business relationship manager.

Multinational corporations (MNCs) are huge conglomerates that operate globally. Typically, MNCs represent the world's largest businesses and have recognizable brand names. Some banks are MNCs as they too operate across borders and these are the banks that can provide banking products and services best suited to MNCs. The geographical coverage a bank reaches through its branch networks or technology, and the ability to provide good local support to the corporate's group companies, are important issues when selecting banking partners for these types of customers. Unlike providing credit to SMEs, larger companies and MNCs expect their banking partners to make commitments and take on some of the corporate risk, especially when economic conditions deteriorate (lending through economic cycles).

In the run-up to the global financial crisis many corporates sought to rationalize the number of banking relationships they held. How many bank relationships a corporate would maintain would depend on a number of considerations, including the availability of credit, costs, services, geographical reach and strategic input.

Depending on their size, most corporates viewed their banking relationships in different ways. Cash-rich corporates may have regarded their banks as suppliers of specific services and banking technology. For these corporates, the relationship with a bank was mostly driven by cost factors. Banking services were viewed more as a commodity, price being the prime differentiator between banks.

Other corporates saw banking relationship management from a wider perspective, taking into account other variables such as:

- customer service and support;
- the breadth of the product and service offering;
- the advisory role that banks can provide.

Whichever view a corporate takes on banking relationships, the power structure of the relationship tends to favour the corporates who are able to demand innovative and sometimes bespoke banking arrangements to support their treasury, cash and liquidity management activities. Banking solutions are provided in response to the unique needs of the corporate.

Following the financial crisis and the subsequent volatility in the financial markets, pressure on banks and corporates increased. Since the crisis and the failure of some financial institutions, the creditworthiness of banks has been a major concern for treasurers and cash managers. A bank's balance sheet considerations and the cost of funds contributed to a tightening of credit standards, reducing access to credit. As such, treasurers and chief financial officers are now much more alert to indications of a bank's creditworthiness.

Banks need to supply their corporate customers with a relationship manager or a relationship team that understands the organization's business and is able to provide consistent service levels. Most treasurers and chief financial officers expect the bank's relationship manager to have comprehensive knowledge of the corporate's needs, as well as a detailed understanding of its business model and developments and challenges in its operating environment.

So, an ideal relationship manager will need to be able to:

- act as a **trusted advisor**;
- provide solutions tailored to the specific requirements of the corporate;
- offer support in challenging times.

Sounds familiar? These are the same requirements as when dealing with all customers. Whether dealing with retail, wealth management, small, medium or large businesses, the relationship manager will need to have the relevant skills to meet the customer's needs.

> **Trusted advisor**   Someone who has the experience, training, knowledge and expertise to build and retain trust with their customers. Their customers will actively seek them out for assistance and accept the advice they offer.

Competences, skills and knowledge

Our individual skills, knowledge and behaviours make us unique and influence the way we react and respond to events and how we perform at work. The first attributes needed by a relationship manager are knowledge and skills.

- knowledge requires understanding of what needs to be done;
- skills are the ability to do what needs to be done.

Skills tell us what types of abilities a person needs to perform a specific activity or role. But skills alone do not describe how well a person can do the job successfully. Competencies, on the other hand do.

A competency describes individual attributes and behaviours needed to do the job successfully. They include individual values, motives, attitudes and behaviours that demonstrate the ability to perform the job requirements competently. So competencies are the behavioural applications of skills and knowledge. They grow through experience and the extent to which an individual is able to learn and adapt.

Traditionally, job descriptions used skills, duties and responsibilities to define the job; however, competencies place the emphasis on the worker, not just the work. Consider the job description below for a corporate relationship manager.

JOB DESCRIPTION: CORPORATE RELATIONSHIP MANAGER

Purpose of the role
- Manage and sustain a portfolio of corporate customers, building long-term relationships founded on efficient and reliable support for their business. This is achieved through making prompt risk decisions and managing the consistency and quality of operational service.

- Maximize income for the bank through retention, growth and the acquisition of new customers.
- Be responsible for business development both with new potential customers and with his/her existing portfolio.

Key responsibilities
- Conduct annual review of customers' borrowing facilities (and interim reviews if customer circumstances or risk profile dictate).
- Consult customer owners/managers on financial/credit issues and general business practice/ideas.
- Deal with, and find resolutions for, customer issues or complaints.
- Determine the products that most effectively meet customer needs and be able to sell them on a proactive or reactive basis.
- Plan and coordinate marketing approaches for new business and actively develop existing relationships.
- Coordinate approaches with other colleagues across the group where required.
- Monitor and ensure adherence to risk, compliance and service standards.

Business management
- Identify priority customers to assess their present and potential contribution.
- Prepare and assess credit applications.
- Sanction applications within personal lending discretion.
- Monitor and control the quality of the portfolio in accordance with bank policy.
- Manage 'early warning list' customers to reduce risk, following head office and regional and line manager guidance.

Staff management
- Day-to-day coaching and coordination of support staff and colleagues in the provision of consistent service quality and risk.

Behaviours required to undertake the role
- Planning and organizing.
- Customer and market perspective.

- Adopting a relationship/partnership approach.
- Drive for results.
- Orientation to learn.

Skills required to undertake the role
- Relationship skills.
- Risk skills.
- General corporate skills.
- Leadership and team skills.
- Product skills.
- Communication skills.

Knowledge of the bank's products, services and policies required to undertake the role
- The jobholder will be required to have a detailed knowledge of commercial and corporate products and services.
- For complex products, a good knowledge will be required sufficient to:
  - recognize the changing needs of the customer;
  - identify product/service that best satisfies customer needs;
  - introduce the product/service;
  - coordinate the introduction of the relevant group product specialists;
  - deal with customers as required.
- A good knowledge of the products and services available in the personal sector is also required to satisfy the individual financial needs of business owners/key individuals.
- The jobholder will require a broad understanding of policies and strategies across the group as they relate to the demands of the customer base.

Applications from individuals with or studying towards Chartered Banker status would be welcomed.

Now let's continue to examine the skills required for this role (that is, what you need to be able to do).

Relationship skills

Resilience and perseverance: clear thinking under stress is a prerequisite for dealing with time-critical customer demands, as is patience. You will need to be able to handle the inevitable disappointments and setbacks that are part of your daily work life.

Likeability: you need to be likeable, but likeability goes beyond having the respect of customers and colleagues. It also relates to personal chemistry, a sense of humour perhaps, and your ability to relate with people at all different levels.

Sensitivity: this is an understanding of the impact you have on others and their responses to you. It means showing respect for customers and colleagues whether inside or outside the work environment and being aware of and reacting appropriately to customer's needs.

Empathy: this is the ability to notice, interpret, and anticipate others' concerns and feelings, and to communicate this awareness to others. Demonstrating empathy involves taking the customer's needs and concerns seriously. It requires excellent listening skills.

Assertiveness: assertiveness and self-confidence is about a high and natural level of openness. It means that you can openly express what you mean and allow others to do the same.

Risk skills

Financial capability: these are skills that you learn over time and through experience. In addition to the ability to read and understand figures, these skills involve analysing, interpreting and communicating information in a language people can understand. Experience will help you to improve your diagnostic abilities, enabling you to identify or anticipate problems and to know how best to deal with them.

Legal acumen: this is an understanding, to an appropriate level, of such things as banking and commercial law, for example, the legal aspects of taking security, law relating to banking, employment and consumer protection. It also requires an in-depth understanding of compliance.

Attention to detail: this relates to thoroughness and accuracy. If customers and colleagues see and sense that you do not pay attention to the smaller issues, then they will doubt your capability to undertake the more important tasks as well.

General corporate skills

Market/business knowledge: the role requires you to keep abreast of what is happening in the general financial environment. You must have knowledge of what is happening in both the national and local business environments.

Networking: you will inevitably build up a network of colleagues during the course of your career as you move through a variety of job functions. These internal networks are just as important as external networks because these contacts are the insiders who can help you to circumvent any barriers that may exist within the bank.

Leadership and team skills

Thinking skills: having well-developed thinking skills will assist you with creativity and problem-solving. You need to have an enquiring mind and be open-minded and receptive to new ideas.

Strategic thinking and long-term planning: thinking strategically is the ability to take a long-term view and to see the bigger picture. You need to understand the difference between taking a long-term view and the day-to-day short-term view, especially when planning. It requires good analytical skills and discipline.

Product skills

Selling skills: selling is not about 'product push'. Selling is based on the relationship and is centred around you understanding the needs of prospects and customers and aligning the bank's products and services to meet those needs in a way that adds value to both the customer and the bank.

Negotiation skills: there are very few times in dealing with other individuals when you are not negotiating in some way or another. The ability to respond well to other people's approaches to an issue is just as important as the ability to put counter-proposals in an open and fair way.

Communication skills

Building rapport: most people see rapport as finding common interests or issues to talk about, but it is broader than that. You will need to observe and analyse the way in which customers communicate and behave, such as their likes or dislikes.

Communication: this is the ability to express yourself clearly in conversations or in writing when interacting with others and ensure that information is passed on to others who should be kept informed.

Administration and organization: these are a collection of skills such as planning, control, diary management, time management, prioritizing and management of resources, including staff.

ACTIVITY 6.2

List the skills that are required in your current job role and compare them to the list above.

Now let us examine the competences required to be successful in this role (that is, how you apply your knowledge, skills and behaviours).

Relationship competences

Interpersonal ability: you will achieve this by understanding, interpreting and responding to others' concerns, motives, feelings and behaviours without any loss of objectivity.

Initiative: you will achieve this by identifying what needs to be done and doing it before being asked or before the situation requires it.

Persuasiveness: this is you being able to convince others to accept ideas and proposals by articulating the advantages and disadvantages and benefits of the solution(s) you propose in order that the recipient can make an informed decision.

Flexibility and adaptability: this is your ability to respond and adapt to a variety of situations whilst maintaining effectiveness. It can be achieved by being open to different and new ways of doing things and being prepared to modify your own preferred way of doing things.

Self-control and resilience: this is your ability to control your reactions to produce behaviours appropriate to the circumstances. You will achieve this by being resilient and maintaining energy, enthusiasm and objectivity through perseverance. It requires you to be able to suspend judgement and to think before you act.

Self-confidence: this is achieved by having faith in your own ideas and capabilities to be successful.

Thoroughness: this requires you to ensure your own and others' work and information is complete and accurate. You will achieve this by carefully preparing for meetings and presentations and following up with others to ensure that agreements and commitments have been fulfilled.

Risk competences

Analytical thinking: this is your ability to anticipate the implications and consequences of situations and to take appropriate action. It is achieved by quickly absorbing and analysing data and information to identify problems, patterns, trends, causes and correlations.

Decisiveness and judgement: you will achieve this by making decisions or putting forward recommendations in a timely manner, based upon sound judgement of the options available, even in the absence of a complete information base.

General corporate competences

Innovation and creativity: you will be required to generate novel and valuable ideas or apply existing ideas in new ways, by using them to help solve problems or by developing news ways to accomplish things. It is the entrepreneurial ability to look for and seize profitable business opportunities, by taking calculated risks to achieve business goals.

Strategic thinking: this is the ability to analyse the organization's competitive position by considering market and industry trends, and the strengths and weaknesses as compared to competitors.

Leadership and team competences

Organizational influencing: you will achieve this by understanding and using relationships from within the organization, by building a network of contacts and using effective strategies to influence decisions.

Building collaborative relationships: you will achieve this by developing, maintaining and strengthening partnerships with others inside or outside the organization who can provide you with information, assistance and support.

Leadership: leaders take responsibility for others and for their actions, by providing purpose, direction, context or vision, as appropriate.

Developing others: this is your ability to help others to reach their potential by delegating responsibility and coaching them to improve their own performance.

Team working: this is the ability to contribute to an effective team by cooperation and participation and a commitment to shared goals or objectives. You will achieve this by providing motivational support and allowing team members the freedom to decide how they will accomplish their goals and resolve issues.

Achievement orientation: this is the ability to take responsibility for improving individual or team performance by committing to challenging standards or objectives, to continually improve quality, efficiency and output. It requires providing feedback and identifying and addressing performance problems and issues promptly.

Managing change: this is the ability to demonstrate support for innovation and for organizational changes needed to improve the organization's effectiveness, by you supporting others to successfully manage organizational change.

Product competences

Product knowledge: this requires having a detailed knowledge of products and services and recognizing the advantages and disadvantages of options available when meeting customers' needs.

Technical and professional knowledge: you will need to have a good understanding of banking systems and procedures and the wider banking marketplace and be able to relate this knowledge to customers' needs.

Customer service orientation: you will achieve this by focusing effort on discovering and meeting customer needs by providing an acceptable solution(s) to their needs.

Communication competences

Planning and organization: this is your ability to plan, organize, prioritize, monitor and control work by making the most effective use of time, money and resources.

Concern for quality: you will show concern for quality by careful adherence to established procedures and practices and being committed to maintaining and improving high standards of work.

ACTIVITY 6.3

List the competences that are required in your current job role, and compare them to the above.

Teamwork

What makes a great relationship manager? Teamwork. The relationship manager does not function in isolation. Relationship managers are dependent upon a variety of colleagues that provide ongoing support and one of the most important functions relationship managers provide is how they support their own support staff, in the wider team.

Teamwork can be described as the managed, planned, systematic coordination of effort by a group of people with a common goal. Teams may be permanent or temporary depending on the nature of the task. Understanding how these teams behave is an important part of the team leader's management skills.

The structure of the day-to-day relationship team will depend on the number and nature of the relationships and the roles that need to be performed. The role of each member of the team will be defined and there is likely to be a hierarchy of authority. Nonetheless, the team needs to be flexible in the way it goes about its business. Think of it as a problem-solving unit dealing with the needs of its customers.

The role of teams

Teams fulfil a number of important formal and informal functions that meet the needs both of the organization and of the individual. Indeed, employees can feel isolated and unhappy if they are not part of a cohesive team.

Question

Working as a team can bring a range of benefits. What do you think they are? Write down your thoughts before reading on.

Some of the benefits of working as a team include:

- task completion based on the combined effort of individuals working together with multiple viewpoints and specialized knowledge;
- making work more enjoyable through cooperation;
- meeting social needs for friendship, support and companionship, and helping to reduce stress;
- providing a means of evaluating opinions and attitudes, and confirming one's identity and status;
- an individual a sense of belonging as well as providing guidelines on acceptable behaviour.

Effective teams need a mix of people with different characteristics, such as those who can get things done, and those who are concerned with the workings of the group. Belbin (2003) identified eight key roles:

- *Chairs*: control the way in which a team addresses the key tasks, recognizing the capabilities of the team members to make best use of their strengths and weaknesses. They are often the leaders responsible for creating the team environment and ethos.
- *Shapers*: direct attention to the setting of objectives and priorities and look to impose some shape or pattern on group interactions in pursuit of the tasks in hand.
- *Company workers:* turn concepts and plans into practical working procedures and carry out agreed plans systematically and efficiently.
- *Plants:* good for new ideas and strategies as they relate to major issues; they are also good at gap analysis (problem-solving) of existing processes.
- *Resource investigators*: tuned in to relevant events outside the team and maintain contacts that may be helpful as the project develops.
- *Monitor–evaluators:* analyse problems and evaluate ideas and suggestions so the team is better placed to make decisions.
- *Team workers:* support members in their strengths and underpin members in their shortcomings to improve communications between members and foster team spirit.
- *Completer–finishers*: ensure that the team is protected from mistakes, look after work that needs a higher level of attention and maintain a sense of urgency in the team.

As Belbin's theories developed, she identified a ninth team role, that of the *Specialist*: they bring in-depth knowledge of a key area to the team.

To be an effective team there should be a balance of all these roles. Some members will adopt a primary role; most will have an alternative secondary role.

ACTIVITY 6.4

Consider the team you participate in. Identify what roles individuals play in this team.

Are there any gaps?

360-degree peer review

How good a relationship manager are you? A very useful (and revealing) exercise is to complete an audit of your capabilities in terms of your own skills and competences (Figures 6.1 and 6.2). This can be enhanced by getting your peers to undertake a review as well.

Figure 6.1 Skills audit

Scores	Exemplar	Skills	You	Line manager	Sub-ordinate
		Resilience Likeability Sensitivity Empathy Assertiveness Financial capability Legal acumen Attention to detail Market/business knowledge Networking Thinking Strategic thinking Selling Negotiation Building rapport Communication Admin & organization			
Totals					

Figure 6.2 Competences audit

Scores	Exemplar	Competences	You	Line manager	Sub-ordinate
		Interpersonal			
		Initiative			
		Persuasiveness			
		Flexibility			
		Self-control			
		Self-confidence			
		Thoroughness			
		Analytical thinking			
		Decisiveness			
		Innovation			
		Strategic thinking			
		Organizational influencing			
		Building collaborative relationships			
		Leadership			
		Developing others			
		Teamworking			
		Achievement orientation			
		Managing change			
		Product knowledge			
		Technical & professional knowledge			
		Customer service orientation			
		Planning & organizing			
		Concern for quality			
Totals					

The exercise is simple. Choose somebody in the same role as you, whom you consider to be an exemplar, and mark their capabilities on a scale of 1–10. This sets the standard and gives you a measure to work with. Then mark your own scores, and have your line manager and a member of your support team score you as well.

The completed reviews

An example of a completed skills audit (Figure 6.3) and a competences audit (Figure 6.4) are given below.

Have a look at the ringed elements in the skills audit where each reviewer has scored the relationship manager differently. Then consider the relationship manager's comments on their own review. They reveal some interesting discussions points:

Relationship manager's comments on skills audit:
On the skills audit, it seems everyone agrees I have work to do on networking. I'm not surprised; I really do not like having to network! Another observation

Figure 6.3 Skills audit: completed

Scores Exemplar	Skills	You	Line manager	Sub-ordinate
10	Resilience	9	9	10
9	Likeability	9	10	10
8	Sensitivity	9	10	10
9	Empathy	9	10	10
10	Assertiveness	9	9	10
10	Financial capability	9	9	10
10	Legal acumen	9	10	10
10	Attention to detail	8	10	9
10	Market/business knowledge	9	9	10
10	Networking	7	5	8
9	Thinking	9	10	10
10	Strategic thinking	9	9	10
10	Selling	8	8	10
10	Negotiation	8	9	10
10	Building rapport	9	10	10
10	Communication	9	8	9
10	Admin & organization	9	10	6
Totals 165		**148**	**155**	**162**

is that my subordinate thinks very highly of me, and has scored me well, apart from administration and organization. My line manager and I think this is a strength and yet my subordinate has only marked me a 6. Having discussed it with him, he explains that on a number of occasions shortly before I go to an appointment, he can see me panicking 'where have I put the file? I can't find the audited accounts!' It's true.

Turning to the competences audit, there are again some revealing observations:

Relationship manager's comments on competences audit:
I have marked myself highly on initiative. My line manager has only marked me 8. After discussing it, she points out that she sees other managers displaying more initiative and reminds me of other colleagues who have undertaken more projects for the team.

Likewise, analytic thinking. Again, she gives me examples of other colleagues who perform better. We agree areas and projects I will undertake to improve. I have already made the point about my planning and organization, and I will be reviewing my time management as part of my personal development plan.

This example is based on the skills and competences of a relationship manager in corporate banking. You can replace the skills section with more

Figure 6.4 Competences audit: completed

Scores Exemplar	Competences	You	Line manager	Sub-ordinate
10	Interpersonal	9	10	10
10	Initiative	10	8	10
10	Persuasiveness	8	8	10
8	Flexibility	9	10	8
10	Self-control	9	9	10
10	Self-confidence	8	8	10
10	Thoroughness	9	10	7
10	Analytical thinking	10	8	10
10	Decisiveness	8	9	10
9	Innovation	9	10	10
10	Strategic thinking	9	9	10
10	Organizational influencing	8	8	9
10	Building collaborative relationships	9	10	10
8	Leadership	9	9	10
8	Developing others	10	10	10
10	Teamworking	10	10	10
10	Achievement orientation	9	8	10
10	Managing change	9	9	10
10	Product knowledge	8	8	10
10	Technical & professional knowledge	9	10	10
10	Customer service orientation	10	10	10
10	Planning & organizing	9	10	7
10	Concern for quality	9	10	10
Totals 223		**207**	**211**	**221**

appropriate skills that apply to your own role (retail banker, wealth management, etc). However, while you can replace the skills, you should not replace the competences, as these remain the same whichever role you are in.

Have fun, it's a very useful exercise and can prompt really helpful discussions with your colleagues to identify your own strengths and weakness and possible improvement areas.

Imagine how powerful it would be if you could arrange for one of your customers to mark you as well!

As we started this chapter you were asked to score yourself (1–10) on what you understood relationship management to be all about. Having almost completed the chapter and the activities, how would you rate your understanding now? Has it changed? Are there any areas you need to review again or discuss further with a colleague or your line manager? How would you rate your own skills and competences in your current role?

My score [   ]

Good relationship managers are those people who understand their customer's needs and desires to a level which allows them to recommend products and services which will help them to deliver on those goals.

Understanding your own strengths and weaknesses is also a critical element, as this can impact how you will interact with others in your immediate and wider teams who also play an important part in delivering an outstanding relationship management experience.

Chapter summary

In this chapter we have explored:

- how relationship managers differ from a traditional salesperson's role;
- the differences between skills and competences;
- customer life cycle stages for both retail customers and business customers;
- the impact of technology on the relationship management role;
- the benefits of working in a team;
- the different roles within a team.

Objective check

1 What are the main differences between salespeople and relationship managers?

2 What impact is the use of technology having on customer relationships?

3 List the seven stages in a personal customer's life cycle. How does this differ from the business customer life cycle?

4 What is the difference between a skill and a competence?

5 What are the benefits of working as a team?

Further reading

Belbin, M (1993) *Team Roles at Work*, Butterworth-Heinemann, Oxford

References

Belbin, RM (2003) *Management Teams: Why they succeed or fail,* Routledge, London & New York

Department for Business, Energy & Industrial Strategy (BEIS) (2016) *Statistical Release – Business population estimates for the UK and regions 2016* [pdf]. Available at: https://www.gov.uk/government/uploads/system/uploads/attachment_data/file/559219/bpe_2016_statistical_release.pdf [accessed 23 October 2017]

Financial Conduct Authority (FCA) (2015) *Occasional Paper No. 8: Consumer Vulnerability 2015* [pdf]. Available at: https://www.fca.org.uk/publication/occasional-papers/occasional-paper-8.pdf

07

Tools and techniques to help relationship managers

This chapter reviews a variety of tools and techniques that can help relationship managers to help their customers, by understanding their customers better.

LEARNING OBJECTIVES

By the end of this chapter you will be able to:

- describe a number of macro-analysis tools (at a market and organizational level);
- analyse businesses and sectors using a number of micro-analysis tools and techniques (at a market and organizational level);
- apply and develop the tools to encourage and stimulate debate with customers and prospects;
- assess the management capability of an organization.

Introduction

There are a number of tried and tested tools and techniques traditionally used by relationship managers with their business customers, especially larger corporates, to identify risk within an organization. These tools and techniques not only identify risk but can be very helpful for relationship managers in formulating and stimulating meaningful discussions with customers and prospects. They provide great talking points where you can add real insight and test business owners about their organization and the markets in which they operate. This chapter outlines a number of the most common and important tools and techniques.

But before we start, how would you mark yourself on scale of 1–10 about your current knowledge of tools and techniques used by relationship managers?

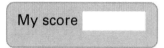

Don't be concerned if, as you work through the chapter, you find that you have never come across any of these. By the end of the chapter you will be able to understand them, and use them with your customers. Indeed, in Chapter 10 there is a case study where you will be asked to practise using some of these tools and techniques and to prepare discussion points when speaking to a real management team. So, let's look at the first tool: PESTEL.

PESTEL

The mnemonic stands for:

Political
Economic
Social/cultural
Technology
Environmental
Legal/regulation

PESTEL looks at the macro-environment in which all businesses operate. The macro-environment consists of the outside influences that affect all businesses. These external factors fall beyond the control of an organization and can be either opportunities or threats to a business; for example, a business cannot change the economy, it can only respond to it.

PESTEL considers potential future changes to an industry and provides a framework for testing reactions to changing events. It can identify trends that may affect the industry, its profitability and therefore its survival in the future.

Consider the changes banks have had to make in terms of regulation and legislation since the 2007–09 financial crisis.

Some of the areas within the PESTEL model you need to consider when you are engaging with your business customers are discussed below.

Political

- Changes in government or government policy (home and abroad) can provide political stability or instability.
- Political stability can aid business planning, whereas political instability can impede it.
- Taxation policy (personal and corporate) can determine business structures and can also impact on investment decisions (is it tax efficient?).

Economic

- Is the economy growing or shrinking?
- What are gross national product (GNP) trends either at home or abroad?
- Economic stability aids organizations whereas economic instability does not.
- Economic stability can boost investor and consumer confidence whereas economic instability provides uncertainty which could lead to reductions or delays in spending.
- Inflation, interest rates, exchange rates and employment levels always affect businesses.

Social/cultural

- Social demographic changes can also affect businesses.
- National population levels and immigration policy all impact businesses, especially in terms of recruitment.
- Lifestyle or lifestyle changes also impact. Consider how much consumers want the latest fashion items or gadgets.
- What do employment trends look like? Do we have sufficient skills?
- What are education trends telling us in terms of levels of education and career expectations?

Technology

- Technology moves on at a pace. Can we keep up?
- How quickly can products or services become obsolete? (Remember fax machines?)
- How reliant is an industry or a business on technology and technological change?
- Consider the power of the internet which can provide access to information and products from around the globe.
- What are the technology risks: cybercrime, technology failures?

Environmental

- Pollution and wastage that have social and legal consequences impact on industries and businesses; eg legislation on greenhouse emissions and emission testing.
- Is the industry/business ecologically sustainable?

Legal/regulation

- Increased legislation (home and abroad), eg legislation to prevent discrimination in the workplace.
- Consider voluntary and non-voluntary codes and regulations and the cost of compliance.
- Consider the trends towards increasing litigation and more onerous rules such as corporate governance or health and safety at work (HASAW).

You may notice that some of these factors are interdependent. There are links and relationships between the factors and it is important to recognize this, because taking action in one area could impact on another. For example, political stability or instability will affect the economic climate. The impact of changes to taxation and employment levels will affect consumer demand through disposable incomes. If taxes rise, the likelihood is that disposable incomes will fall. Similarly, the threat of unemployment can also impact as consumers may delay or cancel spending plans. These influences can impact on demand for products or services, or on the cost of producing them, or both.

> ### ACTIVITY 7.1
>
> Prepare a PESTEL analysis of the banking sector and identify what you consider to be the most important influences that affect it. Once you have completed your analysis compare your answer to the one provided at the end of this chapter (Appendix 7.1).

Porter's five forces

Michael Porter is Professor of Strategy at Harvard Business School. In his book *Competitive Strategy* (Porter, 1980) he defines an attractive industry as one that offers sustainable, superior returns for its participants and identifies five forces that affect any industry. Porter argues that the collective impact of these five forces must be taken into consideration when deciding on the relative attractiveness of an industry because the greatest threat to an organization comes from inside the industry in which it operates.

Professor Porter identifies these five forces as:

- the threat of new entrants;
- the power of suppliers;
- the power of buyers;
- the threat of substitutes;
- competitive intensity.

Threat of new entrants

To enter and compete in a market where **economies of scale** are significant, new entrants must either quickly achieve large volumes, or accept significant cost disadvantages. If there are no significant economies of scale, new players can become competitive with relatively small volumes.

Economies of scale   Where a larger size of output leads to a lower cost per unit of output.

Large-scale capital investments can act as a barrier. A business entering a market with high start-up costs increases risk, especially if those costs are only partly recoverable or non-recoverable (eg advertising or research & development, both of which are 'sunk' costs). If entering a market incurs only minor set-up costs, the risk is significantly reduced.

If distribution channels are closely integrated with existing players, new entrants will face several barriers. They may be forced to pay a premium, find alternative channels, or spend time and money developing their own. If distribution channels are readily accessible to all participants, newcomers will not be disadvantaged, which could encourage them to enter the market.

If participants can differentiate their products/service and develop an image or brand that customers value, it can generate high levels of customer loyalty. If customer loyalty is strong enough, even aggressive pricing may not tempt customers away from the incumbent supplier. If there is no product differentiation or brand loyalty, new entrants will be more likely to acquire new customers.

Government regulations, licence requirements or demand for skilled personnel can make it difficult for new players to enter a market. The costs of compliance can act as a barrier. If there are no such regulatory barriers, any player can enter the market. This would enable even poorly prepared or inadequately equipped businesses to supply the marketplace, which could have an impact on the reputation and profit margins of existing participants.

When margins in an industry are low compared to the risks involved, it is unlikely that new players will consider entering the market as they would be unable to achieve acceptable returns, particularly after start-up/sunk costs are taken into account. If margins are high, new entrants are likely to be attracted to the possibility of good returns.

To assess the impact of the threat of new entrants into a sector, the barriers to entry must be identified. In general terms, where the barriers to entry into a market are high, the threat of new entrants will be low.

Power of suppliers

The more suppliers there are in an industry, the stronger bargaining position a purchaser will be in, as they will be able to compare alternative sources of supply. If there are only a few suppliers, a purchaser's bargaining power will be limited because there are fewer suppliers to choose from. If there is only one supplier, the ability to bargain is severely limited and opens the purchaser to significant risk, should the supplier fail.

If a purchaser were able to identify alternative substitutes, even if they were not exact substitutes, a purchaser would be in a stronger negotiating position with a supplier. If suppliers rely on the purchaser's business volumes and would struggle without these volumes, the purchaser would be in a stronger position to negotiate advantageous terms. Bargaining power is weaker when the cost and inconvenience of switching suppliers would impact on the purchaser and could deter the purchaser from switching to alternative suppliers.

Within the **supply chain,** a participant's existing supplier could decide to try to deal directly with the supplier's own customers, cutting the current provider out of the equation (forward integration). Conversely, a customer could leapfrog the participant to try to secure their own source of supply (backwards integration) direct from the participant's own suppliers (Figure 7.1).

> **Supply chain** All the steps, factors and items from raw materials through to finished product/service to the point where the customer will purchase.

Power of buyers

Having a large customer base puts a supplier in a better position to negotiate terms. With no single customer able to dictate terms, bargaining power rests with the supplier. If a business has a small number of customers it will have less bargaining power, especially if the volume of business increases.

A supplier will be in a strong position if buyers cannot use alternative or substitute products. If there are no viable substitutes for the product/service, buyers will find it difficult to find a replacement supplier. If a substitute product does exist, the supplier could be at risk of being replaced, meaning the buyer has more power.

Figure 7.1 Forward and backward integration of the supply chain

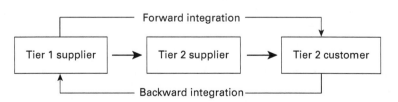

Buyers are less likely to switch if the costs of switching to another supplier are high; buyers are tied into the supplier, making it easier for the supplier to negotiate advantageous terms. Where switching costs are low the supplier is more vulnerable to losing their business.

When the supplier's products/services represent only a small fraction of the customer's costs, the supplier could have an advantage as the customer could be less price sensitive and less likely to bargain hard for discounts. However, if the products/services are a more significant cost to buyers, they will be more likely to compare prices and shop around.

If the products/services form an integral part of a customer's own products/services, the primary concern will be quality. When quality is critical to the quality of the customer's own products/services, the supplier will have an advantage. If the quality of the products/services has minimal impact on the customer's products/services the buyer will be more likely to shop around for the best price and/or terms.

Threat of substitutes

If potentially substitute products/services are in the process of being developed, even if they are not yet viable, it will be only a matter of time before they become a real threat. If potential substitutes are unlikely to fulfil buyers' needs better than the current product, then the threat to suppliers will be minimal. If potential substitute products are likely to be more attractive in the future, then a supplier could become increasingly vulnerable.

Competitive intensity

When a market is made up of a large number of business, competition tends to be fierce for all participants. In a concentrated market with a small number of large participants, the larger players can more or less dictate the market.

When an industry has high fixed costs, participants will aim to fill capacity as often as possible, which can lead to fierce price competition as competitors undercut rivals to fill capacity. If fixed costs are relatively low, price competition is less likely to be as aggressive.

When an industry's products are not greatly differentiated, the market is often subject to fierce price competition. If products are viewed as commodities, price competition can be aggressive as buyers make their decisions on price alone. If products can be differentiated, price becomes less of an issue as quality and brand loyalty are considered to be important in the decision-making process.

When the cost of leaving an industry is high, unsuccessful operators might continue to operate, because they find it too difficult to leave. They may resort to tactics that can affect the profitability of the industry as a whole, reducing the prospects for everyone. Conversely, if the cost of exiting an industry is low, unsuccessful businesses will be able to stop trading at an early stage, leaving more room and opportunity for the remaining players.

If the market is growing quickly, participants tend to find it easier to generate new business and to retain existing customers. If the market is growing slowly or contracting, participants will find it harder to find new customers, or retain their existing ones. Large competitors will be able to use their purchasing power to take business from smaller players in an attempt to squeeze them out of the marketplace.

ACTIVITY 7.2

Prepare a five forces analysis of the banking sector. Identify the most important influences that affect the banking sector. Compare your answer to the one provided at the end of this chapter in Appendix 7.2.

Competitive advantage

Porter contends that in order to be profitable in an industry an organization must have sustainable **competitive advantage**.

Competitive advantage An advantage over competitors gained by offering customers greater value either by lower prices or by providing greater benefits and services that justify higher prices.

There are two basic types of competitive advantage: lower costs than competitors, or a differentiated product or service that is unique and commands a premium price. Porter also states that, by pursuing competitive advantage, an organization must choose its scope, that is, it chooses which aspect of the market to operate in: either to go for a broad industry-wide market or a narrower part or particular segment within the market. When the picture of overall market attractiveness has been explored and determined, the choice of which strategic position to take should emerge. Primarily, there are two options: cost leadership and differentiation.

Figure 7.2 Strategic approach matrix

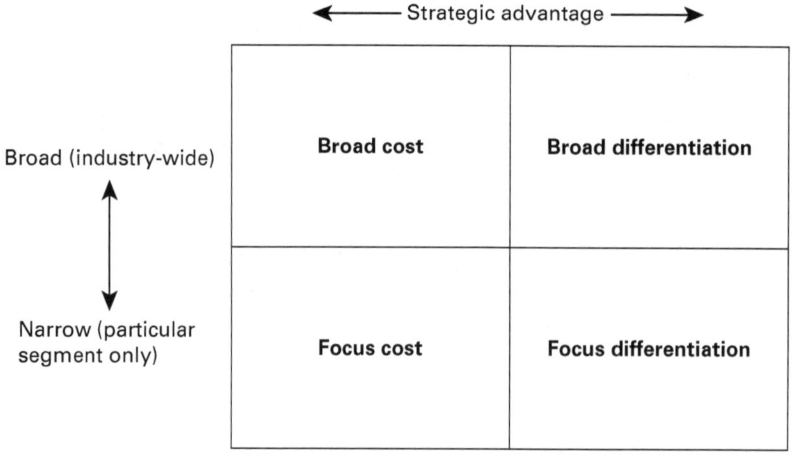

Strategic advantage

	Broad cost	Broad differentiation
Broad (industry-wide)	Broad cost	Broad differentiation
Narrow (particular segment only)	Focus cost	Focus differentiation

Cost leadership means being the lowest-cost producer in the industry. This strategy is usually associated with large-scale businesses offering standard commodity-type products with relatively little or no differentiation.

Differentiation is producing a product or service which customers value and believe to be unique. It assumes that competitive advantage can be gained through particular, unique characteristics of a product or service. This strategy is usually associated with charging a price premium.

A *focus strategy* is a hybrid of both cost leadership and differentiation. Under a focus strategy an organization focuses its effort on one particular segment of the market, pursuing a strategy of cost leadership or differentiation within that narrow segment.

According to Michael Porter, the choice of the scope will define four basic approaches: broad cost, broad differentiation, focus cost and focus differentiation (Figure 7.2).

Broad cost

A cost strategy begins with a good product that is acceptable in quality and features. Instead of having a unique product, the organization seeks advantage by opening up a sustainable cost advantage over its competitors. It does so by managing the areas in the business that are critical to costs. To achieve cost leadership an organization will usually need large-scale production so that they can benefit from economies of scale. Achieving cost leadership normally involves eliminating all extra product functionality and customer service (no frills).

Broad differentiation

Broad differentiation starts by identifying the needs that a buyer perceives are valuable and views as important. The business then seeks to meet those needs better than any other competitor. In achieving this it attempts to command a premium price.

Focus cost

Organizations can also achieve cost advantage by focusing on a particular target sector (segment) where they can be more cost-efficient than more broadly targeted competitors. These organizations achieve competitive advantage by dedicating themselves to serving the distinct needs of a particular segment, and no more.

Focus differentiation

Here the differentiator chooses a narrow market and concentrates on servicing it better than its more broadly targeted competitors. The important issue for any business adopting this strategy is to ensure that customers really do have different needs and wants and that existing competitor products do not meet those needs and wants.

'Stuck in the middle'

Some organizations will attempt to implement all three strategies: cost leadership, differentiation and focus. A business adopting all three strategies is known as being 'stuck in the middle'. It has no clear business strategy and is attempting to be everything to everyone.

ACTIVITY 7.3

Consider these four businesses:

1 Rolls Royce

2 Tesco

3 Primark

4 Ford Motors

Where would you place them in the strategic approach matrix?
Compare your answer to the one provided at the end of this chapter in Appendix 7.3.

The strategic environment matrix

The strategic environment matrix is a generic strategy model created by the Boston Consulting Group (BCG). It follows on from the work of Michael Porter on competitive advantage.

This matrix is based on the two dimensions of competitive advantage: sources of competitive advantage (differentiated versus cost leadership); the potential size of competitive advantage (large or small).

The model categorizes the outputs into four descriptors (Figure 7.3):

- fragmented;
- specialized;
- stalemate;
- volume.

Volume: in this market there are economies of scale and few opportunities for differentiation. This is where organizations strive for economies of scale to become cost leader. The benefits from large-scale economies help to lower production and service costs by spreading out the cost over a larger number of units. For example, consider computer software. The initial cost investment to develop a software program is substantial but once developed production costs to supply subsequent copies are negligible. In this environment average unit costs fall quickly as volume increases.

Stalemate: here there is little opportunity to differentiate, and therefore the source for competitive advantage is limited. However, there is the opportunity to benefit from economies of scale. The main means of competition are to reduce costs of production.

Fragmented: the participant is differentiated and there are numerous ways to gain competitive advantage. The industry is well suited to niche

Figure 7.3 Strategic environment matrix

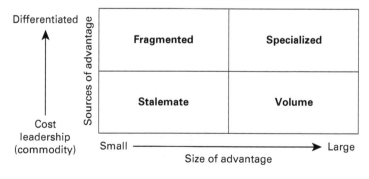

players and profitability may not be linked directly to size. Organizations grow by offering a range of niche products to their chosen segments.

Specialized: these organizations do not gain benefits from economies of scale but chose differentiation in a smaller segment. Profitability and size are not automatically related.

The characteristics and success factors required in each category are summarized below.

Fragmented

- market size varies;
- competition is often locally based;
- many competitors and highly competitive;
- low entry and exit barriers;
- high variety of products and service;
- opportunity for price premiums.

Specialized

- small, highly segmented market;
- high perception of quality;
- premium prices;
- strong brand perceptions and customer loyalty;
- few market players;
- restricted customer base;
- customized products/services.

Stalemate

- basic, mature, well-established marketplace;
- often cyclical as tied to levels of economic activity;
- commodity-type products;
- competes on price and low switching costs;
- when supply exceeds demand prices tend to weaken.

Volume

- standardized products;
- strong economies of scale;
- mass market with large sales volumes;
- mass manufacture;
- dominated by a few large competitors;
- strong brand names.

ACTIVITY 7.4

Consider these industries:

- textiles;
- volume car manufacturers;
- restaurants;
- branded foods;
- supermarkets;
- shipbuilding;
- housebuilding;
- cosmetics.

Where would you place them on the strategic environment matrix?
Compare your answer to the one provided at the end of this chapter in
Appendix 7.4.

ACTIVITY 7.5

Now let us consider retail banking.

In which environment would it appear?
Compare your answer to the one provided at the end of this chapter in
Appendix 7.5.

Product portfolio matrix

The Boston Consulting Group's (BCG) product portfolio matrix is designed to assist with long-term **strategic planning**. It can help an organization to consider growth opportunities by reviewing its portfolio of products or strategic business units (SBUs) in order to decide whether to invest, discontinue or develop new products.

> **Strategic planning** An organization's process of defining its strategy, or direction, and making decisions on how to allocate its resources in pursuit of its strategy.

The BCG model is styled for products rather than services, but it does apply to both (Figure 7.4). It is based upon two factors:

- market share (does the product have a high or low market share?); and
- market attractiveness (are the numbers of potential customers in the market growing or not?).

Stars (products in high-growth markets with high market share)

Stars are high-growth businesses or products competing in markets where they are relatively strong compared with the competition. Stars are those products that have not yet reached their full potential and tend to need continuous investment during their development in order to sustain their growth. Typically, they are still expanding their product line, expanding into new geographic markets, helping grow the overall market and attracting

Figure 7.4 BCG product portfolio matrix

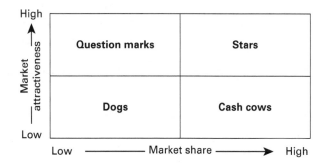

first-time consumers while defending their market share against competitors. Eventually their growth will slow and, assuming they maintain their market share, they will become cash cows. Stars can be the cash cows of the future.

Cash cows (products in low-growth markets with high market share)

Cash cows are mature, successful products/businesses with very little need for ongoing investment. They still need to be managed for profit so that they can continue to generate strong cash flows needed for developing the stars.

Question marks (products in high-growth markets with low market share)

Question marks (sometimes referred to as 'problem children') have potential, but may need substantial investment to grow market share. Management have to consider whether to invest in them or allow them to shrink or fail. Exit barriers (difficult or easy) within the industry will help to make this judgement.

Dogs (products with low growth and low market share)

Dogs may generate enough cash to break even, but they are rarely, if ever, worth investing in. Dogs are usually sold or closed as they are a drain on resources. They generally have a number of competitive weaknesses, and their level of profitability is relatively minor when compared to stars or cash cows.

Product portfolio strategies

An organization's product portfolio often starts with question marks, which eventually grow and become stars. Afterwards, as products mature and growth slows, they could either become cash cows or end up as dogs.

Once an organization has classified its SBUs or products it must decide what to do with them. Conventional strategic thinking suggests four possible strategies:

- Build and share: here the organization can invest to increase market share (eg turn question marks into stars).
- Hold: invest just enough to keep the SBU/product in its present position.
- Harvest: reduce the amount of investment in order to maximize the short-term cash flows and profits from the SBU/product. This may have the effect of turning stars into cash cows.

- Divest: the organization can divest the SBU/product by phasing it out or by selling it in order to use resources elsewhere, eg investing more in the promising question marks.

Ansoff's growth matrix

The Ansoff growth matrix examines strategies in terms of the products and services offered and the markets a business competes in (Figure 7.5). There are four different strategies:

- market penetration;
- market development;
- product development;
- diversification.

Each strategy carries its own inherent risks. The concept is that each time an organization moves into a new quadrant (horizontally or vertically), risk increases.

Market penetration

A market penetration strategy involves increasing sales to existing customers and increasing the frequency of purchases. This can be achieved by a combination of competitive pricing strategies, advertising, sales promotions, loyalty schemes, etc.

This is the lowest risk strategy as the organization knows the product and knows the market. It is likely to have good information on competitors and on customer needs and buyers' behaviours.

Figure 7.5 Ansoff's growth matrix

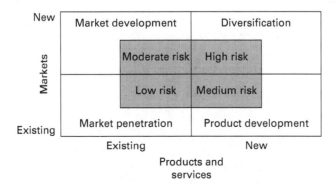

Product development

Product development is needed when an organization has a good customer base but knows that the market for its existing products has, or is reaching, saturation point. This is slightly more risky, because the organization is introducing a new product into an existing market. Risks include the cost of product development and the costs of new product launch.

A product development strategy could be suitable where an existing product needs to be differentiated in order to remain competitive. Consider how often Apple rejuvenates or updates its iPhone products.

A successful product development strategy places the marketing emphasis on:

- research and development;
- innovation;
- detailed insights into customer needs (and how they change);
- being first to market.

Market development strategy

This strategy is used when an organization targets a new market with existing products and is most often considered when existing markets offer few growth prospects.

The most common forms of a market development strategy are entering new international markets for expansion, for example exporting to a new country. Another method relates to accessing new distribution channels such as selling the products via e-commerce or mail order. Selling through e-commerce can capture a larger customer base and in the digital arena most people access the internet to purchase goods that could be sourced from anywhere in the world.

Market development is a more risky strategy than market penetration because the organization becomes involved in new markets. Risks to consider are lack of market knowledge, a lack of knowledge of buyer behaviours and potential reactions by competitors who will inevitably retaliate.

Diversification strategy

This involves entering new markets with new products and is adopted when new product development is unlikely to be effective and when the existing market is static or saturated with few/no prospects for growth. This strategy carries the highest risk because it involves introducing a new, unproven product into an entirely new market that might not be fully understood.

A good example of diversification is offered by Richard Branson's companies. He took advantage of the Virgin brand and diversified into a number of different industries such as entertainment, air and rail travel, food and banking. While diversification carries the highest risk profile, with an equal balance between risk and reward, then the strategy can be highly rewarding.

Now we have looked at some of the tools and techniques, how can they be applied to assessing management capabilities? If you understand the industry/sector your customers, or prospective customers, operate in, the better-quality discussions you can have with them. It will therefore allow you to test (and challenge) a management team's own knowledge of their industry/sector.

Management teams have an obvious focus on the day-to-day running of the business and are not always in a position to stand back and look at the wider picture. Most will welcome an outside view and the chance to discuss what is happening now and what could happen in the future. So, your discussions will add value and help them to make the right decisions, for the right reasons.

Assessing management capabilities

This is considered to be one of the most important, if not the most important, role of a relationship manager. When dealing with customers and potential customers, you must be able to assess the competence of the people running the organization. The tools and techniques previously described can assist in this process and should feature as part of the preparation needed before visiting customers or prospects.

When engaging with customers or prospects, you will be seeking to understand a number of things such as:

- what the organization does and how long they have been doing it;
- what they sell and who they sell to;
- what the organization has achieved in the past and what it wants to achieve in the future;
- how successful the management team are, now and are likely to be in the future.

When looking at any organization, one of the most important areas to focus on is the management team that runs it. As a relationship manager, you will need to understand the abilities and capabilities of those running the business. It is also important to understand the roles and responsibilities of the management team. Completing an **organizational structure** chart can be very useful.

> **Organizational structure chart**   A diagram that shows the structure of an organization and the roles, responsibilities and functions of key personnel, including the directors of the organization.

Management assessment goes hand-in-hand with the business's financial statements. The financial statements show how well or otherwise a business is doing; management assessment tells you why. It's the management decisions and actions that drive the numbers, not the other way round.

A successful management team will be able to demonstrate a broad range of competences and disciplines in the following key areas:

- Governance:
  - structure;
  - leadership;
  - strategy;
  - teamworking/effectiveness.
- Business functions:

  - production;
  - sales and marketing;
  - finance;
  - risk management;
  - management information;
  - internal controls;
  - planning (forecasting/budgeting);
  - people management.

One early step in the process of understanding a business is to find out who carries out certain key functions and who has responsibility for them.

Figure 7.6 A simple organizational structure

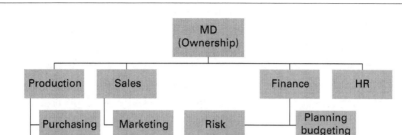

Organizational structure

It is important to explore the appropriateness of the organization's structure to understand how the business is organized. It can be useful to prepare an organizational structure chart as part of this process (Figure 7.6). Here you will be looking at who within the business undertakes the key functions.

Larger organizations are more likely to have clearly defined structures and hierarchies, while smaller organizations may be more fluid, with some roles combined.

It is also important to understand the part played by external parties who could help the business. These could be non-executive directors, consultants, advisors and auditors. These are people unconnected to the day-to-day running of the business, but who can also influence its direction.

Leadership

Leadership provides guidance, direction, control and supervision. Commonly, in a hierarchical structure, this comes from the top down; however, leadership can exist at any level within the organization. Discussions with your customers should help you to identify who it is that motivates people: a good leader will, whereas a poor leader will not. Similarly, it is useful to get an understanding of the culture of the organization and whether the organization's cultural values permeate throughout the entire workforce.

Strategy and goals

A strategic plan sets the organization's goals and objectives and the tactics that will be used to achieve these goals. It shows where the organization is heading and how it will get there. It will also identify the priorities and resources available to it, ensuring that employees and other **stakeholders** are working towards these common goals. As a relationship manager you will be examining whether the members of the management team have the skills and ability to implement their strategic plan and to modify it as business conditions dictate. The strategic plan should be designed to maintain and build upon the organization's competitive advantages. You should also explore who drives the plan and how it is communicated to employees.

> **Stakeholder** Anyone who has an interest in a business who can affect or be affected by the organization's actions, objectives and policies.

Teamworking and effectiveness

Effective management teams will demonstrate a number of qualities such as participation, mutual cooperation, good communication and trust. Teams need clear objectives and a clear understanding of each individual's role and how this fits in with the roles of others. Here you will try to establish that the management team has the right balance of skills and the desire to succeed together. In effective teams, communication between management and staff should be a two-way activity with no one person dominating the discussions or outcomes.

Having looked at the governance elements of the organization, we can now turn to the more functional aspects, which will be determined by the organization's structure. Here you will examine a number of key operational areas which are common to most organizations.

Production

Operational management is concerned with designing and controlling the process of production of goods and services. It involves the most efficient use of resources to deliver goods or services, on time and of the required quality that is valued by their customers. It would be important to identify how production is controlled, who controls it and how production links to sales.

Sales and marketing

Management teams with good marketing skills understand the markets that their organization sells into. They understand their position in the market and who their competitors are, now and in the future. They should recognize the organization's competitive advantages and be able to capitalize on them. They should also know whether they are competing on price, quality, brand or a combination of all three.

Finance

This is obviously important to you as a relationship manager and the management must understand the factors that affect the financial performance of the organization. Management need to plan their financial resources. There should be a routine monitoring of cash flow, profitability and overall financial performance. Well-managed organizations will have a detailed knowledge of financial matters and will anticipate their funding needs, and all in good time. Poorly managed organizations will not.

Risk management

This part of the assessment is concerned with the effectiveness of the risk management processes. Risk is ever present in business and needs to be managed well. The management team should be fully cognisant of the risks they face now and in the future and must be compliant with relevant regulations and legislation. A good test of this would be your discussions based on Porter and PESTEL.

An understanding of how the organization manages risk is paramount to any lender. Well-managed organizations will have robust risk controls and procedures in place, poorly managed organizations will not.

Internal controls

The management team are responsible for ensuring the organization's systems are sufficiently robust to identify all the activities and procedures that are needed to get the job done. As a relationship manager you will need to know who reviews internal controls and how often they are reviewed.

Planning

Planning is the ability to see where the business is going, and all areas of the organization should be involved in the planning process. Many smaller organizations place a lot of emphasis on the day-to-day running of the business and sometimes pay less attention to planning for the future. You will want to understand how your customer's planning process works, how often plans are reviewed and whether they are realistic and coordinated.

People management and human resources

People management is concerned with managing employee relationships. It involves recruiting and retaining the right people with the right skills, enabling them to carry out their job functions efficiently and effectively. It ensures that work is being done correctly and to a consistently high standard. A well-run organization will have clear reporting lines in place and people will be sufficiently skilled to carry out their duties. Successful organizations will be able to identify and address any gaps in knowledge or skills.

Once roles and responsibilities have been identified and understood, you will need to look at the management team to gauge their competence in a number of other important areas.

How experienced are the team? It would be valuable to know how long they have been involved with the organization and what particular knowledge or skills they bring to the party. You will be trying to determine whether the team has been together through a number of economic cycles and whether they have been tested through any challenging scenarios or situations.

If the performance of the organization is dependent on the knowledge or skills of a small number of personnel, the organization should be concerned with the risk and be able to plan for it in the event that key staff are unable to carry out their duties. Situations like this carry a higher risk to the organization because they affect the continuity and consistency of the business.

The decision-making unit (DMU)

Each organization will have its own unique decision-making process which can include several parties, depending on the scale of the decision to be made. In large organizations this is often referred to as the decision-making unit (DMU). When dealing with a management team you will need to identify who the ultimate decision-maker is. It may not always be the person you are talking to or negotiating with. Sometimes decisions may have to be referred to a higher authority for sanction.

Now we will look at a tool which summarizes all of the previous tools and techniques.

SWOT analysis

SWOT is an acronym for Strengths, Weaknesses, Opportunities and Threats. It can be used with the other tools reviewed in this chapter to summarize the organization's overall strategic position (Figure 7.7).

SWOT analysis can be used at a number of different levels:

- the organization as a whole;
- a strategic business unit (SBU) or a division within the business;
- a specific market segment;
- product lines.

The internal analysis (SW) should look at strengths and weaknesses relative to competitors in the main business functions of:

- sales;
- marketing;
- production;
- operations;
- risk management;
- finance;
- people (HR) management.

When an organization completes a SWOT analysis on itself it should then benchmark itself against its strongest competitor or rival (Figure 7.8).

The aim of a SWOT analysis is to identify and minimize weaknesses and threats and to match strengths to the opportunities available. The idea is to turn weakness into strengths and threats into opportunities.

Figure 7.7 SWOT analysis

Internal	Porter's competitive strategies
Strengths & Weaknesses	Product portfolio matrix Ansoff's growth matrix
External	PESTEL
Opportunities & Threats	Porter's five forces Strategic environment matrix

Figure 7.8 Turning weaknesses and threats into strengths and opportunities

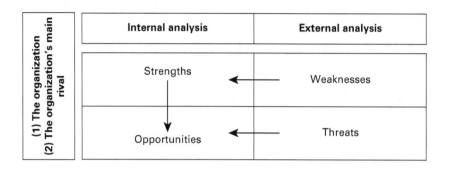

Strengths

Strengths are those positive internal capabilities that give the organization a strategic advantage. Strengths must be a source of clear competitive advantage over rivals and should serve as a cornerstone of strategy. Strengths should be protected and built upon. The test of a strength is whether it improves sales or margins. If it doesn't, it's not really a strength.

Examples of strengths could include:

- a unique product or service;
- a unique location;
- intellectual property rights (IPR) such as patents, design rights, copyright, etc;
- a unique brand;
- unique skills or capabilities.

Weaknesses

In most cases, weaknesses are the opposite of strengths and are a source of competitive disadvantage. The organization should seek ways to reduce or eliminate weaknesses before they are exploited by rivals. Weakness should be seen as areas for improvement.

Examples of weaknesses could include:

- low market share;
- low productivity;
- poor quality;

- inadequate financial resources;
- outdated technology;
- a weak brand;
- a poor reputation;
- poor skills;
- the lack of a new product.

Strengths and weakness are internal to the organization, whereas opportunities and threats (OT) are external to the business and need to be acted upon.

Opportunities

An opportunity is any feature of the external environment that creates positive potential for the organization to achieve its objectives. Key questions to ask to identify opportunities include:

- what opportunities exist?
- what is their profit-making potential?
- can we exploit these opportunities?
- what would we need to do this?

Examples of opportunities could include:

- higher economic growth;
- technical innovation;
- new markets;
- new demand;
- market growth;
- the development of new distribution channels (eg e-commerce);
- changing consumer lifestyles that potentially increase demand for the organization's products;
- partnering, mergers, joint ventures, strategic alliances, or potential acquisitions;
- vertical or horizontal integration within the supply chain.

Horizontal integration Acquiring a company in the same industry.

Vertical integration A company acquisition in the supply chain.

Threats

Threats are any external developments that may hinder or prevent the organization from achieving its objectives.

Examples of threats could include:

- new entrants;
- new substitute products;
- changes in consumer demand/taste;
- demographic changes;
- consolidation along the supply chain;
- new regulation;
- vulnerability to an economic downturn (eg recession) or a deterioration in the business cycle;
- loss of key staff;
- a technological change that could make existing products become obsolete.

This chapter has detailed a number of tried and tested models that can be used to stimulate debate with customers and prospects and identify any potential risks the organization could face in the future. We will return to these tools later when we examine the case study in Chapter 10, where you will be able to see how these tools can be used to secure new business.

The thought processes used with these tools will provide you with information and evidence of the management team's capabilities. Used intelligently, through a combination of observation and conversations, you will be able to demonstrate your own skills and competences as a financial professional who is looking to support the management team, helping it to become even more successful in the future.

As we started this chapter you were asked to score yourself (1–10) on your knowledge of the tools and techniques used by relationship managers. Having completed the chapter and the activities, how would you rate your understanding now? Has it changed? Are there any areas you need to review again or discuss further with a colleague or your line manager?

> My score

Chapter summary

In this chapter we have explored:

- a number of macro and micro tools and techniques used with business customers;
- how to apply these tools to your business customers and prospects to help them manage risk, and open up valuable discussion points during your meetings with them;
- how to assess a management team's capabilities.

Objective check

1 What is the starting point for assessing the size of the threat of new entrants into a market?

2 Having completed a Porter analysis, what are the two options for strategic position?

3 Taking a business you are familiar with, map its product portfolio in the BCG strategic environment matrix.

4 For the same business, consider which of the four strategies identified by Ansoff is being applied by the business. What level of risk does each carry?

5 Why would you as a relationship manager need to understand how decisions are made by a business's management team?

Further reading

Porter's Five Forces – Strategy Skills, www.free-management-ebooks.com
Ansoff Matrix, AnsoffMatrix.com (2013) *Your Guide to Ansoff Matrix Analysis*
    [online]. Available at: http://www.ansoffmatrix.com/ [accessed 28 October 2017]
Boston Consultancy Group Matrix, www.free-management-ebooks.com

References

Porter, ME (1980) *Competitive Strategy*, The Free Press, London

Appendix 7.1

PESTEL

The banking sector is inextricably linked to government policy and the economy. Banks are dependent on the economy and the economy is dependent on banks because of the need to access credit and payment services. Whether the economy is prospering or contracting (recession) directly affects access to capital and therefore the ability of the sector to generate profits. More capital means more lending and more lending, if done correctly, leads to greater profits.

Following the global financial crisis, governments in the UK and abroad have intervened by introducing a raft of regulations and legislation which have impacted the sector considerably. The cost of compliance and the penalties of non-compliance have damaged the levels of profitability within the sector. This level of intervention is unlikely to go away in the foreseeable future.

In recent times, the banking sector has changed in response to consumer demands and the development of new technologies (digital banking). New entrants (challenger banks/FinTechs) have disrupted the marketplace, although the level of disruption remains dependent on overcoming the regulatory hurdles demanded by the authorities to gain banking licences.

These innovative banking solutions allow banks to provide bespoke customer experiences and facilitate faster access to banking products and services. More importantly, they ease the interaction between banks and their customers, who are able to search further and faster for the best deals, advice and value, when and how it suits them.

Appendix 7.2

Porter's five forces

The events of the global financial crisis during 2007–09 demonstrated the vulnerabilities of a number of banks, including:

- business models that depended heavily on uninterrupted access to financing, with many banks overreliant on excessive short-term financing of long-term, illiquid assets; and

- weaknesses in corporate governance, incentives and infrastructure which undermined the effectiveness of risk controls.

Since the crisis, the banking sector has also been plagued with a number of mis-selling and non-compliance events, all of which have contributed to a collapse in trust in banks.

These events have opened the way for a number of *new entrants* to enter this lucrative market. New participants (challenger banks/FinTechs) have all successfully taken market share from the established banks. These new entrants compete on brand image, service quality, restoring trust and price competition, all of which were perceived to be key customer issues. Furthermore, these new participants are not burdened by the legacy technology systems and cumbersome branch networks that impede the more traditional players.

Once these new challenger banks overcame regulatory and capital/liquidity hurdles, they were able to take their place in the market, increasing competition and reducing the larger players' dominance in the sector.

The digitalization of the banking sector has also led to the *emergence of substitutes*, with peer-to-peer lending and crowdfunding now commonplace, allowing personal customers and small businesses to lend to, and borrow from, each other. This has taken significant market share for lending services from the traditional banks and it continues to grow, year on year.

The *power of buyers* in the banking sector throws up some interesting dichotomies. On one hand an individual retail bank customer has no significant power other than to move banks. Personal customers still, in the main, remain complacent and lethargic when it comes to moving banks. Many just don't bother.

Large corporate and global MNCs, on the other hand, can wield considerable buyer power. Large multibanked conglomerates use banks differently from retail customers and most SME customers. They use their banks to enter the financial markets, raising capital, for example, in mergers and acquisitions and using complex derivatives as part of their own internal treasury functions. This element of banking is extremely remunerative and attractive.

The *power of suppliers* in banking concerns the prime suppliers to the banking sector who provide capital and liquidity for their operations. Banks traditionally source capital and liquidity from a combination of customer deposits, profitable trading, lending and investors including other financial institutions in the financial markets. Following the global financial crisis, access to capital and liquidity became a challenge for some banks as providers became more cautious.

Another important supplier to the banking sector relates to *human capital* (talent). The banking sector invests considerable amounts of time and money in its employees in terms of recruitment, retention, incentives and compensation (rewards).

Finally, as *competitor intensity* increases, the banking sector is lucrative, extremely profitable (if done right) and highly competitive. The sector has extremely high entry and exit barriers.

Conclusion

The banking market is considered to be attractive, particularly if a participant can differentiate themselves in some way. New entrants have intensified competition within the sector and while remaining lucrative, it has experienced downward pressure on profitability given the regulatory requirements of compliance, the cost of non-compliance (fines) and the cost of capital and liquid adequacy.

Appendix 7.3

Strategic advantage

Broad cost: Tesco
Broad differentiation: Ford Motors
Focus cost: Primark
Focus differentiation: Rolls Royce

Appendix 7.4

Strategic environment matrix

FRAGMENTED	SPECIALIZED
Restaurants	Branded foods
Housebuilding	Cosmetics
STALEMATE	VOLUME
Textiles	Volume car manufacturers
Shipbuilding	Supermarkets

Appendix 7.5

Strategic environments

There are features of retail banking which could lead to either stalemate or volume. On close examination stalemate appears to be the most appropriate, although this could change over time.

Banking is a mature, well-established market and its fortunes are undoubtedly linked to the economic climate and are therefore subject to cyclability. Most banks' offerings can be described as being commodity-based. There are occasions where a bank introduces a new product but this first-introducer status is soon matched by fast followers who are able to replicate the product. In banking, new products do not last long.

The industry is price competitive and pressures on margins (particularly for lending) do weaken when supply exceeds demand.

Successful banks manage their assets (people) productively with tight spans of control, given the regulatory and compliance demands. Most banks focus on cost-to-income ratios closely. In an attempt to reduce costs many banks have used offshoring for non-essential departments to reduce costs even further.

So, on balance, it could be argued that UK retail banks are currently in a 'stalemate' situation. But this could change as new entrants become established and take volume from the established players. New entrants can develop and exploit strong brand names as they are not tainted with the reputational risk issues that some of the traditional players have experienced following the global financial crisis and subsequent non-compliance and mis-selling penalties.

New entrants do not have access to cumbersome and costly branch networks and in some cases large branch networks are no longer considered to be essential. Technology and the digitalization of the industry have seen to that.

08

Customer service and portfolio planning

This chapter reviews service levels, service quality, key account management and portfolio planning, all of which need to be at the forefront of relationship management.

LEARNING OBJECTIVES

After completing this chapter you will be able to:

- define a customer;
- describe the customer value proposition;
- define service quality and describe how it is measured;
- identify service quality gaps and how they can be identified;
- assess a customer complaint and state the timescales for dealing with them;
- value and manage key accounts;
- evaluate Cope's Seven Cs of Consulting and apply them to relationship management.

Introduction

In this chapter we explore what is meant by customer service, and what can happen when service quality gaps appear that may threaten the banking relationship. We look at everyone's role in customer service and how that can impact on relationship management and customer perceptions. Things can and do go wrong so we examine complaint management and service recovery. We also look at how relationship managers and their teams plan the management of their portfolios and the need to have a consultative mindset when interacting with customers. Finally, we review what it means to become a trusted financial professional, which is where the relationship manager has such a good relationship with their customers that they can lock in customers and lock out the competition.

Before we start, how would you rank yourself on a scale of 1–10 about your understanding of customer service, and what this means to both customers and your bank?

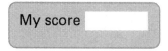

My score

We'll come back to this at the end of the chapter, so now let's start by looking at what is meant by customer service.

Customer service

A customer is somebody who buys something from a supplier. It may be a one-off purchase or a series of repeat purchases. If the customer repeatedly comes back to purchase more, a degree of satisfaction exists, to the point where the buyer and supplier develop a mutually beneficial relationship. Providing great customer service is a way to ensure customers return to purchase more. Without great customer service, they won't.

> When was the last time you received great customer service? Why did you consider it to be 'great'?
>
> Now compare it to a time you received very poor customer service. What were the differences? Did you complain?

As well as great customer service, other important factors that form part of the **customer value proposition** are:

- price;
- perceived value;
- branding.

> **Customer value proposition** The reason that a customer buys a product or uses a service. It is a statement that convinces potential customers why your product or service will add more value or solve a problem better than those offered by your competitors.

Pricing is important, but less important than perceived value. When a customer's expectations are met, or exceeded, at what they consider to be a fair price, value is realized. Value is a subjective assessment that the customer makes about the overall worth of the product or service. Customers will undoubtedly seek out the best price but they still look for, and expect, value for their money.

Perceived value is personal to the customer because they believe your offer will add more value or solve a problem more effectively than the products or services offered by rivals. It is important to remember that it is the customer's perception of value that is important, and what the customer considers valuable may be different from what the bank considers valuable. Furthermore, what one customer may value, another may not.

Branding is not just the perception of a bank that has been created by its marketing campaigns. It encompasses the personal experience that the customer has enjoyed or endured, whenever they make contact with the bank. So it is essential that a high quality of service is delivered consistently across the bank at every level whenever contact is made. Gaining customer attention and approval is the essence of customer service and this has to be achieved by all employees throughout the lifetime of the relationship.

> **Branding** The process of creating a unique name, image and perception for a product. It aims to establish a significant and differentiated presence in the mind of the customer. A strong brand makes the offering stand out from the crowd.

Service quality

Excellent **service quality** plays an integral part in attracting and retaining customers and there can be no doubt that it plays an important role in the customer experience.

Service quality   Meeting or exceeding a customer's expectations at a price that is acceptable to the customer and at a return that is acceptable to the supplier.

Question

How does your bank measure service quality?

Many banks have focused on service quality as a potential source of competitive advantage and have implemented organization-wide programmes to improve performance. Many are finding that being nice to customers is not enough and that customers' expectations continue to rise remorselessly; indeed, customers' expectations may rise the more favourably disposed they are to the bank.

Service quality is not without cost, so there must be a point beyond which it becomes uneconomic. The challenge is to supply a service that the customer recognizes as being of good value and the bank considers to be profitable. In effect, it's a contract of mutual value and it's important that the customer understands what is part of the contract and what is not. As a relationship manager it is particularly important that you get the balance right, because the risk is that you can end up over-servicing an account to an extent that is not justified by the income the relationship generates.

You may have heard the term **service level agreement (SLA)**.

Service level agreement (SLA)   Part of a service contract in which the level of service is clearly defined.

We commonly think of SLAs as formal or informal contracts that exist between different departments of the bank; for example, an advances department may agree that all credit applications are dealt with within a 48-hour turnaround timescale. But SLAs are much more than that and they are not always formal or even visible.

You and your customer will have a service level agreement; it is implied. It's what the customer and the bank expect of each other. If these expectations become misaligned, service quality gaps will appear. If they go unnoticed or ignored, the relationship will suffer.

Service quality gaps

Service quality gaps can arise from the differing perceptions and expectations of customers and bank personnel. It is not just the relationship manager's responsibility; it is the responsibility of everyone who has contact with the customer. As a relationship manager you may not even know a problem exists.

Consider the scenario where a business customer telephoned a call centre to trace a foreign payment they had made. It appeared to have gone missing. After being kept waiting, and transferred from department to department, the call centre member of staff said they would get back to them. They didn't and the matter was not resolved until the following day. The customer was annoyed but didn't think it was so significant to ask you to intervene. Nevertheless they were still irked.

Service quality gaps can emerge because of misunderstanding, misinterpretation or mismanagement. They can also emerge because activities are not fully aligned or focused in a way that puts the customer first.

In the context of service quality, a model frequently referred to for helping to identify the gaps between the perceived service quality that customers receive and their expectations, was developed by Berry and Parasuraman (1991). Their research identified five key gaps:

- *Gap 1*: this exists because there is a difference between the levels of service that the customer expects to receive and supplier's interpretation of the customer's expectations. An example might be the size and scope of a bank. Bank executives may see size as a service strength, whilst a customer might see this as a disadvantage because it may imply that the bigger the bank, the more impersonal the level of service.

- *Gap 2*: this may result from management being unsuccessful in translating the customer's requirements of service quality into service quality standards for the bank for staff to follow. For example, managers might think customers will want to see a manager when they have a complaint but customers may just want the complaint to be dealt with remotely, quickly and with little or no fuss.

- *Gap 3*: this exists because the actual service delivery, before or after an event, has failed to meet defined standards. It is not possible to ensure exactly the same quality of delivery because of the people element. People can cause problems, intentionally or unintentionally.

- *Gap 4*: this arises if the levels of service are not properly communicated or understood by the customer. Setting the expectations and communicating these at the outset is an essential requirement. Remember it is always better to under-promise and over-achieve than over-promise and under-achieve.

- *Gap 5*: this exists if the customer's perception of the service that is being provided falls short of what they hoped for. An example here might be a relationship manager failing to provide adequate information on a particular service which they and the customer had previously discussed.

In reality, some gaps are inevitable; the challenge is not to make them transparent to customers.

Customer satisfaction

Banks measure customer satisfaction in a number of ways:

- By using independent surveys undertaken by professional research organizations that may give market share data as well as generic product usage and satisfaction levels.
- Internal surveys can be undertaken and can be based upon how customers perceive the bank at both a team and individual level.
- Banks are learning to harness the capability of social media (Facebook, Twitter, etc) to solicit feedback on a one-to-one basis. This is important as relationships can only be measured in terms of the impact of one individual on another.

> How does your bank measure customer satisfaction? How often is this carried out and how can satisfaction levels be increased? What role do you play in this?

Staff work tremendously hard to attract customers to the bank and it is high-quality service that will retain them. Of course, things can go wrong, and when a customer lets you know they are unhappy, they expect a satisfactory response and outcome. So you have to reach a mutually beneficial outcome, otherwise you could risk losing the customer.

Many research organizations have studied why customers defect and report that the primary reason why customers defect is *perceived indifference* by a staff member.

Complaints play a part here. A high percentage of all defecting customers said they would never return because of staff indifference, particularly when dealing with complaints. Getting complaint handling wrong can be costly and it is generally accepted that only one in ten dissatisfied customers even bother to complain.

The process of dealing with complaints

Every bank has a formal complaints management system to ensure that a complainant is kept informed throughout the process and that staff understand the complaint process and follow it rigorously. The complaints management system should ensure complaints are taken seriously and that staff are trained and empowered to find an acceptable solution.

The process for dealing with complaints is illustrated in Figure 8.1 and includes eight stages from receipt of the complaint through to resolution and review.

Responding to complaints

The rules for how financial services organizations should deal with complaints are set out in the Financial Conduct Authority's complaints-handling rules (FCA, 2018). The FCA expects regulated firms to resolve all complaints they receive properly and in line with these rules. In particular they expect financial services organizations to:

- investigate the complaint competently, diligently and impartially;
- assess fairly, consistently and promptly:
  - what the complaint is about;
  - whether it should be upheld; and
  - what action or redress should be taken.
- provide fairly and promptly:
  - a clear assessment of the complaint; and
  - an offer of redress or remedial action, if appropriate.
- ensure any offer of redress or remedial action that is accepted is settled promptly;
- resolve complaints by close of the third business day after receiving the complaint.

Figure 8.1 The process for dealing with complaints

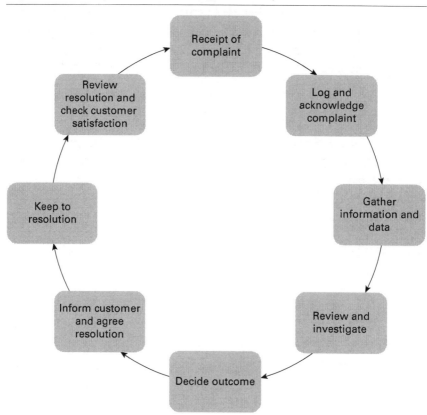

If a complaint has been resolved in line with the FCA rules by close of business on the third business day following receipt of the complaint, then, providing the customer has accepted the response, the financial services organization does not need to take any further action.

The financial services organization must send a final response to a complainant within eight weeks of receiving the complaint. A final response is a written response that:

- states whether the complaint has been upheld;
- where appropriate, offers redress or remedial action;
- encloses a copy of the Financial Ombudsman's Service's (FOS) standard explanatory leaflet (FOS, 2017); and
- informs the complainant that if they remain dissatisfied they may now refer their complaint to the FOS and must do so within six months.

If a financial services organization is not able to provide a final response at this stage, they must write to the complainant explaining why and indicate when the financial services organization expects to be able to provide a response. They must also inform the complainant of their right to refer the complaint to the FOS and enclose a copy of the standard explanatory leaflet.

Where problems persist and customers remain dissatisfied with the way an organization has dealt with their complaint, the independent FOS will arbitrate. The FOS deals with complaints from consumers against financial institutions that are regulated by the FCA. If a bank and a complainant cannot resolve a complaint themselves, the FOS will decide whether the complainant has been treated unfairly. They have legal powers to put things right which can require the bank to pay compensation.

Financial Ombudsman Service: small business complaints

The FOS receives complaints from smaller businesses, charities and trusts and well as private individuals. FOS can also look at complaints brought by 'micro-enterprises', those that have an annual turnover of up to €2 million and fewer than ten employees.

Sole traders and people running small businesses don't always register a complaint with FOS as a business dispute. People often see problems as personal rather than commercial. FOS statistics indicate that around 5,000 complaints come from small businesses each year.

Small businesses have different degrees of knowledge and experience of dealing with financial matters. Some businesses may be relatively small, but have expertise of dealing with financial matters and may have arrangements in place for getting financial or legal advice. When the FOS looks into complaints from these businesses, they usually expect them to have approached their affairs in a way that reflects their knowledge and experience. But smaller businesses usually do not have advisors and might have less experience of dealing with financial or legal matters. FOS takes this into account when dealing with cases from businesses like these.

ACTIVITY 8.1

Read the case studies for business customers from *Ombudsman News* on the FOS website: http://www.financial-ombudsman.org.uk/publications/ombudsman-news/108/108-smaller-business.html.

Carried out well, complaints handling represents a valuable opportunity for banks to rebuild and enhance their relationships with customers. When something has gone wrong, **they can use** the information gathered to make changes that deliver fair outcomes for their wider customer base, for example, by changing their product design or sales processes.

ACTIVITY 8.2

Obtain a copy of your own bank's complaints processing procedures. *How well are they aligned with the requirements of the FCA?*

Managing complaints

Customers will often regard the way in which a complaint is dealt with as being as important as the resolution itself. The art of dealing with complaints is part mental attitude and part skill. Employees who deal well with complaints tend to share similar characteristics. They:

- remain reasonable and thoughtful;
- realize something has caused the behaviour and the problem;
- are good at assessing people's needs and concerns quickly;
- are good listeners and display strong empathetic skills – they are quick to sense the mood of the customer;
- remain calm and collected throughout the discussions;
- help to separate the customer's feelings from the facts.

If a complaint is dealt with well, it is likely the bank will retain the customer's future business. Complaints should be seen as an opportunity to strengthen a relationship rather than an occasion to weaken it.

Service recovery

As a rule, customers dislike complaining because it costs them time, effort and can cause emotional stress. Stewart (1998) found that retail banking customers normally made some effort to resolve a service issue by contacting their branch or other point of contact. The fact that banking customers tended to make such an effort rather than merely defecting was probably because of the perceived high switching costs involved when switching banks.

In Stewart's study, the most frequently stated cause of customer dissatisfaction was the sense of frustration, anger, disappointment or other negative emotion caused by the bank's failure to respond positively to a complaint. It is the failure of service recovery that leads to defection rather than the initial failure itself.

Effective service recovery is based on four principles:

- *Make it easy to complain*: in order to overcome customers' natural disinclination to complain, procedures for customer complaints should be as clear and as flexible as possible. Complaints-handling staff should be trained in the interpersonal skills necessary to set customers at ease.

- *Establish the grounds for the complaint*: customers will be more willing to complain if they are confident that they will be successful. The publication of a simple, comprehensive guarantee, a customer charter or a similar definition of acceptable service levels, will provide such confidence.

- *Offer immediate redress where possible*: until the complaint is resolved, the customer will experience negative emotions concerning the cause of their grievance. The more quickly the complaint is resolved, the lower the negative impact on the customer's attitudes and therefore the easier the customer will be to placate. Where possible, it is advisable to delegate authority and responsibility for resolving complaints to customer-facing staff, so that problems can be resolved immediately as they arise.

- *Communicate*: Seiders and Berry (1998) note that customers' negative perception of a service failure is intensified if they feel that the failure could have been prevented. Often, all that is needed in order to defuse customer dissatisfaction is an apology, together with an explanation of why the failure occurred, and the steps that will be taken to ensure that it does not reoccur.

Mishandling complaints can also be very costly. In January 2011 the Financial Services Authority (now the FCA) fined Royal Bank of Scotland and its parent bank NatWest £2.8 million for multiple failings in the way the banks had handled customers' complaints (*The Guardian*, 2011).

Net Promoter Scores®

Following the global financial crisis, trust in banking fell to an all-time low. The banking sector is still recovering and whilst trust is being rebuilt it has not reached anywhere near the level it was at before the crisis. Whilst consumers still might not trust the sector as a whole, levels of trust are improving, which may be a reflection of a customer's day-to-day experiences with their own banks.

This is demonstrated by the individual banks' Net Promoter Scores.

Net Promoter Score (NPS) was introduced by Reichheld in his 2003 *Harvard Business Review* article 'One Number You Need to Grow'. Reichheld contends NPS is a management tool that can be used to measure customer advocacy. The NPS is calculated based on responses to a single question: on a scale of 0–10, how likely is it that you would recommend our company/product/service to a friend or colleague?

Those who score 9 and 10 are called Promoters.

Those who score 7 and 8 are called Passives.

Those who score between 0 and 6 are called Detractors.

Promoters are customers who are loyal and enthusiastic about doing business with the organization. They may buy more, remain customers for longer and are happy to share their experiences with family, friends and colleagues and to make recommendations or referrals.

Passives are those consumers who are neither pleased nor displeased, and can easily be convinced to defect to another competitor because of the apathetic nature of the relationship.

Detractors are those consumers who are displeased or dissatisfied and have a poor relationship. They are the ones who are most likely to defect.

One positive indicator in recent years that banks are rebuilding trust is that customer NPS scores are, generally, strongly positive.

ACTIVITY 8.3

Compare your own bank's NPS with two other direct competitors.
Why do you think they are different?

Reichheld also argues that there is a clear correlation between NPS scores and the sales and profitability of a financial institution. The higher the score, the better the sales and higher the level of profitability.

However, the real benefit of NPS does not stop with scoring; the system relies on doing follow-up research to understand the motives behind the score. Follow-up conversations and research should uncover what it is the organization is doing very well (promoters), doing less well (passives) and what it is doing badly (detractors). These conversations should inform the organization how to convert passives into promoters and move detractors into passives. Additional questions can also be included to help gain a better understanding of customers' perceptions on product lines, service levels and quality. Some proponents of NPS also contend that the same methodology can be used to measure, evaluate and manage levels of employee loyalty.

Customer satisfaction versus customer loyalty

Many banks have invested heavily in understanding customer satisfaction and point to recurring surveys giving satisfaction levels of more than 90 per cent. Unfortunately research shows that there is no comfort here. Satisfied customers are just as likely to defect.

How many times have you sat in a restaurant eating your meal with family or friends? After the meal has been served the waiter or waitress comes to your table and asks, 'is everything all right with the food?' A common response is 'yes, it's fine'. Then the waiter/waitress walks away safe in the knowledge that the customers are satisfied. Out of earshot one of you replies 'actually my steak isn't very nice. I won't be coming here again'. There are two failings in this situation. The waiter or waitress believes they have satisfied customers, when in fact they haven't. Why was the person with the steak less than honest in their response?

Studies show that up to 80 per cent of customers who defected to competitors had scored themselves as being 'satisfied' or 'very satisfied' in customer satisfaction surveys (Bain and Co, 2007). So, customer satisfaction can be described as a passive state; the customer is only willing to stay until something better comes along.

On the other hand, customer loyalty is the positive intention to stay. A loyal customer will make regular purchases and will purchase across all product lines. They become more immune to any approaches made by competitors and are more forgiving of any mistakes made. They also tend to be less price sensitive and therefore more profitable. Loyal customers may become advocates who will be willing to refer new business to you.

Customers who become your advocates promote your business on your behalf and are so happy with your product/service that they tell others. They are also willing to provide you with testimonials or take part in your customer success stories and case studies.

Achieving customer loyalty should be the aspiration of any relationship manager. However, there are other influences that you also need to understand:

- Customer loyalty does not always mean superior profitability; loyal customers may not be your most profitable ones, particularly if you over-service them.

- Loyal customers can be more forgiving of mistakes and this can distract attention away from what is usually the biggest problem: poor service and not handling complaints correctly. These are the things that drive customers away. For some companies, fixing the basics of poor customer service should have a higher priority than seeking customer loyalty.

- Customer loyalty is maintained by continuing to delight customers. Exceeding customer expectations is important; however, once a surprise is repeated, it is no longer a surprise.

What brands or businesses are you an advocate of? What makes them so special? Why are you loyal to them?

Customer data and key account planning

What makes a customer attractive? One could assume it is loyalty, advocacy or levels of income generation, but attractive customers may not just be your most loyal ones. Customer attractiveness can be rated on a number of factors such as:

- *size*: volume, value and profit opportunity;
- *growth potential*: value, profit opportunity;
- *financial stability*: industry and individual risk factors;
- *ease of access*: geography and location.

A customer who is split-/multibanked may be attractive if the bank has the lead position, but less attractive if it has a junior or secondary banking role. Your own bank's circumstances will determine the selection and the relative weighting given to these individual factors.

> Question
>
> How does your bank define customer attractiveness? What factors do they take into account?

Key account customers

Key accounts are the most attractive customers. Donaldson (1998) notes that key account customers are likely to possess some of the following characteristics:

- They account for a significant proportion of existing or potential business for the organization.
- They form part of a supply chain in which efficiency is enhanced by cooperation rather than conflict.
- Working interdependently with these customers, rather than independently, can represent benefits in lower transaction costs, better quality or joint product and service development.
- Supply involves not just the product itself but other service aspects, such as technical support or after-sales service.
- There are advantages to both parties in loose, open relationships rather than a focus on transaction efficiency.

Key account management

According to Hise and Reid (1994), the six most critical conditions that are needed to ensure the success of key account management are:

- integration of a key account programme into the organization's overall sales effort;
- senior management's understanding of, and support for, the key account unit's role;
- clear and practical lines of communication between outlying sales and service units;
- the establishment of objectives and goals;
- compatible working relationships between sales management and field sales personnel;
- clear definition and identification of customers to be designated for key account status.

Advantages (and disadvantages) of key account management

Jobber and Lancaster (2000) note that there are a number of advantages with key account management:

- *Close working relationships with the customer*: the salesperson knows who makes which decisions and who influences the various individuals involved in the decision-making process (the decision-making unit).

- *Improved communication and coordination*: the customer knows that a dedicated salesperson or sales team exists and who to contact when a problem or opportunity arises.

- *More efficient follow-up on sales and service*: the extra resources devoted to the key account mean that there is more time to follow up and provide service after a key sale has been concluded.

- *More in-depth penetration of the decision-making unit*: there is more time to cultivate relationships within the key account. Salespeople can pull the buying decision through the organization from the users, deciders and influencers to the buyer. A more traditional sales approach faces the difficult task of pushing it through the buyer into the wider organization.

- *Higher sales*: most organizations that have adopted key account selling techniques claim that sales have risen as a result.

- *The provision of an opportunity for advancement for career salespeople*: a tiered salesforce system with key account selling at the top provides promotion opportunities for salespeople who wish to advance within the salesforce.

However, Burnett (1992) points out that key account management is not without potential dangers:

- When resources are channelled towards a limited number of buyers, the supplier runs the risk of increased dependence on, and vulnerability to, relatively fewer customers.

- There is a risk of pressure on profit margins if a customer chooses to abuse its key account status.

- There is the danger of a customer making ever-increasing demands for higher levels of service and attention once they know that they have preferred customer status.

- Focusing resources on a few key accounts may lead to neglect of smaller accounts, some of which may have a high long-term potential.

> ### Question
>
> How does your bank manage its key accounts? What characteristics do
> your key accounts have?

Portfolio planning

Portfolio planning is used at relationship management team level to identify who the key accounts are within the relationship manager's portfolio
of customers. The Boston Consultancy Group's product portfolio matrix
model (as discussed in Chapter 6) can be used to analyse the current status
of the portfolio:

- It can identify those customers that are generating core income (cash
  cows) and those that require further investment of time and resources
  (stars).
- It can also identify those customers that, on the face of it, should be
  discontinued (dogs/question marks).
- It can help to determine how resources should be allocated and prioritized.

Time is one of the most precious and valuable commodities you have as a
relationship manager. It has to be used wisely. As part of reviewing your
portfolio it is essential to examine just how much time is being spent on
these different customer classes:

- *Stars*: good credit risk, with good growth potential and more potential to
  cross-sell products and services.
- *Cash cows*: as above but with little growth potential or the ability to
  cross-sell any more products, but still generate good levels of income.
- *Question marks*: weaker relationships that may still be developing. It
  could be a minor banking partner or a customer where you have a small
  element of their share of wallet but with good potential if the relationship
  can be developed.
- *Dogs*: this could be a customer who sees the bank as a pure supplier
  where pricing overrides everything else or it could be a customer who is
  a habitual switcher. It might also be a customer that is considered to be a
  poor credit risk.

How much time should you spend on these customers? Inevitably, some relationship managers end up spending most of their time on the dogs, particularly when they are experiencing credit problems. These customers may require daily intervention and examination of their bank account conduct and even having to review whether or not to pay items being presented each day. This can take up an inordinate amount of time and may also require more frequent credit reports having to be produced to justify the decisions taken.

If the dogs or question marks take up the majority of your time you will be depriving your better customers of your time, effort and resources. Bear in mind that inadequate attention to your existing accounts is often a key reason for the competition being successful.

If, say, 70 per cent of time is spent on dogs and question marks and only 30 per cent on cash cows and stars, the time equation gets out of balance. Some banks have recognized this and addressed it by moving problematic accounts to specialist business support managers who are better able and better resourced to manage the relationship back into health, or to exit the relationship entirely. Moving the management of these problematic customers to specialist support should free up more of your time to spend where you should be spending it: with those customers and prospects that have the most potential.

The dilemma some relationship managers experience is that, despite these customers causing them problems, they still want to cling on to them. They may have developed strong relationships during the better times and still believe they are the best people to provide support during the bad times. The question they really need to ask themselves is based upon how much time they are spending with these problem customers and whether they can justify ignoring their better customers at the expense of these time bandits.

The degree of resources allocated to each account should be proportional to its potential to generate income. In this context it is useful to compare **sales efficiency** and **sales effectiveness**.

Sales efficiency   Getting in front of the right customers, at the right time, for minimum cost.

Sales effectiveness   Maximizing business development and sales potential once you are in front of the customer.

Often, there is a conundrum about what to do with the low-value accounts:

- how do you allocate resources in an attempt to make the low value more profitable?
- do you migrate low-value customers away from the bank or manage them to a less personal, more cost-efficient delivery channel? or
- do you accept their lower contribution and reprioritize their needs and the levels of service provided?

Your bank or line manager will probably determine the strategy on how to handle the low-value accounts in the most cost-effective way. Perhaps consideration could be given to choosing to delegate the management of them to more junior, but still capable members of the team. This would enhance their capabilities and therefore their career prospects and leave you more time to devote your efforts to the higher-value accounts, whilst keeping a watching brief on the more junior member of the team.

If they cannot be managed cost-effectively they may have to be managed away, particularly if credit quality has been compromised.

Developing a contact programme

People in the team, including product specialists, need to understand that their roles and efforts need to be coordinated. Generally the more points of contact between the customer and the bank, the better the quality of the relationship.

Face-to-face customer visits are the most effective means of interacting with customers but they are also the most expensive. Face-to-face visits may be justified if:

- personal service is considered essential;
- an important new contact is being made;
- a difficult and sensitive problem needs to be resolved;
- a complicated presentation needs to be delivered;
- in-depth diagnostic work needs to be carried out;
- the customer requests a visit;
- on-site research is required;
- you are closing a deal.

Customer contact programmes

On a regular basis, and at least annually, you should audit what you are seeking to achieve with any particular relationship. The level of formality that this review takes will depend very much on the nature of the customer relationship. The aim is to get an understanding of where the customer is going in business terms and understand what opportunities there may be for you to improve your share of their wallet.

When meeting customers on a face-to-face basis you need to prepare thoroughly and follow up effectively. Make sure you have the key people from the customer's side at the meeting. It is best practice to prepare an agenda for the meeting as part of your visit planning. This will help to keep you and the customer focused on what needs to be discussed. And remember that it's not just your agenda; the customer will have their own agenda as well. A typical agenda may include:

- updates of industry sector (PESTEL);
- updates of markets (Porter);
- individual personal and business objectives and strategies – has anything changed?
- do they need any help?
- what is their view on the quality of the service you and your team provide?
- an agreed set of action plans with timescales.

Most of the time you spend with the customer should be looking forward. The aim of the meeting should be to stimulate an open and honest conversation. This forms part of the process of building trust and moving towards a relationship that is a true partnership.

The consultative mindset

Cope (2010) outlines the components of a consultative model which can be adopted by relationship managers (Figure 8.2).

Customer: getting it right from the start

Often, customers are grappling with a problem (or opportunity) that they have not yet clearly defined in their own minds. There is a need to consider the following:

Figure 8.2 The seven Cs of consulting

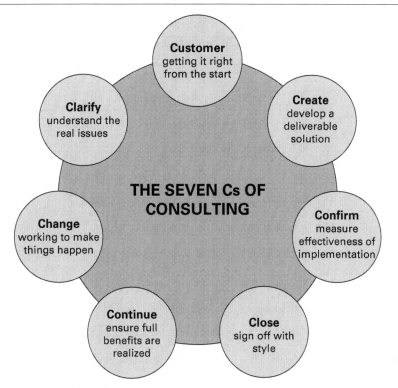

SOURCE Adapted from Cope

- viewing the issue as the customer sees it;
- testing the clarity of the desired outcome in terms of what the customer wants;
- removing the clutter from the issue by focusing on where and what might be needed;
- ensuring the issue can be successfully resolved and that the timings are right;
- having a clear picture of the decision-makers who can influence the initial stages of the buying process (DMU);
- having a clear agreement that sets out a framework for action and measurement.

Clarify: understand the real issues

The real risk is that you go into a 'one size fits all' product mode before having a clear understanding of the customer's needs or how the product may need to be modified to get the best fit. Your role is not to solutionize, but to facilitate a solution. You can achieve this by:

- Gathering sufficient information to determine the real source of the problem and not just the symptoms. This is where good questioning techniques and active listening skills come to the fore.

- Having a clear appreciation of the background and of any unspoken issues affecting the situation.

- Having a clear map that indicates who can influence the outcome of the issue or problem, ie who else do you need to involve?

- Determining the extent to which known and unknown factors will have an impact. This might range, for example, from environmental and competitive factors (Porter's five forces and PESTEL could help here).

- Clarifying how the customer wants to be kept in the information loop as the solution(s) develop.

Create: developing a deliverable solution

One of the core roles of the relationship manager is engineering the fit between customers' needs/wants and the bank's capabilities. This may not always be a particularly comfortable role; for example, the shuttle diplomacy between the customer, you and your credit function. You will need to:

- Ensure you can actually deliver any solutions that you come up with.

- Understand if there are any potential creative blockages for the customer. This is particularly relevant if the customer has a more traditional outlook and tends to be resistant to new ideas.

- Find solutions from the experience and work of others. This may include seeking advice from other colleagues such as product or market specialists or from your line manager.

- Have a clear process for deciding on the solution. This would involve understanding how decisions are made within the company and who has the most powerful voice (DMU).

- Understand the resources required for the potential solution to ensure the option is viable. This may require the involvement of market or product specialists.

- Establish who will own the solution both internally and at the customer level and that everyone has the capability and willingness to own the solution.

- Consider the potential threats to adopting the solution. You may have to use your influencing skills to reposition some of the perceived negative aspects of your solution(s) as positive ones.

Change: working to make things happen

This relates to the difference between thinking and doing. It also highlights the coordinating role you will have between the customer and the internal functions of the bank. It means:

- Having a clear understanding of how the desired outcome will be managed.

- Having a clear appreciation of where the impetus for action will come from and how it will be shared across the different parties.

- Knowing how people can be encouraged to be involved in the effective and continuing implementation.

- Understanding how systems and processes, both externally with the customer and internally with the bank, can cope with the proposed activity.

- Checking the planned solution is flexible enough to operate in a dynamic and uncertain environment.

Confirm: measuring the effectiveness of implementation

Ahead of measuring the benefits of implementation is defining what these might be. A key part of the role of the relationship manager is setting these expectations. In particular:

- Establishing ownership and management of the measurement process.

- Deciding at which point or points the measurement will take place.

- Understanding the relationships between qualitative measures (based on attitudes and opinions) and quantitative (numbers-based) measures are clear.

- Ensuring your own personal performance is of the standard expected by the customer.

- Having a clear view of the costs of the solution and any ongoing support costs required.

Continue: making sure the full benefits are realized

Often there is a positive halo effect after successful completion of a piece of business, but there is a risk that customers may subsequently become disappointed for some reason. There is a need for you to continue to manage both the perceptions and the reality of the solution that has been delivered. You will need to:

- Have a plan to ensure slippage does not occur once the solution has been provided and that the expected benefits have been delivered.
- Ensure that the customer will derive the full benefits from the solution you promised. The risk is that if this is not the case it may rebound against you or the bank.
- Ensure the knowledge created as part of the project is captured by both the customer and any other parts of the bank that may have been involved (file note/contact report, case study or testimonials).

Close: signing off with style

Memories fade. Usually formal correspondence between the customer and the bank will relate to technical and procedural issues rather than capturing the real benefits at the time. Make sure there is a record on the file that reflects the success between you, your customer and the internal support areas. Better still, write up the event as a success story that can then be featured in your internal communications and intranet. You can achieve this by:

- Forming a view of the success for the business.
- Encouraging the customer to reflect on their view before presenting your own view of the outcomes.
- Helping the customer/bank to consider what has been learned.
- Identifying any tangible improvements to the operational or commercial viability of the customer and the bank.
- Identifying what future opportunities may exist.

You can see there are a number of quasi-consultant roles in relationship management. As a relationship manager you will be a:

- *Facilitator*: having the skills to help the customer explore the problem and solve it themselves. It may be that you do not have a product that meets the customers' needs and therefore have to refer them to another provider.

- *Problem-solver*: using investigative skills to break down the problem and provide a solution.

- *Trusted financial professional*: making use of, and reference to, your experience from the range of customers you have dealt with, to put forward ideas for your customer to consider.

In your role you will need to identify and understand the real issues. You will need to listen well. Active listening and good questioning techniques are vital for you to undertake a relationship management role effectively.

The trusted financial professional

The journey from relationship manager to trusted financial professional is not made quickly; it takes time. From the very first meeting, the customer or prospect will be assessing your levels of confidence, ability and professionalism. Trust is built around knowledge and experience and through being able to articulate this to customers and prospects. In meetings it is evidenced by the extent of disclosure and the willingness of the customer to share information, including any bad news. The best relationship managers develop skills and knowledge necessary to build and retain trust. They know how to communicate their knowledge and experience in such a way that they become recognized as the experts in their chosen field: they become *the* choice rather than *a* choice.

Being a trusted financial professional means you have the ability and confidence to diagnose a customer's problems in a non-hostile environment. The customer will actively seek your assistance.

Customers who feel comfortable in their relationships can be expected to act as advocates for you and the bank. They can make referrals to you or support you with other customers by providing testimonials for other customers who may be facing similar issues. For example, if a customer is looking to import for the first time, you could ask one of your existing importers to talk to them to affirm the quality of the bank's international services when importing (Gremler and Gwinner, 2000; Price and Arnould, 1999).

By earning trusted financial professional status, you will have access to all the business development you need because customers are advocates who may be happy to refer new business opportunities to you. This is the most effective and rewarding way to generate new business.

So what does a trusted financial professional look like? Remember when we discussed skills and competences in Chapter 6. They are the same, namely:

Professionalism:

- have integrity and are considered both trustworthy and ethical;
- are fair and honest;
- love their job and are proud of the bank they work for.

Expectations:

- understand the different needs/wants of different types of customers;
- manage, meet and exceed customer expectations.

Resolution:

- provide first-time/right-time resolution for problems or opportunities;
- take responsibility for complaint resolution seriously;
- provide proactive progress updates;
- demonstrate concern for the individuals involved.

Time and effort:

- anticipate and pre-empt the next step and any potential problems;
- minimize unnecessary pain points;
- proactively manage the customer's time;
- are always accessible and easy to get hold of.

Empathy:

- build rapport;
- build personal connections and networks with those who could help their customers.

Chartered Banker Institute's Code of Professional Conduct

Having integrity, being honest and trustworthy, and acting ethically are core principles of the Chartered Banker Institute's Code of Professional Conduct. The Chartered Banker Institute is the largest professional body for bankers in the UK. It believes that, to enhance public confidence and trust in banks and bankers, and pride within the banking profession, individuals working in banking should make a personal commitment to a higher standard of professionalism (Chartered Banker Institute, 2018a, 2018b). The Institute's view is that professionalism can be demonstrated through attainment of a professional qualification or professional standard, as well as membership of a professional body and an ongoing commitment to continuing professional development. All members of the Institute are expected to demonstrate the highest standards of professionalism and a commitment to ethical conduct, and are bound by its Chartered Banker Code of Professional Conduct which sets out the ethical and professional values and behaviours expected of them. You can view the Institute's Code of Professional Conduct at https://www.charteredbanker.com/resource_listing/knowledge-hub-listing/chartered-banker-code-of-professional-conduct.html.

As we started this chapter you were asked to score yourself (1–10) on your understanding of customer service and the importance this has on customer relationship management. How would you score yourself now? Have your views changed? What have you learned that you didn't know before? Are there any elements of the chapter you need to review again or discuss further with a colleague or with your line manager?

My score

The importance of providing great customer service is critical to the customer/banking relationship. You should appreciate that this is not simply down to you as a relationship manager, but everyone from the bank that has contact with the customer. Obviously part of your role is to coordinate activities to make sure everyone is aligned and puts the customer first.

By achieving this on a regular and consistent basis, you may become perceived by your customers as their trusted financial professional. This will enable you to lock in customers and lock out competitors. After all, why would a customer go elsewhere when they have their own personal trusted financial professional?

Chapter summary

In this chapter, we explored:

- customer service;
- service quality;
- complaint management and service recovery;
- portfolio planning and portfolio management;
- the need to have a consultative mindset;
- the trusted financial professional.

Objective check

1 What is a customer?

2 How does your work influence your organization's customer value proposition?

3 How is service quality measured in your organization?

4 Consider the overall service you provide to your customers. Are any of the five key service gaps visible to your customers?

5 Why do you think it has been necessary for the FCA to set out timescales for dealing with customer complaints?

6 Which are your key account customers and how do you identify and manage them?

7 How can you incorporate Cope's Seven Cs of Consulting in your management of customers?

Further reading

Financial Conduct Authority (2017) *How to Complain* [online]. Available at: https://www.fca.org.uk/consumers/how-complain [accessed 29 December 2017]

Henderson, B (1970) *The Product Portfolio* [online]. Available at: https://www.bcg.com/publications/1970/strategy-the-product-portfolio.aspx [accessed 11 February 2018]

Michael, J, Maxwell, MN and Taraporevala, Z (2017) A consumer-centric approach to retail banking sales [online]. Available at: https://www.mckinsey.com/industries/financial-services/our-insights/a-consumer-centric-approach-to-retail-banking-sales [accessed 11 February 2018]

References

Bain and Co (2007) *Turning your consumers into die-hard fans* [online]. Available at: http://www.bain.com/publications/articles/turning-your-consumers-into-die-hard-fans.aspx [accessed 29 December 2017]

Berry, L and Parasuraman, A (1991) *Marketing Services: Competing through quality* The Free Press, New York

Burnett, K (1992) *Strategic Customer Alliances: How to win, manage and develop key account business,* Financial Times, London

Chartered Banker Institute (2018a) *Chartered Banker Code of Professional Conduct* [online]. Available at: https://www.charteredbanker.com/resource_listing/knowledge-hub-listing/chartered-banker-code-of-professional-conduct.html [accessed 16 May 2018]

Chartered Banker Institute (2018b) *Professionalism in Banking* [online]. Available at: https://www.charteredbanker.com/culture-and-conduct/professionalism-in-banking.html [accessed 16 May 2018]

Cope, M (2010) *The Seven Cs of Consulting,* Pearson Education Ltd, Harlow

Donaldson, B (1998) *Sales Management: Principles, process and practice,* Palgrave Macmillan, London, New York

Financial Conduct Authority (2018) *Dispute Resolution: Complaints* [pdf]. Available at: https://www.handbook.fca.org.uk/handbook/DISP.pdf [accessed 5 July 2018]

Financial Ombudsman Service (2017) *Our Consumer leaflet* [online]. Available at: http://www.financial-ombudsman.org.uk/publications/consumer-leaflet.htm [accessed 29 December 2017]

Gremler, DD and Gwinner, KP (2000) *Customer-Employee Rapport in Service Relationships* [pdf]. Available at: http://www.gremler.net/personal/research/2000_Rapport_JSR.pdf [accessed 29 December 2017]

The Guardian (2011) Nat West and RBS fined £2.8m over complaint handling failures [online]. Available at: https://www.theguardian.com/money/2011/jan/11/natwest-rbs-fined-complaint-handling-failures [accessed 29 December 2017]

Hise, R and Reid, E (1994) *Buying Behavior,* Macmillan, London

Jobber, D and Lancaster, G (2000) *Selling and Sales Management,* Pearson Education Ltd, Harlow

Price, L and Arnould, E (1999) *Commercial Friendships: Service Provider – Client Relationships in Context* [online]. Available at: https://manchester.rl.talis.

com/items/B308CB72-592B-8D3F-BC5F-8B97F83176B4.html [accessed 29 December 2017]

Reichheld, FF (2003) *The one number you need to grow* [online]. Available at: https://hbr.org/2003/12/the-one-number-you-need-to-grow [accessed 5 July 2018]

Seiders, K and Berry, L (1998) *Service Fairness: What it is and why it matters*, Academy of Management [online]. Available at: https://www.jstor.org/stable/4165454 [accessed 29 December 2017]

Stewart, K (1998) An exploration of customer exit in retail banking, *International Journal of Bank Marketing*, **16** (1), pp 6–14 [online]. Available at: https://doi.org/10.1108/02652329810197735 [accessed 29 December 2017]

09

Relationship strategies

Customer retention, development and acquisition

This chapter looks at relationship strategies, consultative selling including questioning techniques, and active listening skills.

LEARNING OBJECTIVES

By the end of this chapter, you will be able to:

- evaluate the three relationship strategies of retention, development and acquisition;
- appraise the benefits of customer retention over an acquisition strategy;
- describe bonding, and the role it plays in retaining valuable customers;
- explain features and benefits;
- evaluate the differences between transactional selling and consultative selling;
- describe a process for acquiring new customers;
- critically analyse the steps in the ladder of loyalty.

Introduction

In this chapter, we look at customer acquisition, retention and development. We examine the economics of customer retention to learn of the economic benefits of retaining your valuable customers in comparison to the cost of acquiring new customers. We also explore questioning techniques and listening skills which are vital components of consultative selling. Whether you are looking to retain customers, acquire new ones or develop the customers you have, you will need to use these questioning techniques and listening skills to do your role effectively.

Before we start, how would you rate yourself on a scale of 1–10 on your knowledge of these core strategies for relationship management? How adept are you at questioning customers and prospects, and how good a listener are you?

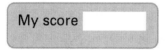

We'll come back to this at the end of the chapter, but before we start to look at relationship strategies, let's understand what we mean about selling.

Selling

Throughout this book we use the term 'selling'. Some banks have disowned this term because of poor behaviours and malpractice demonstrated in the past. This has been evidenced by a number of mis-selling scandals (PPI, LIBOR manipulation, interest rate hedging products, packaged bank accounts, etc) that have plagued our industry.

When we refer to the term selling we make a distinction between transactional selling and consultative selling. Transactional selling is based on pushing product. Consultative selling is based upon earning the right to have a conversation with a customer to explore and then satisfy their needs. It involves asking the right questions at the right time to determine what the customer's needs are and then finding the best way to meet those needs for the customer. Transactional selling is all about pushing product. Consultative selling pursues something more; it is about creating real value for the customer. That is what relationship management in banking is all about.

Customer retention, development and acquisition

The customer life cycle consists of three core relationship strategies: customer retention, customer development and customer acquisition.

1 The objective of a customer retention strategy is to keep a high proportion of your most valuable customers. The emphasis here is 'valuable customers'; these are the ones you need to defend and protect. They are your highest priorities rather than those customers who have little or no value. Your valuable customers will be the ones that will be targeted by the competition.

2 A customer development strategy aims to increase the value of your existing customer base by selling them more of your products and services that they need. This in turn will make your customers more valuable

3 A customer acquisition strategy concerns winning new business for the bank.

Which strategy your bank will prioritize will depend on its own strategic objectives. In practice, banks will adopt all the strategies, but some will place a higher emphasis on one particular strategy over another. For example, if your bank is long established with a significant customer base the priority will be to defend and protect its customer base so a retention strategy will be important. In contrast, a new entrant challenger bank will want to build market share so it will pursue a customer acquisition strategy as a priority.

> What kind of strategy does your own bank pursue?

At a portfolio level, the make-up of a portfolio may also determine where your priorities lie. Take, for example, the three portfolios illustrated in Figure 9.1.

Abigail has managed her portfolio for more than 10 years. She knows her customers well and they know her well. Given this is a long-established portfolio Abigail is able to spend far more of her time on acquiring new customers, while at the same time keeping a watchful eye on her existing customer base.

Bernadette is new to her portfolio as she has just inherited it from another manager. Her priority will be to get to know her customers so her immediate objective will be more about retaining her customers and then developing them, before embarking on an acquisition strategy.

Figure 9.1 Portfolio priorities

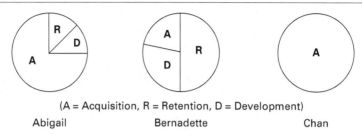

(A = Acquisition, R = Retention, D = Development)

Abigail   Bernadette   Chan

Chan is new to the bank, having joined from a competitor. He does not have a portfolio of customers. His brief is to start one. So his time will be spent exclusively pursuing an acquisition strategy and most likely from the customers he managed at his previous bank.

At the same time, no doubt the manager from his previous bank who inherited his customer portfolio will be pursuing a retention strategy in order to protect and defend their newly inherited portfolio from any approaches.

Customer retention

Retaining valuable customers is an imperative in today's business environment. Many organizations may appreciate that customer retention is important, but relatively few understand the economics of customer retention within their own organization.

The economics of customer retention

There are many commentators who argue that there are a number of benefits a retention strategy has over an acquisition strategy. For example:

- Relatively small increases in retention rates can have a significant effect on long-term profitability (Reichheld and Sasser, 1990).

- Having a customer retention strategy in place is economically more important than having a customer acquisition strategy (Fornell and Wernerfelt, 1987).

- The average cost of dealing with existing customers is lower compared to new customers (Reichheld, 2003).

- Studies across a number of industries have revealed that the cost of acquiring new customers can be up to five times greater than the cost of satisfying and retaining existing customers. Furthermore, a 2 per cent increase in customer retention has the same effect on profitability as cutting costs by 10 per cent (Stevens, 2002).

The reasons why retention has such a significant effect on profitability has been highlighted by Reichheld and Sasser (1990):

- The costs of acquiring new customers can be significant and it could take some years to turn a new customer into a profitable customer.
- As customers become more satisfied and confident in their relationship they are more likely to give you a larger proportion of their business.
- As the relationship with a customer develops, there is greater mutual understanding and collaboration, which produces efficiencies that reduce operating costs.
- Satisfied customers are more likely to refer others, which reduces the cost of acquiring new customers.
- Loyal customers can be less price sensitive and may even accept premium pricing if they value the relationship. This is because they view value as being more important than price.

So it makes good economic sense to have a retention strategy in place.

When we think about customer defection we assume that it's about those customers that move to a competitor. We should also realize that defection is also concerned with those customers that stop buying from you. If your customers stop buying your more profitable products you may be left with a customer who is actually costing you more to service them. For example, consider a customer who has significant balances held on deposit with you. Because interest rates are low, they decide to move the majority of their balances away to a competitor who is paying more interest. You may not be aware the funds had been moved. So what you thought was a valuable customer is no longer so.

Should a retention strategy embrace all customers? Not really. Not all customers are worth the time and effort involved in building a relationship. Some may be habitual switchers, difficult to deal with and may not generate sufficient income to justify the expense of acquiring and maintaining them. So you need to identify those customers with whom you want to develop a long-term relationship and those with whom you do not.

A retention strategy must answer the following questions:

- Which customers do you want to retain?
- What retention strategies are you going to use?
- How will you measure the success or otherwise of the strategy?

A retention strategy should be built around bonding, staff education, promise fulfilment, trust and service recovery. We'll now go on to consider each of these in turn.

Bonding

Retention strategies vary in the degree to which they bond the parties together. It is generally accepted that there are three levels of bonding.

- Level 1 (low) – the bond is primarily through financial incentives such as discounts and loyalty schemes. Many airlines and supermarkets compete in this way, but some consumers have got wise to this and have learned to join more than one scheme, playing suppliers off against each other, which contradicts the whole idea of loyalty.

- Level 2 (medium) – a wider variety of communication through new or different channels such as social media or websites. In corporate banking this could also include enhancing your relationship by using educational or entertainment activities such as seminars or visits to sporting events.

- Level 3 (high) – this is the most important level. This is about building financial, social and structural bonds to lock in customers by providing solutions to their problems or helping them to maximize their opportunities. Done well, it will lock out your competitors.

Staff education

This involves training, communicating with and motivating internal staff. Staff need to be trained to be technically competent at their job as well as to be able to handle service encounters with customers. A high-quality service is fundamental to customer retention and this depends on high-quality performance from all employees, at every level.

Promise fulfilment

This is the cornerstone for maintaining relationships. It involves making realistic promises and enabling staff and systems to consistently deliver on the promises made. Remember, always look to under-promise and over-achieve, not the other way around.

Building trust

This is particularly important for any service organization because services are intangible. It is difficult to evaluate a service before buying and experiencing it, so an element of trust has to be involved. To build trust into any relationship you need to keep in touch with customers by regular two-way communication, which will develop feelings of closeness and openness which is mutually beneficial for both parties.

Service recovery

When things go wrong, as they sometimes do, effective service recovery mechanisms need to be in place to remedy the situation and restore the customer's trust in the organization. If things do go wrong it is very important to keep the customer informed about what you are doing and what needs to be done to put things right. Good communication and providing regular updates will strengthen the relationship as will finding the right solution for both sides.

When the customer experience (which is unique to them) exceeds expectations you will find the relationship has developed into a trust partnership based upon customer delight. This makes it very difficult for competitors to compete on a level playing field. They may well compete with very similar products and services but because they cannot see 'customer delight' their efforts will go unrewarded no matter how hard they try. It becomes almost impossible to break the partnership. Customer delight locks in the customer and locks out the competitors.

Customer development

In mature markets, like banking, where customer acquisition can be difficult or expensive, customer development is an important source of additional revenues. Customer development is the process of growing the value of customers. It means developing less profitable customers, to make them more valuable, ie to increase the share of the customer's wallet by providing more products and services that they need. Existing customers give relationship managers a prospect base for cross-selling and up-selling the bank's products to improve the share of the customer's wallet.

The objective of **cross-selling** and **up-selling** is to increase income levels and to protect the relationship. The more products the customer has, the more likely they are to stay. However, it is essential to ensure that any additional products or services sold enhance the perceived value the customer gets from them.

> **Cross-selling** The practice of selling additional products or services to an existing customer.
>
> **Up-selling** A sales technique whereby a seller persuades the customer to purchase more expensive items, upgrades or other add-ons in an attempt to make a more profitable sale.

Up-selling can also be achieved by providing the customer with other options that they had not previously considered. An example would be to discuss how to protect a customer from currency fluctuations which could impact on their costs and profitability, if currency rates moved against them. If you discussed forward currency contracts that would be cross-selling; however, if you suggested an additional and alternative way of protecting themselves, such as using a currency option, that would be considered to be an up-sell.

> How comfortable do you feel in a sales environment?

Some relationship managers may feel uncomfortable in a selling environment, but if they recognize that selling banking products can help to protect their customers, then they should not be concerned about selling; they are actually helping the customer to mitigate risk. This adds value to the relationship. In today's competitive banking arena relationship managers must have a positive attitude that selling is a legitimate banking activity. If they don't sell to a customer, a competitor will. At the most basic level, failure to cross-sell is a failure to develop a consultative mindset.

Consultative selling

The term 'consultative selling' first appeared in *Consultative Selling: The Hanan formula for high-margin sales at high levels* (Hanan, 2011). Here, the author explores a selling technique in which the salesperson acts as an expert consultant for his or her customers or prospects. It involves asking the right questions at the right time to determine what the prospect needs. Whereas transactional selling is about pushing product, consultative selling pushes value.

In a transactional sale, value lies within the product and price becomes the main selection criteria. Consultative selling is all about selling value. It has less to do with what the customer is buying and more to do with why the customer wants to buy. It places more onus on the salesperson's questioning skills rather than simply discussing the product features and price. It requires the salesperson to make connections between the product and the value it creates more effectively and efficiently than the competition. It requires the salesperson to know more about the customer, the goals they have, changes they want to make and the results they hope to achieve. Consultative selling identifies the benefits of the product or service and not the product features.

Product features and benefits

Features are the characteristics of a product or service; it is something your product or service does. Customers may still want to know what features the product has because that can help them to make comparisons but it is the benefits they really want to understand because that is why they buy.

Benefits are the things that create value. Understanding how the product or service benefits them personally is what is important. It might be by helping them solve a problem or simply just making life easier. Defining benefits is an important part of your role as a relationship manager. Let's take mobile banking as an example.

Question

List the features of mobile banking. Once you have completed the list compare your answer with the one provided at the end of this chapter (Appendix 9.1).

Now list some of the benefits of mobile banking. Once you have completed the list compare your answer with the one provided at the end of this chapter (Appendix 9.2).

One way to determine whether a benefit is really a benefit is to determine whether it gives the customer what they want. Benefits deliver a positive change and create a measurable impact on the customer. Benefits are exclusively defined in the mind of the customer because it's personal to them. Unless a customer recognizes that a product or service creates benefits for them, then benefits do not exist. Your role, as a relationship manager, is to help your customer or prospect to realize and recognize the benefits that will create value for them.

Examples of benefits for a business customer might include:

✓ increased profitability;

✓ increased productivity;

✓ increased efficiencies;

✓ increased market share;

✓ increased consumer awareness;

✓ increased safety (risk reduction);

✓ improved response times.

or

✓ reducing down-time;

✓ reducing maintenance costs;

✓ reducing operating expenses;

✓ reducing the cost of financing.

Any product or service will be of value to the customer at that point where the benefit outweighs the price of the product or service. If benefits do not outweigh the price the customer will see little or no point in purchasing it.

In consultative selling the customer is not solely concerned about price, or solely concerned about benefits. They are concerned with the combination of cost and benefits because together they will determine the customer's perception of value. Customers always want value regardless of cost or benefits.

Transactional selling characteristics include:

- placing emphasis on product features;
- price is the most important aspect;
- the salesperson adds little value;
- closing the sales is the most important objective for the salesperson.

Whereas consultative selling has these characteristics:

- the emphasis is on value as defined by the customer;
- price is less important than value;
- the salesperson defines value through benefits (not features);
- delivering value and creating trust is the most important objective of consultative selling.

There are two particular skills needed for consultative selling: questioning techniques and listening skills. You cannot do one without the other.

Questioning techniques

Good questioning techniques enable the listener to elicit the information they need. Good questioning techniques can collate information quickly and efficiently, whereas poor questioning techniques will lead to poor information, on which poor judgements will be made.

Basically there are two main types of question: **open** and **closed**.

> **Closed questions**   Those questions that can be answered by a simple 'yes' or 'no'.

Closed questions are used to gather factual information and are also effective when summarizing a conversation such as closing a sale. For example: 'Are we agreed and can we go ahead?' Answer: 'Yes' (or 'No').

> **Open questions**   Questions that cannot be answered by a simple 'yes' or 'no'. They generally start with words such as: why, what, when, who, where, which and how.

When building rapport with customers the majority of questions tend to be open because the questioner wants the customer to talk so they can learn more about them. Open questions encourage a more informative response and allow the questioner to explore the subject further, for example:

- 'How would you feel if…?'
- 'What would that mean to you?'
- 'Why do you see that as a problem?'

'Why' and 'what' are useful when seeking clarification. 'When', 'who', 'where' and 'which' are used to seek additional information, and 'how' can be used to confirm a choice.

The response you receive may be verbal or physical (a nod, a gesture, a shrug or some other form of body language). You need to listen carefully with your eyes as well as your ears. And bear in mind that persistent questioning may make some people feel uncomfortable; questioning should never become an interrogation.

Probing questions

Probing questions are used to clarify what has been said or to find out more detail. They are also useful for building rapport. Examples of probing questions are as follows:

- 'Why do you think that is?'
- 'Could you be more specific?'
- 'What are your concerns?'

Reflective questions

Reflective questions are also used to check and clarify understanding. You take some of the information you have just learned and repeat it or paraphrase it in the form of a question. Reflective questions can work very well, because they show that you have been listening, and help you to focus on determining the exact needs of your customer. For example: 'You're looking for some way to mitigate your foreign currency risk, is that correct?'

Do you consider yourself to be a good listener?

Listening skills

There is no point in asking questions unless you are capable of truly listening to the answers. Hearing is a physical ability while listening is a skill. Effective listening enables you to understand what the speaker is saying rather than merely hearing what has been said. An effective listener encourages the speaker by showing interest and indicating they have heard and understood what has been said.

The following are tips for effective questioning and listening:

- ✓ be attentive and alert (participate fully);
- ✓ use open body language (good posture: no slouching, lean forward, uncross your arms);
- ✓ use eye contact (but don't stare);
- ✓ focus on what is being said (nod, smile);
- ✓ ask open questions;

✓ ask closed questions;

✓ ask probing questions;

✓ ask clarification/reflective questions;

✓ paraphrase what the customer says;

✓ reflect feelings;

✓ take notes;

✓ summarize what has been said.

Transactional salespeople are interested only in the product sale and do not typically spend their time asking the right questions that uncover the customer's needs. They feel they have done their job once they ask a few basic questions, then provide the customer with information and only one solution. They spend most of their time talking and not listening. On the other hand, a good relationship manager will think of themselves as a consultant first and a salesperson second. When talking to their customers, relationship managers may uncover additional needs, unrelated to the first, that the customer has and then offer to meet these needs as well. They listen more than they talk.

Customer acquisition

Every business or organization needs to acquire new customers. Even organizations with high retention rates lose customers, so they need to acquire new ones continually. Some of your customers may get taken over or be purchased by larger competitors. In most cases this would result in a lost customer if the acquirer insists they move their banking to their own bank. Similarly, some customers are lost because the business fails or gets wound up.

So relationship managers must always be on the lookout for new, replacement customers and make sure they are of the right type and quality. You wouldn't want to take on a competitor's problem account. Customer acquisition is concerned with acquiring the right kind of customers.

Lead generation

Various surveys have identified that over 60 per cent of corporate banking customers are likely to have received an approach from another bank or financial institution during the last 12 months. This statistic reinforces the need for relationship managers to be proactive in identifying and targeting good-quality prospects.

They should build referral networks within the local community. This is an integral part of the lead-generation process. Leads are the raw material for the sales process and they need to be managed in a cost-efficient and effective way.

Most banks have invested in prospect CRM systems that include a wide range of published and unpublished sources. They use this data to produce prospect lists for business development teams and relationship managers. If your bank has such a system, you must be aware of the characteristics that drive the prospect selection to understand what sources are used and what filters need to be applied to refine the outputs.

Identifying the best prospects

A typical process for sifting leads and identifying the best prospects might work in the following way:

- Working with readily available lists of companies provided by specialist database organizations such as Dun & Bradstreet, MINT, Lotus One Source and Experian that generate lists of potential prospects based on location, size and industry.

- The relationship manager would then need to eliminate those industries or businesses that do not fit the bank's product portfolio or business strategy.

- Filter based on geographical location, close to where the relationship manager works. If you were based in the North East, you wouldn't want to be travelling to London to visit a prospect. Prospects want a local manager who can respond to their needs quickly.

- Filter based on risk. Eliminate prospects that are a poor credit risk, either of themselves or because of the sector they operate in. Your credit policy will give you a steer here.

- Filter based on profiling. A review of current customers might determine the level of business generated by each one. From this information, a common profile of the most desirable customers can be established and used to identify and target prospects with a similar type of profile who will hopefully generate similar relationship opportunities.

An example: Caitlyn

A new relationship manager, Caitlyn, has been appointed in the North West, working in the corporate banking part of the bank looking after customers in the £2–£25 million range. She has inherited a small portfolio of customers who are predominantly involved in the glass manufacturing sector. Caitlyn has some experience of the glass manufacturing sector from her previous role when she worked in Southampton.

Caitlyn's line manager has given her a brief to 'use your experience dealing with the glass manufacturing sector and go out there and get more customers of the right quality'. The line manager provides her with a database of all limited companies within her new geographical patch.

Question

What should Caitlyn do with the database and how might she start filtering it to make her prospecting list more manageable?

Caitlyn's list contains the name of *all* limited companies in her patch so she needs to apply an industry filter to identify those companies involved in glass manufacturing. She would start by using an industry filter such as the Standard Industrial Classification codes (**SIC codes**).

SIC code   A system for classifying industries by a four-digit number.

Caitlyn applies the SIC code range of 3211–3231 (glass manufacture). The resultant list has now shrunk to 145 local businesses involved with glass manufacturing.

Question

What could she do next to filter the prospect list more?

Caitlyn needs to apply a turnover filter for customers in her range £2–£25 million. The list shrinks again to 63 businesses.

Question

What other filters could she use?

Caitlyn sees her list contains some prospects who are loss-making or are too highly geared for the bank's credit policy. So she filters the list to exclude those prospects that are loss-making or whose **gearing** levels are more than 100 per cent.

> **Gearing**   A measure of the proportion of debt a business has in relation to its overall net worth. The higher the gearing ratio the greater the risk being assumed by the lenders rather than the shareholders.

The list shrinks again to 25 prospects.

Question

Is there anything else Caitlyn could do to focus on these best prospects?

The database information also includes who the prospects bank with and who their auditors are; this can be very useful information. Caitlyn would therefore remove those prospects that already bank with her bank, as they are already customers. Alternatively, she may choose to target a particular banking competitor, if she has reason to believe her bank has some form of competitive advantage over the rival.

The database also includes details of the prospects auditors. So Caitlyn scrutinizes the information to see who the prospects' auditors are and whether she or any colleagues knows anyone in the audit firm. That way she might be able to obtain an introduction from the audit firm at the appropriate time.

Caitlyn ends up with a prospect list of 25 potential customers who are:

- businesses within her patch;
- businesses involved in a sector she knows well;
- good-quality targets (not loss-making or highly geared);

Caitlyn is now ready to proceed to the next stage: nurturing them. This involves a lot more research, so she starts by obtaining the financial statements of the prospects from Companies House to get a better understanding of them. The financial statements contain a lot more information than just the numbers, as you will find out when you reach Chapter 10. Notes to the accounts provide a wealth of information.

Acquiring customers can take a long time and during that time new information may come to hand that turns a prospect back into a suspect or takes them off the prospect list completely. Consider the position when a relationship manager obtains more up-to-date financial information, such as the latest set of audited accounts, which shows the business has now become loss-making. As they would no longer fit the preferred criteria they are moved off the prospect list.

Prospects may be well entrenched with their current bank and may be entirely happy with their relationship manager. Patience, tenacity and perseverance are required as you may have to wait quite a long time before the present incumbent relationship manager leaves the relationship or the bank. On most occasions, it can be worth the wait.

Potential versus difficulty

Some prospects will be difficult to acquire, some will not, but they will all offer either high or low potential to the bank.

A business that has been with a competitor for a very long time and is on record as valuing the relationship – for example, an article about them that appears in the local press which extols the virtue of the incumbent bank – would be difficult to prise away. Conversely, a business that feels its present bank has let them down in some way would be less so and possibly more amenable to moving banks.

If sufficient information gained by detailed research can identify both the difficulty and potential, then the relationship manager can build a better picture of what approach to use. Figure 9.2 illustrates how prospects can be categorized in terms of their potential and difficulty.

The boxes in the matrix are as follows:

A = this is where you would want all your prospects to be. The task here is to identify needs and to build acceptance.

Figure 9.2 Potential versus difficulty matrix

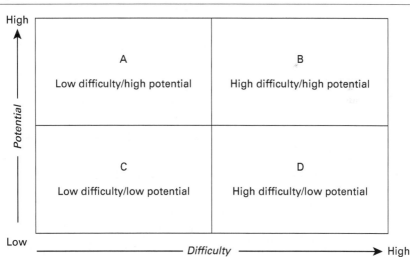

SOURCE Abley and Goulding, 2012

B = known as the sales graveyard. They are long-term prospects only. They may offer great potential but are extremely difficult to win. The previous example of a business extolling the virtues of a rival is a prime example.

C = they may be easier to obtain, but are not really worth the effort as the rewards are so low. Perhaps a business that has a track record of switching banks quite often or one that is just looking for the lowest prices. If they are taken on then they should be managed using cost-efficient, low-touch delivery techniques so that they are not costly in terms of servicing.

D = why bother at all? They are difficult to win, with little or no value in having them. They could be businesses with credit issues. If so, either ignore them or wait for their circumstance to change for the better.

Not all leads are equal, so you may employ some form of rating system to categorize their potential and focus your effort appropriately. This may be a relatively sophisticated system or it may simply be based on the relationship manager's intuition, such as using a simple traffic light system of red, amber and green, or short-, medium- or long-term prospects.

Referrals

It is generally recognized that the most cost-effective way of building a prospect base is through customer referrals. This is often referred to as word-of-mouth or viral marketing. Referrals can be made by customers or by those within your own network of contacts.

As part of the search for a new supplier or bank, it is human nature to ask family, friends and respected business colleagues. Prospects want to know what people like them think about the service and products offered by the organization. This may be positive when a customer is happy to provide a referral, but it may also be negative if they have had a bad experience.

Assuming a customer is happy to provide a referral, you need to ask for one. It will rarely happen without asking. General consensus suggests that up to 80 per cent of loyal customers would refer if asked, but only 30 per cent are ever asked. In the challenge to provide a solution to a customer and then move on quickly to another opportunity, you can often risk missing out on what is an excellent source of new business.

Good relationship managers know when to ask for a referral and what to ask for. They will personally ask for a referral on each occasion they have done something good for the customer. If a customer offers a compliment this should be a trigger to ask for an introduction or referral.

The relationship manager does not ask for a name, but will steer the customer towards referring a similar business to theirs or a business that has a similar need to them. Even if the referral proves to be unproductive, the relationship manager should always thank the customer for the referral. However, some customers, particularly recently acquired ones, are not always keen to offer referrals in case things go wrong and their own standing with a valued supplier could be compromised.

Most customers are not trained in banking so they are not always sure of exactly what type of referral is required. They might refer someone whose business does not match your criteria. If they do, you must still thank them for the referral. The most successful referral strategies are those where the relationship manager has done most of the work and the client has to do as little as possible. An example might be identifying a key local prospect with whom your customer has had dealings previously and may be able to make an introduction. It is always preferable to have someone who is known and trusted to help open a door as opposed to a pure cold call which has no introduction.

The ladder of loyalty

The ladder of loyalty is a visual representation of the journey from suspect to partnership (Christopher *et al*, 1991), and is illustrated in Figure 9.3.

Figure 9.3 The ladder of loyalty

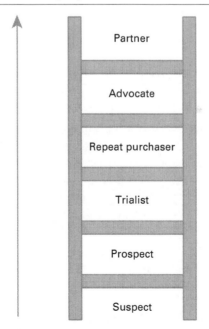

SOURCE Abley and Goulding, 2012

There are six rungs on this ladder:

1 It begins at the *suspect* stage when someone discovers your business.

2 If they are interested in what you provide, the suspect becomes a *prospect,* which means they are now in your target market as a potential customer.

3 Moving up the next rung of the ladder, prospects become customers, purchase a product or service from you for the first time, and are known as *trialists.*

4 If they come back to purchase more they are *repeat purchasers.*

5 They then may become *advocates* who are willing to recommend you and make referrals.

6 Eventually, they buy no other brand. They see the relationship as a true partnership, becoming your strategic *partner* and a champion of you and your brand.

The key to moving up the ladder is the value you create and the amount of customer delight you can generate.

As we started this chapter you were asked to rate yourself on a scale of 1–10. How would you rate yourself now? What have you learned that you didn't know before reading this chapter? How have your views changed? Is there anything you need to review or revisit?

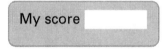

My score

As a relationship manager, you will at some point in your career adopt all three of these relationship strategies – retention, development and acquisition – although given your type of portfolio you will place more emphasis on one rather than another. You will definitely be tasked with acquiring new customers. The way you achieve a successful strategy will be in the quality of your communications with customers and you will need to use excellent questioning techniques, great listening skills and a consultative mindset.

Chapter summary

In this chapter, we have explored:

- consultative selling;
- the economic benefits of each of the relationship strategies;
- cross-selling and up-selling;

- the importance of good questioning techniques and active listening skills;
- lead management and prospecting;
- the importance of referrals.

Objective check

1 Which of the relationship strategies of retention, development and acquisition offer most value to a bank?

2 In what circumstances might an acquisition strategy be preferable to a retention strategy?

3 Explain the three levels of bonding. Which of the levels would have most impact in a retention strategy?

4 Appraise features and benefits from the perspective of a customer.

5 What is consultative selling, and how does this differ from transactional selling?

6 If you were appointed to a portfolio which required an acquisition strategy, how would you plan for success?

7 Describe how a prospect progresses from a suspect to a strategic partner on the ladder of loyalty.

Further reading

Defining the Consultative Sales Approach (Richardson.com). Available at: https://www.richardson.com/sales-resources/defining-consultative-sales/ [accessed 11 February 2018]

Jobber, D and Ellis-Chadwick, F (2016) *Principles and Practice of Marketing*, McGraw-Hill, New York

Marketing Features vs. Benefits (Entrpreneur.com, 2000) [online]. Available at: https://www.richardson.com/sales-resources/defining-consultative-sales/ [accessed 11 February 2018]

References

Abley, R and Goulding, S (2012) *Corporate Relationship Management*, IFS School of Finance, Canterbury

Christopher, M, Payne, A and Ballantyne, D (1991) *Relationship Marketing: Bringing quality, customer service and marketing together*, Butterworth-Heinemann, Oxford

Fornell, C and Wernerfelt, B (1987) Defensive marketing strategy by customer complaint management: A theoretical analysis, *Journal of Marketing Research*, **24** (4) November 1987 [pdf]. Available at: http://www.jstor.org/stable/3151381?seq=1#page_scan_tab_contents [accessed 1 Jan 2018]

Hanan, M (2011) *Consultative Selling: The Hanan Formula*, American Management Association, New York

Reichheld, F (2003) *The Loyalty Effect*, Harvard Business School Press, Boston, MA

Reichheld, F and Sasser Jr, W (1990) Zero Defections: Quality comes to services, *Harvard Business Review*, September–October 1990 [online]. Available at: https://hbr.org/1990/09/zero-defections-quality-comes-to-services [accessed 1 Jan 2018]

Stevens, M (2002) *Extreme Management: What they teach you at Harvard Business School's Advanced Management Program*, Harper Collins Business, London

Appendix 9.1

Features of mobile banking

Mobile banking allows you to:

- check account balances;
- transfer money from one account to another;
- set up text alerts to notify you if an account balance has hit a certain threshold;
- view account statements;
- deposit cheques by using your camera phone;
- pay bills;
- send money to another person or business;
- transfer credit card balances.

Appendix 9.2

Benefits of mobile banking

- You are able to do most, if not all, of your banking on the move whenever you want (24/7).
- It means being able to manage your finances without having to visit a branch during opening hours which can save you time and effort.

- It helps to keep you in control of your finances.
- It can show you where your money is being spent.
- It enables you to monitor your account whenever you want. The majority of identity fraud is discovered by people monitoring their own accounts, so it makes you safer.
- With text alerts, you can know if your account falls below a certain threshold. You can then instantly transfer money into that account to avoid overdraft fees or interest.
- You can deposit cheques by using your phone camera instantly without having to visit or post the cheque to your branch.
- You can get reminders when to pay bills so you will never have to pay late fees or penalties.
- You can set up recurring bill payments so you don't even have to think about when a bill is due.
- Even if you lose your phone, you're still safe. Bank data is guarded with encryption, passwords and other ID checks.

10

Case study

Gaining new business

This chapter takes you on a quest to gain a new business customer. It consolidates the learning from the entire book.

LEARNING OBJECTIVES

By the end of this chapter you will be able to:

- assess the reasons for undertaking detailed research prior to meeting customers/prospects;
- apply good negotiation techniques in interview with prospective customers;
- analyse why excellent questioning techniques and listening skills are essential to relationship management;
- appraise the worth of having an agenda with clear objectives;
- review the skills of a good relationship manager;
- review the competences of a good relationship manager.

Introduction

This case study is fictional, but is based on true experiences throughout a career in relationship management.

This final chapter will take you on a journey to gain a new business customer. Along the way you will experience the highs and lows that relationship managers experience when they are trying to gain new business.

Sometimes the journey can be long and arduous, but it's all worth it when you gain new business of the right quality.

Throughout the case study you will be asked to consider your response to certain situations, the Activities, as the journey progresses. How you respond and the decisions you make should be based on the learning you have gained from this book. You will be shown how a fictional relationship manager in the case study reacted at certain stages of the journey so that you can compare your own responses and reactions to a variety of situations.

All the information you need to undertake the Activities can be found in the Appendices at the end of this chapter. These are followed by suggested Activity Answers. However, you are advised not to look at the answers until you have completed the various exercises in writing.

Background

You once had a customer whom you and the bank supported through very difficult times. The business was Water Reclamation Services UK Ltd (WRS). It was established in 1984 by Asfar Nazir. Their main markets were agricultural sheds, car parks, petrol station forecourts and car washes. They provided:

- filtration systems;
- biological treatments; and
- disinfection services.

In the late 1990s the UK agricultural sector was struck by bovine spongiform encephalopathy (BSE), commonly known as 'mad cow disease'. This caused fatal neuro-degenerative disease in cattle which in some rare cases was transmitted to humans. It devastated the UK agricultural sector for a number of years.

Unfortunately WRS was heavily impacted by the crisis as it experienced a collapse of its agricultural market overnight. The bank supported the business through this difficult time by increasing its facilities to help the business recover. The period back to recovery took its toll on the managing director who had many sleepless nights. In 2004 the business was acquired by Woodville Water Treatment Solutions PLC (WWTS group) and WRS's banking was lost to WWTS's bank.

You have met Asfar on many occasions at your local Chamber of Commerce meetings and he is always complimentary and grateful for the bank's support. Recently you were giving a lecture on the global financial crisis and met Asfar again. You asked about WRS (UK) and Asfar told you everything was going splendidly and how selling his business was the best thing he had done. Not only did he make a lot of money, he is still the MD of WRS and welcomes the involvement of his co-directors in the wider group. He has a board position on the group's board of directors.

He mentioned WWTS and suggested you might like to speak to them as they do have some issues with their bank. He did not elaborate but suggested you research the group and if you would like a meeting, he would arrange for you to meet the chief executive of WWTS. Asfar said he was due to be out of the country for a few weeks but he would contact you upon his return. You thanked him and said you would have a look at the group and would welcome the opportunity to meet them.

Once back at the office you looked at WWTS's website and ordered its latest sets of accounts from Companies House. The website and financial accounts provide a wealth of information (especially the notes to the accounts) some of which is relevant and some less so. Nevertheless, as a relationship manager you have to read all the information in order to extract that which is relevant.

Appendix 10.1 provides extracts from WWTS's website. Appendix 10.2 provides the financial accounts from Companies House.

You have sent the financial information to a credit analyst in your Advances department and have received the analyst's credit report. Appendix 10.3 contains this credit report. The credit analyst confirmed that this looks to be a business that the bank would like to take from a competitor. (Note: you are not required to undertake any credit analysis as this has been done for you.)

ACTIVITY 10.1

Using information from the website (Appendix 10.1) and the accounts (Appendix 10.2), prepare PESTEL, Porters five forces, and strategic environment analyses to identify discussion points for a potential first meeting with the chief executive. Then compare your answer with the one found in Activity Answer 10.1.

Now you have undertaken some research and collated your thoughts, you can turn to the credit analyst's report (Appendix 10.3).

ACTIVITY 10.2

Read the credit analyst's report and accounts to see if there are any questions you would like to ask in the first or any other subsequent meetings. Then compare your answer to the one found in Activity Answer 10.2.

ACTIVITY 10.3

From the information contained in the financial accounts draw up an organizational structure chart for WWTS group. Then compare your answer to the one found in Activity Answer 10.3.

Great news! Asfar has telephoned you and confirmed that the chief executive would like a meeting. It has been arranged for early next week for a one-hour chat.

ACTIVITY 10.4

Prepare a short agenda for the meeting, then compare your answer with the one found in Activity Answer 10.4.

How are you going to approach it? You will only have one hour, which is only a short amount of time to make a great impression.

For the purpose of this chapter we have introduced a fictional relationship manager called Kate. This will enable you to compare your own responses to a number of exercises which appear throughout this chapter, with the way Kate approached the same exercises. Please ensure you undertake the exercises before referring to the suggested answers.

The journey begins.

Meeting 1

The meeting takes place and the following are extracts of the conversation between Kate, the relationship manager, and David Wood, the chief executive.

Extracts from Meeting 1

The meeting is held in David's office. His PA sits Kate down, offers her a drink and informs her that David will be with her shortly.

David enters.

DAVID: Hello Kate, thanks for coming to see me. Asfar speaks very highly of you and your bank. What would you like to know?

KATE: Thanks for agreeing to meet me. I understand we have an hour together, so I'll keep it brief. I have looked at your website and your accounts and done some research on the sector, so I do have some information, but I would really like to know more.

David nods.

KATE: Basically there are three things I'd like to understand:

  1 What is it you do?

  2 How well do you do it? and

  3 How could we help you do it better?

David smiles.

KATE: I know the business is involved in water treatment, in particular manufacturing specialized membranes as part of the water treatment processes, and that you operate in a number of different countries. As I understand it, there are four different filtration processes and that you design and produce four types of membranes for each different process. I also understand that you are working on a new type of membrane based on graphene. What can you tell me about that?

DAVID: Not a lot I'm afraid. It's all quite confidential. But yes, we are working with Manchester University to develop a new product using graphene technology. We believe it could have incredible potential which could revolutionize the water treatment sector. At the moment, as you rightly say, we make different membranes for each of the processes, but imagine if you only needed one!

KATE: The nature of the industry would totally change. How would customers react?

DAVID: They would probably buy us out. You see we wouldn't have the resources to exploit the technology ourselves, unless of course you could offer us hundreds of millions. Joking apart, we would probably look to sell up; none of us are getting much younger! But until then we'll just carry on.

KATE: Doing what you already do, and from your accounts, doing it very well.

David smiles.

KATE: One thing that did jump out at me was what happened in 2015. Your accounts show a large fall in turnover.

DAVID: Yes 2015 was a strange year. But so were 2014 and 2016. You see, in 2014 we had a late surge in sales which we had expected to come onstream in 2015. So the turnover in 2014 was much greater than we expected. Conversely, in 2015 where we had expected a decent performance, towards the end of the year we suddenly experienced delays in projects, which had the effect of pushing sales into 2016. As a result we decided to forgo a dividend.

Kate nods.

DAVID: Whether it was the Brexit effect or even the US election, most likely both, there seemed to be a slowdown in confidence and projects kept getting pushed back. Thankfully things do seem to have settled down now.

KATE: I guess that's fairly typical of the sector. When you are dealing with large capital projects delays can impact significantly, making turnover 'lumpy'.

DAVID: Yes, that's the nature of our game. It was one of the reasons we acquired WRS. Asfar and his business had been on our radar, and we knew they were experiencing difficulties. It took a brave bank to stand by them given the situation.

Kate smiles.

KATE: Well we knew it would come good, they just needed time to recover.

DAVID: Well I'm glad you did because the acquisition gave us the opportunity to complete our product portfolio. WRS were very strong in ceramic membranes so adding that to our portfolio made perfect sense and made the group much stronger.

KATE: You mentioned the group. I did put a group structure together. How successful was I?

Kate hands David a copy (see Figure 10.1).

DAVID: Yes that looks good. Woodville Group, the management company, is where the dividends are paid, the rest are the trading companies, all of which are wholly owned apart from graphene which is an associate. And you've got the US division – we use that to cover the Americas and Asia.

KATE: The German company, that's dormant isn't it?

DAVID: Yes, but probably not for much longer when we exit the EU. In all likelihood, we'll reactivate it to cover our European markets. It was quite fortunate really; it's an office that my father had when he was working at BASF. We don't use it, but now I think we are going to have to reactivate it after Brexit happens.

KATE: I couldn't tell which countries you operate in, from your accounts. You don't give any details.

DAVID: I know, we're not too keen on our competitors knowing where we operate. They soon find out, but we don't volunteer it. I can let you have a list of our operations' coverage if you'd like.

KATE: That would be great because I could then see what currencies you use. I know you hedge some of the currency exposure by using forward contracts.

DAVID: Yes, but you'll need to speak to Neville our finance director for the details. He tends to look after that side.

Kate nods.

KATE: I'm conscious of the time we have. I haven't asked my final question yet. How do you think we can help you?

DAVID: Well for a start you seem well informed, so you have done your homework. I think our banking needs are relatively straightforward. We don't have a lot of debt, so we don't need much in the

Figure 10.1 WWTS's organizational structure chart

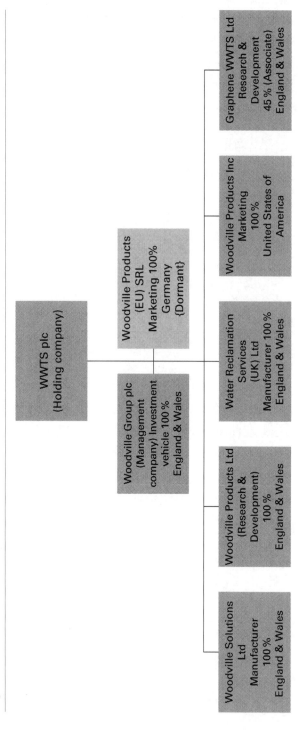

way of borrowing, so it's unlikely you'll make a fortune from our banking needs.

KATE: That's not what banking is all about. It's more about developing good relationships with our customers so we can help them when they need it.

DAVID: Our relationship with XYZ Bank is OK, but we have had a couple of issues.

KATE: Really?

DAVID: Yes, well they didn't come out of the financial crisis with their reputation intact, and that has seemed to change the way they do things.

KATE: In what way?

DAVID: Well over the last four or five years, I think we've had five or six relationship managers. Before the crisis we had an excellent relationship with a lady called Christine Chamberlain. Do you know her?

KATE: No, can't say that I do.

DAVID: Well Christine was quite close to us and we relied upon her for everything. Unfortunately, she retired and since then the turnover of relationship managers has been quite dramatic. Whilst I understand banks have changed, it can be really frustrating to have to keep explaining our business to yet another relationship manager. In fact, we had one manager, and when we tried to contact her, we found out she had been moved to another department and we had no idea who was looking after us. So, continuity of relationship is important, and so is making sure the bank's systems work properly.

KATE: So you've had problems with what exactly?

DAVID: Computer outages, where we don't have access to the banking system. It's happened a few times and it really impacts us, especially when you are dealing with different countries. I know of one time when Neville couldn't even send payments abroad to one of our suppliers.

KATE: Thankfully (*touching the table*) touch wood; we've not had any problems in that area. And as far as banking relationships go, I've no plans to go anywhere. But I would like to learn more about the business.

DAVID: I know our time is up. I'll send you the information I promised, and if there is anything else you'd like, just let me know.

KATE: Great, I'll drop you an e-mail if that's OK.

DAVID: OK, how about next time you visit some of our sites? I can arrange for my production supervisor to give you a tour of our facilities and if you want, my lab technician can walk you round some of our labs?

KATE: That would be really great, I'd appreciate that. Thanks for your time, I'll be in touch.

DAVID: Thank you, I've enjoyed the hour. Thinking about it, I'd also like you to meet Neville. Our latest financials should be ready next month. I'll get Neville to meet you to go through the latest figures.

KATE: Great, thanks again for your time.

Meeting ends.

Observations from the meeting

Kate's objectives were to:

1 make a good impression;

2 learn more about the business;

3 secure a further meeting.

Did Kate achieve her objectives?

Objective 1: make a good impression

Kate made a very good impression. The meeting was positive and both Kate and David appeared comfortable with each other. They clearly had rapport and there were plenty of smiles and nods (body language).

Who talked more, Kate or David? In the early stages Kate tended to talk more than David, but soon after, it was David who talked more. Indeed, David spoke for two-thirds of the time and Kate one-third.

Note Kate's use of open and closed questions which she used to draw out information from David. From the extracts, David used three open questions and two closed, whereas Kate used 10 open questions and only two closed questions. This is why David did the majority of the talking.

Objective 2: learn more about the business

ACTIVITY 10.5

What did Kate learn from the meeting? Write down your thoughts then compare your answer with the one found in Activity Answer 10.5.

Objective 3: secure a further meeting

Kate's third objective was to secure another meeting. She succeeded because David has lined up three more meetings with:

1 the production supervisor;

2 the senior lab technician;

3 the finance director.

What are Kate's next steps?

Having reflected on the meeting, Kate should complete a file note of the meeting detailing her own observations and next steps. She should send David an e-mail which could include any further requests for information such as the geographical coverage of customers David said he would send. She should also thank him for his time.

Over the next two weeks David sent Kate information on where their customers operated from. He also included information on their key suppliers. Their largest customers are based in:

- Canada;
- North America;
- Mexico;
- France;
- China;
- Japan;
- Australia.

Their suppliers are based in:

- Germany;
- France;
- UK;
- Canada;
- Mexico;
- China;
- India.

David set up meetings with Mahmoud Ali, the production supervisor at their Warrington production facility, and Ayame Mai, the senior lab technician who works in another one of their laboratories based at Liverpool University.

Meeting 2

Kate met Mahmoud at the production facility. Mahmoud was very friendly and throughout the tour explained each of the processes of manufacture in simple language that Kate understood. Quality assurance was very high on Mahmoud's agenda and he emphasized how critical it was to the operation. He confirmed the water sector is heavily regulated and he saw this as an opportunity, given their long experience in the industry; indeed they undertake regulatory audits for customers when they commission new water treatment plants.

Mahmoud also introduced Kate to a number of key staff, in production, sales and IT. Kate had time to chat with the sales team who confirmed that given their expertise and technical assistance they got a lot of repeat business from customers. It also enabled them to charge premium pricing for their goods and services. Customer loyalty was considered to be strong.

Meeting 3

The third meeting was held at the WTTS laboratory based in Liverpool University. Ayame introduced Kate to a number of her technicians, some of whom had been seconded from the university to gain workplace experience as part of their studies. Kate considered them to be very bright, enthused and highly motivated.

Ayame explained that talent recruitment was very important and they were able to recruit from universities such as Manchester and Liverpool. She explained a lot of the students were from all around the world and after qualification some did return to their home counties. She did not think this was an impediment because students would work in their own countries' water treatment companies, where more often than not, they became 'customers of the future'.

Later that month Kate received an e-mail from Neville, the finance director, suggesting a meeting time and place as the latest draft accounts had become available.

Meeting 4

Kate was sitting in a meeting room and in walked Neville clutching a batch of papers. He sat opposite Kate and slid the draft accounts over to her.

NEVILLE: David told me to give you a set of the 2018 figures; they're not finalized or audited and they are not for public consumption.

The draft 2018 figures can be found in Appendix 10.4.

KATE: Don't worry, everything here is confidential.

Kate glanced at the headline figures, which looked good:

- *turnover had increased to £28.8 million;*
- *net profit was posted at £5.3 million;*
- *after tax, retained profits were £4.4 million;*
- *the net worth of the business had increased to £14.1 million after dividend payments of £2 million;*
- *There was no Statement of Cash Flows, but Kate could calculate that herself when she got back to the office. Cash at the bank was now £8.7 million.*

NEVILLE: So how much are you going to lend us?

Kate was surprised.

NEVILLE: I want to build up a war chest for acquisitions, so how much are you going to lend us?

Kate was taken aback at Neville's tone which seemed aggressive and almost hostile. She had to respond immediately.

ACTIVITY 10.6

In a real-life scenario you cannot prevaricate; you have to reply to the direct question. How would you respond to Neville's question? Write down what you would say then compare your response to Kate's, which can be found in Activity Answer 10.6.

The meeting continued.

NEVILLE: I'll tell you upfront I'm not keen on changing banks. David and the rest of the board might see it as a good thing, but they don't have to deal with all the fallout of moving banks. That would land on me and my team and I don't need all that hassle and additional work.

KATE: Don't worry about that, if we get to the position of where you wish to move banks, we will have a team on hand to make everything goes smoothly, it's what we do. But I think we are at a very early stage yet and I'm not even in a position to know what services and lending facilities you need. I have some ideas but it would be really helpful if you could let me have an idea of what products and services you currently use from your existing bank and what lending limits are currently in place. I can then start to understand how we can help.

NEVILLE: I'll send you a list of what we have already but I'm not going to let you have details of pricing or conditions, that's up to you.

KATE: Sure, that's fine. I'll take the figures away and have a proper look at them. If you let me have the banking details then we can get together to chat through my proposals.

NEVILLE: OK, give me a ring when you're ready.

The meeting ends.

What products and services do you think WWTS could benefit from?

ACTIVITY 10.7

From the information provided, list the products and services you think would be beneficial to the business. Ignore any lending limits; just concentrate on the products and services that might be attractive. Compare your answer to the one provided in Activity Answer 10.7.

A week later Neville e-mailed Kate the details of their banking facilities:

- £1 million overdraft (in case of need – never used);
- £1 million combined limit for forward currency contracts and documentary letters of credit;
- £187,000 medium-term loan (two years remaining);
- security comprises inter-company cross-guarantees and debentures.

Kate thanked him by e-mail and suggested a further meeting with herself and her local international manager who wanted to review their international banking requirements.

Neville responded and informed Kate that his colleague John Baldwin, the sales director, will also attend the meeting.

Meeting 5

Kate met with Neville and John and introduced Denise, her international manager.

They confirmed that payments for exports are undertaken using letters of credit and they operate euro and US dollar currency accounts. They also confirmed they off-set currency balances as customers were largely based in the same countries as their suppliers.

Denise also asked them if they have any bonds, indemnities and guarantees. John and Neville looked at each other and said, 'What are they?'

ACTIVITY 10.8

Explain what bonds, indemnities and guarantees are, then compare your answer with Activity Answer 10.8.

JOHN: That would be useful. I wonder why our bank has never mentioned them? That is definitely something we should consider.

KATE: It would form part of your lending arrangements and now I know what they are I can proceed to prepare my credit report for your banking facilities. Could you let me have copies of your latest management accounts and forecasts?

NEVILLE: Sure, I'll send them to you. We already prepare this information for our existing bank so I'll copy you in as well.

The meeting ends.

The following week Neville sends Kate their latest management accounts package which comprises:

- a Statement of Comprehensive Income (profit and loss account);
- the Statement of Financial Position (balance sheet);
- their cash flow forecast (prepared on a monthly basis);
- aged lists of receivables and payables (debtors and creditors).

Kate submitted a credit proposal and was pleased to learn that it had been sanctioned. She telephoned David who agreed to arrange a further meeting with the board where Kate could present her proposals.

Meeting 6

Kate meets the board. She already knew David, Neville, John and Asfar and she was introduced to Erica Wood, the production director and Henry Wood, David's father, who is a non-executive director. Henry informs Kate that he is a private banking client of Kate's bank and can vouch for the quality of service he receives.

Neville was not at the meeting. David explained he had been delayed because the bank's systems went down again yesterday which caused problems for the finance team. Then Neville appeared and apologized for keeping everybody waiting.

Kate outlined her proposal, which was similar to the facilities provided by their existing bank. The terms and conditions appeared acceptable. However, a question was raised about the pricing.

NEVILLE: The margin on the overdraft is more expensive than what we have already, why is that?

KATE: I've used our standard pricing for the overdraft and that's the margin we calculated. It's based on our perception of risk and the security package we propose. Our view is that the bank regards you as a low-risk customer and the margin reflects that.

        I'm also conscious you don't actually use the overdraft and it is there 'in case of need'. I thought it was more appropriate to concentrate on the margins for your credit balances which are slightly higher than our standard rates for credit balances. I could drop the margin on the overdraft a little but I would have to drop the margin for your credit balances by the same amount.

NEVILLE: No leave it as it is, I'd prefer to earn more on our credit balances.

KATE: And don't forget the VAT deferment bond will help cash flow.

The board liked the idea of a VAT deferment bond.

David said the package looked acceptable and the board would discuss the banking later on in the afternoon. He said that he would telephone Kate the next day with the decision.

One thing Neville did seek clarification on was the mechanics of transferring all the accounts and facilities. Kate explained that, should they decide to go ahead, she will establish an 'on-boarding' team of colleagues who would project-manage the transfer, liaising with members of the finance team as appropriate. This was welcomed by Neville and the rest of the board.

The meeting ended.

The following day Kate received a telephone call from David, who confirmed they would like to transfer their banking and asked Kate to 'get the ball rolling'. Kate requested the signed facility letter and David confirmed he would send it to her the following day. He also mentioned that he would have to inform his current bank and ask for their cooperation. Kate suggested it might be better to wait until everything was in place as there was a lot of work that needed to be completed. Once the bank was ready she would let David know when to make the call. Kate also offered to liaise with their current relationship manager to effect a smooth transfer.

Kate managed their expectations well.

Kate and the on-boarding team met with people from the finance team and undertook all the account opening procedures including the customer due diligence (CDD) and KYC formalities, payroll systems, currency accounts, etc.

Four weeks later the banking transfer for WWTS was completed.

Over the forthcoming months Kate and her team kept close to the people at WWTS who began to form strong bonds and relationships with David, Neville and his team. Over the next few months both David and Erica became private banking clients with Kate's bank.

ACTIVITY 10.9

Highlight the skills and competences Kate demonstrated that stood out to you. What areas could Kate have improved upon? Then compare your answer with Activity Answer 10.9.

At the start of this book we said this final chapter was based on the journey of gaining new business. It's a bit more than that. Once the business has been on-boarded, it must be looked after for the lifetime of the relationship.

Understanding your own strengths and weaknesses is critical to delivering an outstanding relationship management experience. Everybody has strengths and everybody has weaknesses. This book will help you to understand yours. If there are any areas you feel might need further clarification then revisit the appropriate parts of the text. And, don't forget there are many of your own colleagues who would be willing and able to help.

In Chapter 8 we asked, 'What makes a great relationship manager?' The answer was teamwork. So don't be afraid to use it.

Enjoy your studies and your banking career.

Chapter summary

In this chapter we have explored:

- the stages of the journey for gaining new business;
- how financial and non-financial analyses complement each other;
- the type of information that can be obtained from examining a set of financial accounts;
- how to undertake Porter, PESTEL and strategic environment analyses;
- how to gain and support new business.

Objective check

1 What are the benefits to undertaking detailed research prior to meeting customers and prospects?

2 Which are the key skills used during effective negotiations?

3 What examples can you see of excellent questioning techniques and listening skills being displayed during the interview?

4 How did having an agenda for meetings assist the relationship manager in their ultimate goal?

5 Which skills did the relationship manager display during the interviews?

6 Which competences were displayed by the relationship manager during the interviews?

Appendix 10.1

Extracts from the WWTS website
HISTORY OF WWTS

WWTS was established in the 1960s by Henry Wood, who was pioneering water treatment membranes for BASF. Ultimately, water treatment services were considered to be a non-core division of BASF and in 1965 Henry got the opportunity to buy the division from BASF and set up WWTS as a result.

His first major project was developing water treatment membranes for the Hoover Dam in America.

Since then WWTS has grown and expanded, developing a whole range of specialized membranes for each filtration process, including polymers, ceramics, metallics, MD and hybrids.

We are currently working closely with the University of Manchester to explore the exciting possibilities provided by Graphene™ for use within the water treatment sector.

PROVIDING SUSTAINABLE WATER SOLUTIONS FOR OUR COMMUNITIES

WWTS is at the forefront of the water industry; supporting our clients in managing and meeting increasingly stringent water and wastewater quality and regulatory requirements, whilst facilitating innovative, cost-effective solutions.

We maintain our leading role by implementing renowned technical and organizational expertise in support of programmes for water quality improvement, environmental restoration, productive reuse and strategic environmental planning.

WWTS is committed to *Sustainable Water Treatments* and this ethos underpins our approach to technical solutions. We strive to produce solutions with the lowest carbon footprint and the highest standards of energy saving solutions to our clients.

THE WATER TREATMENT PROCESS

The water treatment process has six different stages and WWTS is at the forefront of the third stage (membrane filtration):

(1) | **Preliminary dosing:** Lime and carbon dioxide are added to the water to improve the water's alkalinity. This ensures the treatment processes work effectively and metallic plumbing is protected from corrosion.

(2) | **Screening:** Water passes through a filter screen which captures particles larger than 2mm before moving into a flocculation tank, where a coagulant is added to bind the finer particles together to make larger particles, which are easier to filter out.

(3) | **Membrane filtration:** Water is drawn through polymer/ceramic membranes to remove the finer particles. The membranes are fine enough to remove many harmful micro-organisms. There are four types of filtration processes: see below. Our water filtration membranes are used for each of the four filtration process types.

(4) | **Ozone contact plant:** Filtered water is mixed with ozone, a disinfectant to break down any compounds which can cause taste or odour problems.

(5) | **BAC filtration:** Biologically Activated Carbon (BAC) removes any remaining taste or odour in the water. The filters are full of activated carbon which absorbs any of the final contaminants.

(6) | **Chlorine contact tank:** Chlorine is added to the water to destroy any remaining bacteria. It is important that chlorine is added at this last stage to ensure the water continues to remain free from bacteria as it passes through the reticulation process.

Since the early 1960s advances in filtration membrane technologies have all but displaced chemical treatment systems in the water treatment and water purification processes. Membranes have become increasingly popular for production of potable (safe) drinking water from ground, surface and seawater sources, as well as for the advanced treatment of wastewater and desalination.

Membrane processes are employed in both drinking water and wastewater treatment for the removal of bacteria and other micro-organisms, particulate material, micro-pollutants and natural organic materials.

Membrane filters are mechanical 'fine sieves'. These sieves consist of porous films with precisely defined pore diameters. The pore diameters define the membrane type and relate directly to the separation rates. All substances smaller than the pores can pass through the membrane whilst larger substances are held back.

TYPES OF MEMBRANES

The common types of membranes are:

- Polymer
- Ceramic
- Metallic
- Nanofunctionalized membranes (Membrane Distillation – MD)

Polymer membranes account for around 75 per cent of the membrane filtration market, with ceramics accounting for the majority of the remaining 20 per cent, along with a small number of other materials such as metallic membranes and nanofunctionalized membranes (MDs).

POLYMERS

The use of polymer membranes is widespread in the wastewater filtration market as they are cheaper to manufacture than their ceramic equivalents; however, polymer systems do require more frequent filter replacements.

CERAMICS

Ceramic filtration membranes require lower pressure (and less energy) to circulate fluid. Ceramic membranes have more strength and rigidity, giving them better stability under pressure than polymer membranes.

Ceramic membranes are also better for high-temperature applications. They can be sterilized or steam-cleaned for specific applications, something that is not possible with polymers. The use of ceramic membranes is common in the agriculture sector (water reclamation) whereas polymers tend to dominate the wastewater treatment sector.

METALLIC MEMBRANES

Metallic membranes are made of stainless steel and can be very finely porous. Their main application is in gas separations, but they can also be used for water filtration at high temperatures or as a membrane support.

NANOFUNCTIONALIZED MEMBRANES – MEMBRANE DISTILLATION (MD)

A more recent development in membrane technology is in the use of nanofunctionalized membranes and Membrane Distillation (MD). MD membranes are fabricated composite hydrophobic/hydrophilic membranes in a multilayered structure. One of the major advantages for MD is the use of waste heat as its feed temperature requirement, which is much lower than conventional distillation processes.

ENGINEERING AND TECHNICAL

Encompassing the entire spectrum of water services, our technical expertise extends from water and wastewater treatment and networks to environmental and natural resources services. We have significant global experience of developing 'signature designs' for clients, utilizing standard components to meet their specific process and operational needs. Operating throughout the world we provide the following Engineering and Technical Services:

- Water Resource Planning and Management
- Process Engineering Services
- Wastewater Treatment Engineering and Design
- Wastewater Network Modelling
- Water Network Modelling
- Process Design and Support
- Conceptual Design & Feasibility Studies
- Engineering & Detailed Design

Appendix 10.2

Financial accounts of Woodville Water Treatment Solutions PLC

Woodville Water Treatment Solutions PLC

Annual Report and Consolidated Financial Statement for the year ended 31st March 2017

DIRECTORS	D Wood
	E Wood
	J Baldwin
	A Nazir
	N Johnstone
SECRETARY	N Johnstone
REGISTERED OFFICE	Woodville House
	Woodville Industrial Science Park
	Manchester Old Road
	Manchester
	M24 4WT
REGISTERED NUMBER	30256
INDEPENDENT AUDITORS	Rhodes Middleton LLP
	Chartered Accountants
	2 King Street
	Manchester
	M1 2PE

Woodville Water Treatment Solutions PLC

**Group strategic report
for the year ended 31st March 2017**

INTRODUCTION

The principal activity of the Group during the year continued to be that of the design and manufacture of specialized filtration membrane products and systems to the water treatment industries.

BUSINESS REVIEW

The Board is delighted to report another excellent performance for the year.

Whilst the UK market has displayed underlying growth, the increase in both turnover and margins has been primarily driven by the level of exports where the group has reaped rewards of the sales effort in the chosen geographies over recent years, being able to capitalize on the market-leading product quality and strength of the 'Woodville' brand.

To maintain the Group's position as market leader, the Board have continued to direct new investment into new complementary product offerings.

PRINCIPAL RISKS AND UNCERTANTIES

Brexit and the inherent uncertainties, particularly surrounding any future trade constraints, presents a potential risk to the business. Exchange rate volatility also has an impact, although the Group's worldwide trading hedges an element of exchange rate gains and losses. The Board believe the group is well positioned to face these uncertainties, with a market-leading brand based on high-quality products, associated 'know-how' and first-class service delivery.

FUTURE OPPORTUNITIES AND STRATEGIC OBJECTIVES

In both our domestic and export markets we continue to target greater product penetration into our existing market sectors. To maintain our competitive advantage and support long-term growth and profitability we continue to invest in new product development and improvements in our technical and on-site service offer.

The board believe the commercial position of the group has become stronger over the past few years and are confident, given the underlying strength of our product and service offer, it will further strengthen in the future.

This report was approved by the Board and is signed on its behalf.

D Wood

Director

Dated   26th September 2017

**Directors' report
for the year ended 31st March 2017**

DIRECTORS' RESPONSIBILITIES STATEMENT

The directors are responsible for preparing the Group strategic report, the directors' report and the financial statements in accordance with applicable laws and regulations.

Company law requires the directors to prepare financial statements for each financial year. Under that law the directors have elected to prepare the financial statements in accordance with applicable law and United Kingdom Accounting Standards (UKGAAP) including Financial Reporting Standard 102. 'The Financial Reporting Standard applicable in the UK and Republic of Ireland'. Under company law the directors must not approve the financial statements unless they are satisfied that they give 'a true and fair view' of the state of affairs of the Company and the Group and of the profit and loss of the Group for that period. In preparing these financial statements, the directors are required to:

1) select suitable accounting policies of the group financial statements and then apply them consistently;

2) make judgements and accounting estimates that are reasonable and prudent;

3) state whether applicable UK Accounting Standards have been followed, subject to any material departures disclosed and explained in the financial statements; and

4) prepare the financial statements on the going concern basis unless it is inappropriate to presume that the Group will continue in business.

The directors are responsible for keeping adequate accounting records that are sufficient to show and explain the Company's transactions and disclose with reasonable accuracy at any time the financial position of the Company and the Group and enable them to ensure that the financial statements comply with the Companies Act 2006. They are also responsible for safeguarding the assets of the Company and the Group and hence for taking reasonable steps for the prevention and detection of fraud and other irregularities.

RESULTS AND DIVIDENDS

The profit for the year, after taxation, amounted to £4,365,249 (2016: £1,282,416).

DIRECTORS

The directors who served during the year were:

D Wood
E Wood
A Nazir
J Baldwin
N Johnstone

Woodville Water Treatment Solutions PLC

Directors' report
for the year ended 31st March 2017

Disclosure of information to auditor

Each of the persons who are directors at the time when this directors' report is approved has confirmed that:

(a) so far as that director is aware, there is no relevant audit information of which the Company and the Group's auditor is unaware; and

(b) the director has taken all the steps that ought to have been taken as a director in order to be aware of any relevant audit information and to establish that the Company and the Group's auditor is aware of that information

Auditors

The auditor, Rhodes Middleton LLP, will be proposed for reappointment in accordance with section 485 of the Companies Act 2006.

This report was approved by the board and signed on its behalf.

N Johnstone

Mr N Johnstone
Secretary

Independent auditors' report to shareholders of Woodville Water Treatment Solutions PLC

We have audited the financial statements of Woodville Water Treatment Solutions PLC for the year ended 31st March 2017. The financial reporting framework that has been applied in their preparation is applicable law including Financial Reporting standard 102 'The Financial Reporting Standard applicable in the UK and Republic of Ireland'.

This report is made solely to the Company's shareholders, as a body, in accordance with Chapter 3 of Part 16 of the Companies Act 2006. Our audit work has been undertaken so that we might state to the Company's shareholders those matters we are required to state to them in an Auditor's Report and for no other purpose. To the fullest extent permitted by law, we do not accept or assume responsibility to anyone other than the Company and the Company's shareholders as a body, for our audit work, for this respect, or for the opinions we have formed.

In our opinion the financial statements:

(a) give a true and fair view of the state of the Group's and parent Company's affairs as at 31st March 2017 and the Group's profit for the year then ended;

(b) have been properly prepared in accordance with United Kingdom Generally Accepted Accounting Practice;

(c) have been prepared in accordance with the requirements of the Companies Act 2006.

Rhodes Middleton

J Ainscough (Senior Statutory Auditor)
for and on behalf of Rhodes Middleton LLP

Kings Drive House
Main street
Manchester
M1 4VP

26th September 2017

Consolidated statement of income and retained earnings (including profit and loss account) for the year ended 31st March 2017

	2017 £	2016 £
Turnover	24,675,016	18,845,240
Cost of sales	(12,634,730)	(10,537,286)
Gross profit	12,040,286	8,307,954
Administrative expenses	(6,871,043)	(6,474,164)
Operating profit	5,169,243	1,833,790
Loss from interest in associated undertakings	(33,847)	(23,468)
Interest receivable and similar income	9,455	7,718
Interest payable and similar charges	(38,127)	(35,866)
Profit on ordinary activities before taxation	5,106,724	1,782,174
Tax on profit on ordinary activities	(741,476)	(499,758)
Profit for the financial year	4,365,249	1,282,416
Retained earnings at the beginning of the year	9,205,670	9,423,254
Profit for the year	4,365,249	1,282,416
Dividends declared and paid	(1,800,000)	(1,500,000)
Retained earnings at the end of the year	11,770,919	9,205,670

Consolidated balance sheet

As at 31st March 2017

	2017 £	2016 £
Fixed assets		
Tangible assets	2,794,425	3,039,011
Investment in associates	(95,696)	(61,849)
	2,698,729	2,977,162
Current assets		
Stocks	1,940,523	1,820,092
Debtors	6,254,482	3,837,307
Cash at bank and in hand	6,797,749	5,075,585
	14,992,754	10,732,984
Creditors: amounts falling due within one year	(5,553,966)	(3,906,347)
Net current assets	9,438,788	6,826,637
Total assets less current liabilities	12,137,517	9,803,799
Creditors: amounts falling due after more than one year	(242,827)	(548,807)
Provisions for liabilities		
Deferred taxation	(274,439)	(300,337)
Other provisions	(251,000)	(195,000)
Net assets	11,369,251	8,759,655

Capital and reserves

Called up share capital	**12,500**	12,500
Foreign exchange reserve	**125,832**	81,485
Other reserves	**(540,000)**	(540,000)
Profit and loss account	**11,770,919**	9,205,670
Shareholders' funds	**11,369,251**	8,759,655

The financial statements were approved and authorized for issue by the Board and were signed on its behalf by

Mr D Wood
Director

Date: 26th September 2017

Woodville Water Treatment Solutions PLC

**Notes to the financial statements
for the year ended 31st March 2017**

1   Accounting policies

The financial statements have been prepared under the historical cost convention and in accordance with Financial Reporting Standard 102, the Financial Reporting Standard applicable in the United Kingdom and the Republic of Ireland and the Companies Act 2006.

The preparation of the financial statements in compliance with FRS 102 requires the use of certain critical accounting estimates. It also requires Group management to exercise judgement in applying the Company's accounting policies.

1.2   Basis of consolidation

The consolidated financial statements present the results of the parent company and subsidiaries ('The Group') as a single entity. Intercompany transactions and balances between group companies are therefore eliminated in full.

1.3   Foreign currency translation

The company's functional and presentational currency is GBP.

Foreign currency risk

The Group's principal foreign currency exposures arise from trading with overseas companies. The Group policy permits but does not demand that these exposures may be hedged in order to fix the cost in sterling. This hedging activity involves the use of foreign exchange forward contracts.

Transactions in foreign currencies are recorded using the rate of exchange ruling at the date of the transaction. Monetary assets and liabilities denominated in foreign currencies are translated using the rate of exchange ruling at the balance sheet date and gains and losses on translation are included in the statement of income and retained earnings.

The results of an overseas subsidiary are translated at average rates in the statement of income and retained earnings. The differences arising from the translation of year-end balances at closing rates, together with restatement of opening Balances, are dealt with as movements on reserves.

1.4   Operating leases

Rentals paid under operating leases are charged to the statement of income and retained earnings on straight-line basis over the period of the lease.

1.5   Research and development

Research and development expenditure is written off in the year in which it is Incurred.

1.6   Pension costs

The Group operates a defined contribution pension scheme for employees. The assets of the scheme are held separately from those of the company. The annual contributions payable are charged to the statement of income and retained earnings.

1.7   Current and deferred taxation

The tax expense for the year comprises current and deferred tax. Tax is recognized in the statement of income and retained earnings, except that a charge attributable to an item of income and expenditure recognized as other comprehensive income or to an item recognized directly in equity is also recognized in other comprehensive income or directly in equity respectively.

Deferred tax is determined using tax rates and laws that have been enacted or substantively enacted by the balance sheet date.

1.8   Leasing and hire purchase

Assets obtained under hire purchase contracts and finance leases are capitalized as tangible fixed assets. Assets acquired by finance leases are depreciated over the short term of the lease and their useful lives. Assets acquired by hire purchase are depreciated over their useful lives. Finance leases are those where substantially all of the benefits and risks of ownership are assumed by the Company. Obligations under such agreements are included in creditors net of the finance charge allocated to future periods. The financial element of the rental payment is charged to the statement of income and retained earnings so as to produce a constant periodic rate on the net obligation outstanding in each period.

1.9   Tangible fixed assets

Tangible fixed assets under the cost model are stated at historical cost less accumulated depreciation and any accumulated impairment losses. Historical cost includes expenditure that is directly attributable to bringing the asset to the location and condition necessary for it to be capable of operating in a manner intended by management.

Repairs and maintenance are charged to the statement of income and retained earnings during the period in which they are incurred

Plant and machinery	5% – 20% straight line
Motor vehicles	25% reducing balance
Fixtures and fittings	25% reducing balance

The assets' residual values, useful lives and depreciation methods are reviewed, and adjusted prospectively if appropriate, or if there is an indication of a significant change since the last reporting date.

Gains and losses on disposal are determined by comparing proceeds with the carrying amount and are recognized within 'administrative expenses' in the statement of income and retained earnings.

1.10   Investments

Investments in subsidiaries are valued at cost less provision for impairment.

Investments in associates are stated at the amount of the parent company's share of net liabilities. The statement of income and retained earnings includes the Company's share of the associate companies loss after taxation, using the equity accounting basis.

1.11   Stocks

Stocks are valued at the lower of cost and net realizable value after making due allowance for obsolete and slow-moving items. The cost of finished goods comprises raw materials, direct labour, other direct costs and related production overheads. Net realizable value is the estimated selling price in the ordinary course of business, less the estimated costs of completion and selling expenses.

1.12   Debtors

Short-term debtors are measured at transaction price, less any impairment. Loans receivable are measured initially at fair value, net of transaction costs, and are measured subsequently at amortized cost using the effective interest method, less any impairment.

1.13   Creditors

Short-term creditors are measured at the transaction price. Other financial liabilities, including bank loans, are measured initially at fair value, net of transaction costs and are measured subsequently at amortized cost using the effective interest method.

1.14   Financial instruments

The Group enters into basic financial instruments transactions that result in the recognition of financial assets and liabilities like trade and other accounts receivable and payable, loans from banks and other third parties and loans to related parties.

1.15   Provisions

The cost of performing any remedial work under warranty where reasonably foreseeable is charged to the statement of income and retained earnings on an accrual basis.

1.16   Dividends

Equity dividends are recognized when they become legally payable. Interim equity dividends are recognized when paid. Final equity dividends are recognized when approved by shareholders at an annual general meeting.

1.17   Employee benefit trust

Assets and liabilities held in Woodville Water Treatment Limited Employee Benefit Trust are recognized as assets and liabilities of the Group until they vest unconditionally in identified beneficiaries. Shares in the company acquired by the Employee Benefit Trust are presented as a deduction from shareholders' funds. When the shares vest to satisfy share-based payments, a transfer is made from own shares held through the Employee Benefit Trust to retained earnings.

1.18   Stock provision

Stock provisions are recognized based on obsolete and slow-moving items with reference to quantity of items sold in the last 12 months.

1.19 Analysis of turnover

The whole of the turnover is attributable to the principal activity of the Group.

A geographical analysis of turnover is not provided as in the directors' opinion this would be prejudicial to their trading activities.

2.0 Operating profit

The operating profit is stated after charging

	2017	2016
	£	£
Research and development expenditure	472,325	530,671
Depreciation	372,345	389,166
Auditors' remuneration	25,000	24,000
Auditors' remuneration in respect of non-audit services	3,100	3,000
Exchange differences	(129,380)	52,743
Defined contribution pension cost	117,083	90,968
Operating lease expense	144,248	147,076
Operating lease – land and buildings	145,000	145,000

3.0 Employees

Staff costs including directors' remuneration were as follows

	2017	2016
	£	£
Wages and salaries	3,685,604	3,476,584
Social security costs	379,381	463,374
Cost of defined contribution scheme	117,083	90,968
	4,182,068	4,130,926

The average monthly number of employees, including directors, during the year was as follows:

	2017	2016
Production, sales and technical staff	62	55
Management, science technical staff and office staff	39	37
	101	92

4.0   Directors' remuneration

The operating profit is stated after charging

	2017	2016
	£	£
Directors' emoluments	168,880	398,708
Company contributions to defined contribution pension scheme	4,357	4,895
	173,237	403,603

During the year retirement benefits were accruing to 4 directors (2016: 4) in respect of defined contribution pension scheme

The highest paid director received remuneration of £90,201 (2015: 109,671)

The value of the company's contributions paid to a defined contribution pension scheme in respect of the highest paid director amounted to £4,267 (2016: £60)

5.0   Interest receivable and similar income

	2017	2016
	£	£
Other interest receivable	9,455	7,718
	9,455	7,718

5.1   Interest payable and similar charges

	2017	2016
	£	£
On bank loans and overdrafts	38,045	34,930
Finance charges	82	936
	38,127	35,866

6.0   Taxation

6.1   Corporation tax

	2017	2016
	£	£
Current tax on profits for the year	764,722	375,051
Adjustments in respect of previous periods	(193,030)	66,885
	571,692	441,936

6.2   Foreign tax

	2017	2016
Foreign tax on income for the year	195,322	30,264
	767,014	472,200

6.3   Deferred tax

	2017	2016
	£	£
Origination and reversal of timings differences	(25,539)	27,558
Taxation on profit on ordinary activities	741,475	499,758

7.0   Parent company profit for the year

The Company has taken advantage of the exemption allowed under section 408 of the Companies Act 2006 and has not presented its own statement of income and related earnings in these financial statements. The profit after tax of the parent Company for the year was £1,800,000 (2016: £1,500,000)

8.0 **Tangible fixed assets**

	Plant & machinery	Motor vehicles	Fixtures & fittings	Computer equipment	Total £
Cost or valuation					
1st April 2016	526,399	366,342	1,060,728		6,690,469
Additions	65,589	27,121	4,828	26,189	123,727
Exchange adjustments	3,494	(1,350)	598		2,742
At 31st March 2017	5,332,482	392,113	1,066,154	26,189	6,816,938
Depreciation					
1st April 2016	2,464,472	234,707	952,279		3,651,458
Chg. on owned assets	308,449	32,067	20,762	8,729	370,007
Chg. on financed assets	2,338				2,338
Exchange adjustments	3,314	(5,202)	598		(1,290)
At 31st March 2017	2,778,573	261,572	973,639	8,729	4,022,513
Net book value					
At 31st March 2017	2,553,909	130,541	92,515	17,460	2,794,425
At 31st March 2016	2,798,927	131,635	108,449		3,039,011

	Investment in associates £
9.0 Fixed asset investments	
Cost or valuation	
At 1st April 2016	**(61,849)**
Share of profit/(loss)	**(33,847)**
	(95,696)
At 31st March 2017	
Net book value	
At 31st March 2017	**(95,696)**
At 31st March 2016	**(61,849)**

9.1   Investments in associated undertakings

The Group has an interest in 45% of the share capital of Graphene WWTS Ltd, a company incorporated in England and Wales.

9.2   Subsidiary undertakings

The following were subsidiary undertakings of the Company:

Name	Country of incorporation	Holding	Principal activity
Woodville Group PLC	England & Wales	100%	Management company
Woodville Solutions Ltd	England & Wales	100%	Manufacture of membranes
Woodville Products Ltd	England & Wales	100%	Research & development company
Woodville Products Inc.	United States of America	100%	Marketing of membranes
Water Reclamation Services (UK) Ltd	England & Wales	100%	Manufacture of membranes
Graphene WWTS Ltd	England & Wales	45%	Research & development company
Woodville Products (EU) SRL	Germany	100%	Marketing of membranes (Dormant)

10.0   Cash and cash equivalents

	Group 2017 £	Group 2016 £	Company 2017 £	Company 2016 £
Cash at bank and in hand	6,797,749	5,075,585	284,167	503,109
	6,797,749	5,075,585	284,167	503,109

11.0   Creditors

Falling due within one year	Group 2017 £	Group 2016 £	Company 2017 £	Company 2016 £
Bank loans and overdrafts	324,949	293,010		
Hire purchase contracts	4,437	17255		
Trade creditors	2,284,898	1,765,369		
Amounts owed to related undertakings	198,594	233,864		
Corporation tax	516,997	422,020		
Taxation and social security	215,067	138,584	5,700	5,700
Other creditors	189,027	8,032	160,612	4,532
Accruals and deferred income	1,819,997	1,028,213	8	8
	5,553,966	3,906,347	166,320	10,240

11.1   Secured creditors

The bank loan and overdraft are secured by way of an unlimited debenture dated 14th November 1995, over all property and assets of the Group.

The hire purchase creditor is secured upon the assets to which it relates.

Included within other creditors is an amount owed to the defined contribution pension scheme of £20,034 (2016: £482).

11.2	Creditors	**Group**	Group	**Company**	Company
		2017	2016	**2017**	2016
	Amounts falling due after more than one year	**£**	£	**£**	£
	Bank loans	**242,827**	548,807		
	Amounts owed to Group undertakings				218,942
		242,827	548,807		218,942

12.0 Financial instruments

		Group	Group	**Company**	Company
	Financial assets	**2017**	2016	**2017**	2016
		£	£	**£**	£
	Financial assets measured at amortized costs	**5,691,652**	3,497,398	**156,080**	
		5,691,652	3,497,398	**156,080**	
	Financial liabilities measured at amortized costs	**(3,244,732)**	(2,866,337)	**(166,312)**	(229,174)
		(3,244,732)	(2,866,337)	**(166,312)**	(229,174)

13.0   Deferred taxation

Group	2017	2016
	£	£
At beginning of year	300,337	272,779
Net movement in year	(25,898)	27,558
	274,439	300,337

The provision for deferred taxation
is made up as follows:

	Group	Group
	2017	2016
	£	£
Accelerated capital allowances	277,557	300,435
Other timing differences	(3,118)	(98)
	274,439	300,337

14.0 Provisions

Group

	£
As at 1st April 2016	195,000
Net movement	56,000
As at 31st March 2017	251,000

The provision represents the director's best estimate of the cost of performing any warranty work where reasonably foreseeable.

15.0 Pension commitments

The Group operates a defined contribution pension scheme. During the year contributions totalling £117,083 (2016: £90,968) were made. Included within creditors due in less than one year are £nil (2016: £nil) due to defined contribution scheme.

16.0 Commitments under operating leases

At 31st March 2017 the Group and the Company had future minimum lease payments under non-cancellable operating leases as follows:

17.0   Assets other than land and buildings

	Group 2017 £	Group 2016 £
Not later than 1 year	183,109	210,774
Less than 1 year and not later than 5 years	83,556	196,162
	266,665	406,936

Land and buildings

	Group 2017 £	Group 2016 £
	145,000	145,000
	145,000	145,000

Appendix 10.3

Credit analyst report

- Strong profit metrics, growth in turnover and evidence of good cost controls.
- NPBT £5,106,724 (2017).
- Consistently cash generative Free Cash Flow (2017) £1,964,676.
- Cash held on balance sheet £6.7 million (2017).
- Debt is being paid down.
- Bank debt £567,776.
- Lightly geared with strong interest cover.

An excellent potential acquisition.

Haley Sternberg (Credit analyst)

Encs:
Financial Analysis
Statement of Cash Flow
Statement of Financial Position
Ratio Analysis

FINANCIAL ANALYSIS INPUT

ACCOUNT: Woodville Water Treatment Solutions PLC

PERIOD END	auto			
DATE AUDITED	31-Mar-14	31-Mar-15	31-Mar-16	31-Mar-17
DAYS	365	365	365	365

STATEMENT OF COMPREHENSIVE INCOME £/£000s				
SALES TURNOVER	19,973,420	15,442,983	18,845,240	24,675,016
COST OF SALES	10,858,475	8,258,825	10,537,286	12,634,730
GROSS PROFIT	9,114,945	7,184,158	8,307,954	12,040,286
ADMINISTRATION COSTS	1,776,155	1,674,505	1,550,469	2,043,413
DISTRIBUTION COSTS				
DEPRECIATION & AMORTIZATION	462,071	406,705	389,166	472,325
STAFF COSTS (EX DIRECTORS)	3,906,009	4,109,317	4,130,926	4,182,068
DIRECTORS REMUNERATION	324,078	402,278	403,603	173,237
OTHER COSTS				
NET PROFIT BEFORE INTEREST & TAX (OPERATING PROFIT)	2,646,632	591,353	1,833,790	5,169,243
INTEREST RECEIVABLE	5,092	11,098	7,718	9,455
OTHER INCOME		(38,426)	(23,468)	(33,847)
INTEREST PAYABLE	54,157	57,014	35,866	38,127
EXCEPTIONAL ITEMS				

NET PROFIT BEFORE TAX	**2,597,567**	**507,011**	**1,782,174**	**5,106,724**
TAX PAYABLE (RECEIVABLE)	628,164	(33,746)	499,758	741,475
DIVIDENDS				
EXTRAORDINARY ITEMS				
PROFIT/(LOSS) ON SALE OF ASSETS				
CAPITAL INTRODUCED				
RETAINED PROFITS	**1,969,403**	**540,757**	**1,282,416**	**4,365,249**

STATEMENT OF CASH FLOWS

STATEMENT OF CASH FLOWS	2015	2016	2017
NET PROFIT BEFORE INT & TAX	591,353	1,833,790	5,169,243
DEPRECIATION	406,705	389,166	472,325
OTHER CASH & NON CASH ITEMS	0	0	0
GROSS OPERATING CASH FLOW	998,058	2,222,956	5,641,568
DECREASE (INCREASE) IN INVENTORY (STOCKS)	21,268	80,858	(120,431)
DECREASE (INCREASE) IN RECEIVABLES (DEBTORS)	1,760,381	73,299	(2,472,836)
INCREASE (DECREASE) IN PAYABLES (CREDITORS)	312,958	423,994	1,624,791
INCREASE (DECREASE) INTER - CO	(744,295)	181,996	(94,818)
NET OPERATING CASH INFLOW (OUTFLOW)	2,348,370	2,983,103	4,578,274
INTEREST (PAID)	(57,014)	(35,866)	(38,127)
DIVIDEND (PAID)	0	(1,500,000)	(1,800,000)
INTEREST RECEIVED	11,098	7,718	9,455
INVESTMENT & OTHER INCOME	(38,426)	(23,468)	(33,847)
TAXATION (PAID) RECEIVED	(164,212)	(2,283)	(672,396)
FREE CASH FLOW BEFORE CAPEX	2,099,816	1,429,204	2,043,359
(PURCHASE) SALE OF FIXED ASSETS	(163,442)	(147,698)	(227,739)
(AQUISITIONS) SALES OF INVESTMENTS	(170,753)	(13,509)	149,056
FREE CASH FLOW	1,765,621	1,267,997	1,964,676

FOREIGN EXCHANGE MOVEMENTS	(66,107)	111,196	44,347
INCREASE (DECREASE) BANK LOANS	(265,023)	(320,272)	(305,980)
INCREASE (DECREASE) BANK O/D	6,368	6,513	31,939
INCREASE (DECREASE) H P & OTHERS	(18,967)	(19,161)	(12,818)
INCREASE (DECREASE) DIRECT'S LOANS	0	0	0
(INCREASE) DECREASE CASH	(1,421,892)	(1,046,273)	(1,722,164)
FUNDING (INVESTMENT) CASH FLOW	**(1,765,621)**	**(1,267,997)**	**(1,964,676)**

STATEMENT OF FINANCIAL POSITION

FIXED ASSETS

FREEHOLD PROPERTY				
LEASEHOLD PROPERTY				
PLANT & MACHINERY	3,372,047	3,081,755	2,798,927	2,553,909
VEHICLES	94,290	105,613	131,635	130,541
FIXTURES & FITTINGS	57,405	93,111	108,449	92,515
OTHER FIXED ASSETS				17,460
SUB TOTAL	3,523,742	3,280,479	3,039,011	2,794,425
INVESTMENTS	45	(38,381)	(61,849)	(95,696)
TOTAL FIXED ASSETS	**3,523,787**	**3,242,098**	**2,977,162**	**2,698,729**

CURRENT ASSETS

INVENTORY (STOCK)	RAW MATERIALS	506,985	483,922	526,487	480,280
	WORK IN PROGRESS				0
	FINISHED GOODS	1,415,233	1,417,028	1,293,605	1,460,243
RECEIVABLES (DEBTORS)	TRADE	3,558,096	2,282,519	2,440,761	4,894,102
	INTER COMPANY	88,130	152,576	204,444	263,992
	PREPAYMENTS	188,961	412,636	339,909	562,830
	OTHER DEBTORS	1,313,246	604,767	445,953	242,527
CURRENT INVESTMENTS		138,000	138,000	138,000	138,000
CORPORATION TAX RECOVERABLE		133,918	47,897	0	0
OTHER CURRENT ASSETS		22,084	231,263	268,240	153,031
CASH AT BANK & IN HAND		2,607,420	4,029,312	5,075,585	6,797,749
TOTAL CURRENT ASSETS		**9,972,073**	**9,799,920**	**10,732,984**	**14,992,754**

(continues)

CURRENT LIABILITIES

PAYABLES (CREDITORS)					
	TRADE	1,442,058	2,013,745	1,765,369	2,284,898
	ACCRUALS & DEF'D	663,319	457,125	1,028,213	1,819,997
	INTER COMPANY	679,849		233,864	198,594
	VAT, PAYE, SOC.SCY	124,325	120,217	138,584	215,067
	OTHER CREDITORS	103,544	95,117	8,032	189,027
DEBT	O/D & BANK LOANS	280,129	286,497	293,010	324,949
	CURRENT HP/LEASE	18,432	17,933	17,255	4,437
	DIRECTORS LOANS				
CORPORATION TAX PAYABLE		257,644		422,020	516,997
DIVIDEND PAYABLE					
OTHER CURRENT LIABILITIES					
TOTAL CREDITORS < 1 YEAR		**3,569,300**	**2,990,634**	**3,906,347**	**5,553,966**

PAYABLES (CREDITORS)

TRADE				
ACCRUALS				
OTHER CREDITORS				
DEBT	BANK LOANS	1,134,102	869,079	548,807	242,827
OTHER LOANS				
HP & LEASING	36,951	18,483	0	0
TOTAL CREDITORS > 1 YEAR	**1,171,053**	**887,562**	**548,807**	**242,827**

PROVISIONS & DEFERRED TAX

PENSIONS				
DEFERRED TAX	299,114	272,779	300,337	274,439
OTHER PROVISIONS	65,000	25,000	195,000	251,000
TOTAL PROVISIONS	**364,114**	**297,779**	**495,337**	**525,439**

(continues)

CAPITAL & RESERVES

CALLED UP SHARES	ORDINARY	12,500	12,500	12,500	12,500
	PREFERENTIAL				
FOREIGN EXCHANGE RESERVES				81,485	125,832
	CAPITAL/NON DIST	(540,000)	(540,000)	(540,000)	(540,000)
	REVALUATON				
	PROFIT & LOSS	8,918,893	9,393,543	9,205,670	11,770,919
MINORITY INTERESTS					
CAPITAL & RESERVES		8,391,393	8,866,043	8,759,655	11,369,251
INTANGIBLE ASSETS					
NET WORTH		**8,391,393**	**8,866,043**	**8,759,655**	**11,369,251**

RATIO ANALYSIS

PROFITABILITY AND COST STRUCTURE

SALES GROWTH	%		-23%	22%	31%
GROSS PROFIT % SALES		45.6%	46.5%	44.1%	48.8%
PBT % SALES		13.0%	3.3%	9.5%	20.7%
PBT CHANGE	%		-80.5%	251.5%	186.5%
ADMINISTRATION COSTS	% OF SALES	8.9%	10.8%	8.2%	8.3%
STAFF COSTS	% OF SALES	19.6%	26.6%	21.9%	16.9%
DEPRECIATION	% OF SALES	2.3%	2.6%	2.1%	1.9%

ASSET UTILIZATION

INVENTORY (STOCK) DAYS ON SALES		35	45	35	29
TRADE RECEIVABLES (DEBTOR) DAYS ON SALES		65	54	47	72
TRADE PAYABLES (CREDITOR) DAYS ON COST OF GOODS		48	89	61	66
NET WORKING ASSETS	% OF SALES	20%	17%	11%	13%
FIXED ASSETS	% OF SALES	18%	21%	16%	11%
TOTAL CAPITAL INTENSITY	% OF SALES	38%	38%	27%	24%

(continues)

BREAKEVEN ANALYSES

BREAKEVEN SALES	14,281,417	14,353,118	14,802,669	14,209,443
MARGIN OF SAFETY (SALES)	28%	7%	21%	42%

LIABILITIES STRUCTURE

EXTERNAL LIAB'S % TOTAL ASSETS	38%	32%	36%	36%
TOTAL DEBT % NET WORTH	18%	13%	10%	5%
CURRENT RATIO	279%	328%	275%	270%
QUICK RATIO	226%	264%	228%	235%

DEBT SERVICE & REPAYMENT

INTEREST COVER	PBIT	4896%	989%	5069%	13494%
TOTAL DEBT / PROFIT	YEARS	0.75	2.20	0.67	0.13
BANK DEBT		1,414,231	1,155,576	841,817	567,776

Appendix 10.4

WWTS draft financial statements 2018

Consolidated statement of income and retained earnings (including profit and loss account) For the year ended 31st March 2018

	2018 £	2017 £
Turnover	28,845,240	24,675,016
Cost of sales	(14,903,405)	(12,634,730)
Gross profit	13,941,835	12,040,286
GP%	48.30%	48.70%
Administrative expenses	(8,632,158)	(6,871,043)
	29.90%	27.80%
Operating profit	5,309,677	5,169,243
Loss from interest in associated undertakings	(35,624)	(33,847)
Interest receivable and similar income	8,578	9,455
Interest payable and similar charges	(30,254)	(38,127)
Profit on ordinary activities before taxation	5,252,377	5,106,724
Tax on profit on ordinary activities	(836,958)	(741,476)
Profit for the financial year	4,415,419	4,365,249
Retained earnings at the beginning of the year	11,770,919	9,205,670
Profit for the year	4,415,419	4,365,249
Dividends declared and paid	(2,000,000)	(1,800,000)
Retained earnings at the end of the year	14,186,338	11,770,919

Consolidated balance sheet
As at 31st March 2018

	2018	2017
	£	£
Fixed assets		
Tangible assets	**3,257,489**	2,794,425
Investment in associates	**(31,849)**	(95,696)
	3,225,640	2,698,729
Current assets		
Stocks	**2,764,591**	1,940,523
Debtors	**7,116,188**	6,254,482
Cash at bank and in hand	**8,700,827**	6,797,749
	18,581,606	14,992,754
Creditors: amounts falling due within one year	**(6,291,487)**	(5,553,966)
Net current assets	**12,290,119**	9,438,788
Total assets less current liabilities	**12,339,817**	12,137,517
Creditors: amounts falling due after more than one year	**(456,258)**	(242,827)
Provisions for liabilities		
Deferred taxation	**(423,163)**	(274,439)
Other provisions	**(450,000)**	(251,000)
Net assets	**14,186,338**	11,369,251

Capital and reserves

Called up share capital	**12,500**	12,500
Foreign exchange reserve	**97,500**	125,832
Other reserves	**(110,000)**	(540,000)
Profit and loss account	**14,186,338**	11,770,919
Shareholders' funds	**14,186,338**	11,369,251

The financial statements were approved and authorised for issue by the board and were signed on its behalf by

DRAFT FIGURES AWAITING AUDITOR'S CONFIRMATION

Mr D Wood

Director

Activity answer 10.1

PESTEL

The group operates globally in many different countries. Political and economic stability will help them; political or economic instability will not. *Do they operate in any geographical locations where this could become a threat?*

The group are technological pioneers. *How do they recruit talent with sufficient skills?* The industry is highly technology-based. *How do they keep up with technical changes?*

Their products are ecologically sustainable and address water pollution and waste.

The industry is heavily regulated both in the UK and around the world. For example, water treatment legislation in the UK:

- The Water Industry Act 1991 sets out the main powers and duties of the water and sewerage companies.

- The Water Resources Act 1991 sets out the functions of the Environment Agency and introduced water quality classifications and objectives for the first time.

- The Environment Act 1995 restructured environmental regulation and placed a duty on water companies to promote the efficient use of water by customers.

- European legislation (which applies to the UK) also sets out important directives for the water and sewerage sectors such as:

  - The Water Framework Directive. The directive sets objectives and deadlines for improving water quality. It looks at both the ecology of the water and its chemical characteristics.

  - The Urban Wastewater Treatment Directive aims to protect the water environment from being damaged by urban wastewater and certain industrial discharges.

  - The Drinking Water Directive sets quality standards for drinking water and requires drinking water quality to be monitored and reported.

  - The Sewage Sludge Directive aims to encourage the use of sewage sludge in agriculture and to regulate its use in such a way as to prevent harmful effects on soil, vegetation, animals and man.

How does regulation and legislation impact on WWTS?

Porter's five forces

- New entrants (low): Regulation and cost of compliance could act as a barrier to entry. Capital requirements and R&D could act as a deterrent to new participants.

- Suppler power (medium): Few suppliers in this niche market.

- Buyer power (high): Large customers and a small customer base give buyers considerable power. The group provides bespoke products and design services which should raise switching costs and strengthen brand loyalty. *Where do new customers come from?*

- Substitutes (low): WWTS are at the forefront of graphene technology – *this needs to be explored further.*

- Competitive rivalry (low/medium): There are a small number of players in the market. Given the differentiation in their products and the fact they have trademarked products that can be applied in each of the different filtration processes, price sensitivity should not be a problem; indeed price premiums should be achieved.

Strategic environment

The business operates in a specialized environment. They have a small and highly segmented market with a high perception of quality which should command premium pricing. The group has been established for over 50 years and should enjoy a good reputation and brand loyalty.

Critical success factors (for discussion) should include:

- scientific research expertise;
- expertise in technology;
- high quality of manufacture;
- access to adequate and suitably qualified skilled labour and technicians;
- available and dependable service and technical assistance;
- design expertise;
- ability to get newly developed products out of R&D and into the market quickly;
- favourable image/reputation with buyers;
- patent/trademark protections.

Activity answer 10.2

Financial accounts (credit analyst report)

The credit analyst report provides a summary which is very positive. However, additional questions would include:

- What occurred in 2015? Turnover fell by £4.5 million.
- Is that why no dividends were paid in 2015?
- Do the group hold any properties or are they 'off balance sheet'?

Activity answer 10.3

Group structure

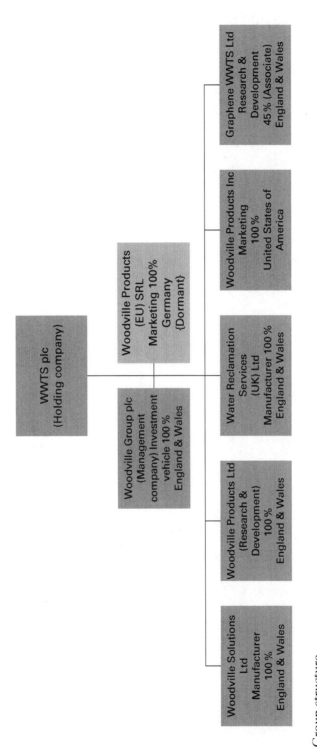

Group structure

Other entities (identified in the notes to accounts):

- Water Treatment Ltd employee benefits trust;
- Defined contribution pension scheme.

Activity answer 10.4

Agenda

Objectives:

1 Create a great first impression

2 Seek clarification on:

- new graphene product and impact on the sector;
- query fall in turnover in 2015;
- query geographical coverage (the accounts are silent);
- confirm group structure.

3 What is it they are looking for from the bank (Asfar mentioned 'issues')?

4 Secure next meeting and next steps.

Activity answer 10.5

What did Kate learn?

Asfar speaks highly of both Kate and the bank and was happy to arrange a referral. David acknowledged that the bank supported WRS in a time of need.

The graphene side of the business, whilst still in development, could change the nature of the industry. Kate also learned that the board's strategy is probably to sell out rather than try to develop this revolutionary product themselves.

David explained the apparent turnover issue in 2015 and Kate learned that this was a timings issue of the contracts and not necessarily a problem. The explanation about the effect of delayed projects (Brexit and the US elections) is very plausible.

Kate learned of the rationale for acquiring WRS and that its products completed WWTS's own product portfolio, ensuring they had a complete product set for each of the filtration processes.

David confirmed the group structure chart Kate presented, which showed Kate had 'done her homework'. He also clarified the role of Woodville Group as a quasi-investment vehicle.

Kate learned of the plans to reactivate the dormant German company in response to the UK leaving the EU and that the US office covered the Americas and Asia. David also promised to let Kate have details of the geographical coverage of their customers and confirmed their currency hedging was via forward currency contracts. This is something she could explore further when she meets with Neville, the finance director.

David confirmed their banking needs as being straightforward with little or no debt, which gave Kate the opportunity to explain that it is the quality of the relationship that is important.

Kate was informed of the 'issues' they have with their existing bank whose reputation was affected by the global financial crisis. Furthermore, David's perception was that their existing bank was changing the way they do business, resulting in frequent turnover of relationship managers. David found it exasperating having to explain what they do to new incoming managers. This underpins the importance of continuity of relationships.

The other main issue was with the bank's computer systems which on occasion meant they couldn't access their bank accounts to pay their foreign suppliers. You should also note that Kate never criticized the existing bank; she turned the conversation around to what she and her bank could do, not focusing on the failings of others.

David appeared to enjoy the discussion and Kate respected the timescale by not exceeding the time allotted. Despite a relatively short amount of time together, by careful questioning and excellent listening skills Kate was able to gain a lot of valuable information and was confident of moving on to the next stage.

Kate wanted to learn more about the business and this was achieved. From the outset Kate had a number of questions, yet there was no interrogation involved. Kate allowed the meeting to flow at David's pace and she was able to address some of the questions raised by her planning and preparation.

Finally, Kate did not present herself as an expert in the water treatment sector; she was well informed and was able to demonstrate her expertise in banking.

Activity answer 10.6

Difficult questions

Kate's response:

KATE: Well the figures look good, but we don't operate like that. We can't provide a blank cheque for acquisitions. It's not the way we do things. If you have any plans for an acquisition then please share it with us, so we can look to assist. Acquisitions are a risky part of lending. I've been involved with quite a few in my time, and I've never known one go exactly to plan. Do you have any acquisitions in mind?

NEVILLE: No not yet, I just wanted to see how you would react.

Activity answer 10.7

Products and services

Bank accounts will be required for:

- WWTS PLC;
- WG PLC;
- WS Ltd;
- WP Ltd;
- WRS (UK) Ltd;
- GWWTS Ltd;
- WWTS pension scheme;
- WTTS Ltd EBT;

Payment services required:

- BACS;
- internet banking;
- standing orders;
- direct debits;
- foreign payments.

Lending facilities required:

- overdraft;
- loan;
- credit cards;
- bonds;
- forward currency contracts;
- documentary letters of credit.

Other products/services identified:

- insurances (eg key person insurance cover);
- currency accounts;
- savings/investment accounts;
- bonds indemnities and guarantees.

Activity answer 10.8

Bonds, indemnities and guarantees

When selling overseas, buyers commonly request bank guarantees or bonds from their suppliers. This provides a means of securing performance or other obligations under the terms of the contract. Banks will act as a guarantor for their customers and will unconditionally pay the importer or exporter a specific sum on demand.

The wording of this demand is included within the guarantee. In return, banks take a counter-indemnity from their customers for the full amount of the guarantee, together with any costs incurred. The counter-indemnity is a legal agreement, under which the bank agrees with its customer that they will reimburse the bank in the event that it has to pay any claims under the bond or guarantee it has issued. For example, the bank may provide a duty deferment bond (also known as a VAT bond or customs guarantee).

KATE: As you are aware, an importer has to pay VAT and import duty on goods imported to the UK from non-EU countries. VAT and import duty must be paid before the importer can have access to their goods. However, the importer can request their bank to issue a guarantee in favour of HMRC covering deferment of import duty and VAT on their regular import business, thereby allowing the payment to be deferred for 28 days. In effect, this allows a period of credit before VAT and import duty payments fall due, thus improving the importer's cash flow. We know you import goods from Canada, Mexico, China and India, so they may be of benefit.

Activity answer 10.9

Skills and competences

Kate displayed some admirable qualities. The core of her success was the in-depth analysis and research she undertook for the first meeting. This was so important because if she had got that wrong, then it would have been her first and only meeting.

Kate had a clear understanding of her objectives for the meeting, which proved to be very successful. We have already discussed Kate's excellent questioning and listening skills which meant David did most of the talking. Kate was able to learn a great deal about the business from David.

Kate demonstrated the following skills:

- sensitivity;
- empathy;
- market/business knowledge;
- building rapport;
- communication.

Kate demonstrated the following competences:

- interpersonal ability;
- self-confidence;
- technical and professional knowledge;
- building collaborative relationships.

In contrast, the fourth meeting with Neville was far more challenging. Neville was quite aggressive and Kate was initially taken aback. But she stood firm and was quick at thinking on her feet. She also addressed Neville's concerns by explaining that she would try to limit the amount of disruption to Neville and his team if they went ahead.

In this meeting Kate demonstrated the following skills:

- resilience and perseverance;
- assertiveness;
- thinking skills.

and the following competences:

- self-control;
- persuasiveness.

Kate also involved others in the process. She introduced her colleague, the international manager, and between them they introduced the idea of a VAT deferment bond that would help the business's cash flow.

Throughout all the discussions Kate never criticized the competitor bank (systems failures, relationship management turnover or the fact they had never discussed bonds, indemnities and guarantees). That would have been unprofessional.

The final meeting with the whole board (the decision-making unit) where Kate presented her proposal was successful. When challenged about the overdraft margin Kate explained her thought process. She considered that improving the margin on the credit balances was more important than the overdraft rate and she gave them an option to lower the margin but explained this would mean she would be unable to provide better rates for the credit balances.

Kate also introduced the concept of an on-boarding team that would project-manage the transfer should they decide to go ahead. This addressed Neville's main concern.

In the final meeting she demonstrated the following skills:

- attention to detail;
- selling skills;
- negotiation skills;
- administration and organization.

and the following competences:

- initiative;
- flexibility and adaptability;
- thoroughness;
- decisiveness and judgement;
- innovation and creativity;
- teamworking;
- achievement orientation;
- customer service orientation;
- planning and organization;
- concern for quality;
- leadership.

So, what could Kate have done better? On reflection, Kate could have benefited from including others. It may have been appropriate to offer to introduce her line manager or a senior bank official to strengthen the relationships, particularly with Henry, the non-executive director, who actually banked with Kate's bank as a private banking client. She could have also met with WWTS's external accountants or any other key influencers she was able to identify.

GLOSSARY

Abridged accounts   Financial statements that cover a full accounting period but omit detailed financial information.

Artificial intelligence (AI)   A term for 'simulated intelligence processes' in machines and computer systems. These machines can be programmed to think like a human and mimic the way a person acts.

Bank stress test   An analysis conducted under unfavourable economic scenarios designed to determine whether a bank has enough capital to withstand the impact of adverse developments.

Bankruptcy   A way for individuals to deal with debts they cannot pay. It only applies to personal customers (including sole traders) and not companies or partnerships.

Board of directors   The individuals who run the organization on behalf of its shareholders.

Branding   The process of creating a unique name, image and perception for a product. It aims to establish a significant and differentiated presence in the mind of the customer. A strong brand makes the offering stand out from the crowd.

Capital requirement (also known **capital adequacy**)   The amount of capital a bank or other financial institution has to hold as required by its financial regulator.

Charity or **not-for-profit organization**   A legal structure where the organization does not earn profits for its owners. All of the money earned by or donated to it is used in pursuing the organization's objectives.

Closed architecture   A product platform where the bank sells only its proprietary products and does not entertain any third-party product.

Closed questions   Those questions that can be answered by a simple 'yes' or 'no'.

Committed facility   A lending facility whereby terms and conditions are clearly defined by the lender and imposed on the borrower. A loan is a committed facility.

Companies House   The UK's registrar of companies. All companies have to be incorporated and registered with Companies House. All registered limited companies must file their annual accounts and annual returns with the registrar. All of these documents are in the public domain.

Competitive advantage   An advantage over competitors gained by offering customers greater value either by lower prices or by providing greater benefits and services that justify higher prices.

Corporate governance   The framework of rules, practices, processes and procedures by which an organization is directed and controlled by the senior management of the organization.

Cross-selling The practice of selling additional products or services to an existing customer.

Crowdfunding Enables individuals to contribute funds to a specific company or project via an online platform.

Customer due diligence (CDD) Requires banks to identify customers. These checks include identity and address verification for every key party to the account.

Customer life cycle Used to map the different stages a customer goes through throughout their life time. It enables banks to market their products and services to customers as they move through each of the life cycle stages.

Customer retention The ability of an organization to retain its customers over the duration of the relationship.

Customer value proposition The reason why a customer buys a product or uses a service. It is a statement that convinces potential customers why your product or service will add more value or solve a problem better than those offered by your competitors.

Data analytics A process of inspecting, transforming and modelling data with the aim of discovering useful information and knowledge. Big data analytics brings benefits of speed and efficiency.

Demand facility An uncommitted lending facility where repayment of the debt can be called upon demand. An overdraft is a demand facility.

Economies of scale Where a larger size of output leads to a lower cost per unit of output.

Fact find An information-gathering form that enables wealth managers to provide the most appropriate advice to their clients.

Financial technology (FinTech) The development of new technology and innovation that aims to compete with traditional financial methods in the delivery of financial services. Those engaged in the industry develop new technologies to disrupt traditional financial markets.

Gearing A measure of the proportion of debt a business has in relation to its overall net worth. The higher the gearing ratio the greater the risk being assumed by the lenders rather than the shareholders.

Hard-core borrowing A term used to describe the part of an overdraft facility that is not cleared each month by payments into the account.

Horizontal integration Acquiring a company in the same industry.

Illiquid assets Those assets held by a bank that cannot be turned into cash quickly.

Joint and several liability When two or more people agree to pay a debt (or similar obligation). It is a joint promise that, if and when the need arises, the partners all agree to pay off the debt together. This means each partner is liable to pay the full amount of the debt, not just his or her own share.

Know your customer (KYC) A legal requirement to verify all bank customers during and after the account-opening process.

Limited company A type of legal structure that provides limited personal liability to the owner(s) of the business.

Limited liability partnership (LLP)   A legal structure that provides its members limited liability for the debts and obligations of the partnership. It is therefore a hybrid between a partnership and a limited company.

Loan-to-value   The ratio of the loan to the value of the property.

Money laundering   The process by which proceeds of crime are converted into assets that seem to have a legitimate origin.

Negative equity   Occurs when the market value of a property falls below the outstanding amount of a mortgage secured on it.

Net promoter score   An index-based system showing the willingness of customers to recommend a company's products or services to others.

Ongoing know your customer (OKYC)   A process of ongoing monitoring, involving scrutiny of transactions to ensure they are consistent with what is known about the customer.

Open architecture   Product platform where a private bank distributes all the third-party products and is not restricted to selling only its proprietary products.

Open questions   Questions that cannot be answered by a simple 'yes' or 'no'. They generally start with words such as: why, what, when, who, where, which and how.

Organizational structure chart   A diagram that shows the structure of an organization and the roles, responsibilities and functions of key personnel, including the directors of the organization.

Partnership   A legal business structure that is formed by two or more individuals to carry on a business as co-owners.

Partnership agreement   A written document that establishes the rights and responsibilities of each party within the partnership.

Peer-to-peer (P2P) lending   Non-bank financial intermediaries that are able to lend money to individuals or businesses through online services that match lenders with borrowers. Sometimes known as 'crowd-lending'.

Probate   Grants authority for an executor or administrator to administer the estate of a deceased person.

Retail bank run   When a large number of customers withdraw their deposits simultaneously due to concerns about the bank. Having large numbers of customers withdrawing their funds means banks could run out of cash (liquidity).

Revolving credit   A type of credit where the debt is not repaid by instalments. A credit limit is agreed and the customer can use the funds up to and including the credit limit agreed.

Sales effectiveness   Maximizing business development and sales potential once you are in front of the customer.

Sales efficiency   Getting in front of the right customers, at the right time, for minimum cost.

Scalability   A system or model that describes an organization's capability to cope and perform under an increased or expanding workload.

Service level agreement (SLA)   Part of a service contract in which the level of service is clearly defined.

Service quality   Meeting or exceeding a customer's expectations at a price that is acceptable to the customer and at a return that is acceptable to the supplier.

SIC code   A system for classifying industries by a four-digit number.

Social responsibility   An ethical framework that acts for the benefit of the society in which an organization operates.

Sole trader   A self-employed person, who is the sole owner of their business. Sole traders may or may not have employees.

Stakeholder   Anyone who has an interest in a business who can affect or be affected by the organization's actions, objectives and policies.

Strategic planning   An organization's process of defining its strategy, or direction, and making decisions on how to allocate its resources in pursuit of its strategy.

Supply chain   All the steps, factors and items from raw materials through to finished product/service to the point where the customer will purchase.

Systemic risk   The risk of collapse of an entire financial system or entire market.

Trust   A legal structure which is designed to hold and administer money or other assets on behalf of another party. There are three key people involved in any trust: the settlor, the person who puts the assets or money into the trust; the beneficiary, the person who benefits from the trust; and the trustee, the person who manages the trust.

Trusted advisor   Someone who has the experience, training, knowledge and expertise to build and retain trust with their customers. Their customers will actively seek them out for assistance and accept the advice they offer.

Up-selling   A sales technique whereby a seller persuades the customer to purchase more expensive items, upgrades or other add-ons in an attempt to make a more profitable sale.

Vertical integration   A company acquisition in the supply chain.

INDEX